A Return to Sunday Dinner

RUSSELL CRONKHITE

Multnomah Gifts™
Multnomah® Publishers *Sisters, Oregon*

In loving memory of my grandmother,
Addie May Ridgway

A Return to Sunday Dinner

© 2003 by Russell E. Cronkhite
published by Multnomah Gifts™, a division of Multnomah® Publishers, Inc.
P.O. Box 1720, Sisters, Oregon 97759

www.sundaydinner.com

International Standard Book Number: 1-59052-091-2

Design and photography by Koechel Peterson and Associates, Inc., Minneapolis, Minnesota
www.koechelpeterson.com

Unless otherwise indicated, Scripture quotations are from:
The Holy Bible, New International Version © 1973, 1984 by International Bible Society.
Used by permission of Zondervan Publishing House.

Multnomah Publishers, Inc., has made every effort to provide proper and accurate source attribution for all selections used in this book. Should any attribution be found to be incorrect, the publisher welcomes written documentation supporting correction for subsequent printings. We gratefully acknowledge the cooperation of other publishers and individuals who have granted permission for use of their material.

Multnomah is a trademark of Multnomah Publishers, Inc., and is registered in the U.S. Patent and Trademark Office.
The colophon is a trademark of Multnomah Publishers, Inc.

Printed in Korea

For information:
MULTNOMAH PUBLISHERS, INC. • P.O. BOX 1720 • SISTERS, OR 97759

Library of Congress Cataloging-in-Publication Data
Cronkhite, Russell.
    A return to Sunday dinner / by Russell Cronkhite.
        p. cm.
    ISBN 1-59052-091-2 (Hardcover)
    1. Dinners and dining. I. Title.
    TX737.C76 2003
    641.5'4--dc21
                                                    2003008420

03 04 05 06 07 08 09—10 9 8 7 6 5 4 3 2 1 0

Table of Contents

Welcome to Our Table

Remember Sunday dinner?

Just hearing the words can take you back—perhaps to a well-loved dining room in your grandparents' house, where a stately oak table is laid with lace and hand-painted china. The table overflows with its Sunday bounty...bowls of steaming, garden-fresh vegetables, crocks of sweet butter and homemade jam, and the succulent Sunday roast, juicy and brown. Incomparable aromas fill the house, laden with the promise of freshly-baked, light-as-a-feather biscuits or warm-from-the-oven peach cobbler.

Perhaps your memories of Sunday dinner are something else entirely. I found this to be the case when I brought up the subject at a recent gathering of friends. Everyone, it seemed, had a favorite Sunday-dinner memory to relate—and everyone was fiercely committed to his or her memory. The delightful sharing soon turned into a debate over whose mother made the best fried chicken, whether or not pot roast should be cooked with turnips, what kind of cheese goes best with macaroni, and whether mashed potatoes should have lumps! My friends are normally well-adjusted and well-educated professionals, but when it came to the topic of Sunday dinner, I had a near riot on my hands.

Why did they get so worked up? I think it's because the subject of Sunday dinner taps into something deep within us. It's about family and faith and meaning and memories—and something even deeper. Can you feel it? Even if your passions are more civilized than my friends'—or if Sunday dinner isn't part of your personal past at all—surely you know the tug of longing for a special day, a weekly refuge of love and laughter, peace and plenty, comfort and tradition.

Sunday dinner was once an American institution, a strong, familiar thread running deeply through our national fabric. I believe it can be that way again. A return to Sunday dinner can help bring us back to a time of craftsmanship, honor, values, and care. It can show us once again that time spent with those we love—enjoying family games, listening to tales of past struggle and glory, sharing our dreams and disappointments, and simply enjoying life together—far outweighs the amusements of the hectic, impersonal world that presses in all around us.

And now is the time to build those traditions anew. The book you hold in your hands is a call to launch your own Sunday dinner heritage, creating fresh and indelible memories for generations to come.

It's a call to rediscover Sunday dinner in your own life.

In a sense, Sunday dinner is a gift we can give to one another and pass on to our children and our children's children. It's a much-needed respite of rest, celebration, and inspiration.

In years gone by, whether in small towns, on the farm, or in great cities, most Americans took Sunday off. And rested. Shops and markets closed their doors. Twenty-four-hour groceries, shopping malls, and so-called convenience stores belonged to the unimaginable future. Life slowed for one day a week: a day for worship and quiet reflection, a day for relaxation and restoration, a day for family, a day apart from the everyday bustle.

Even in past centuries, setting apart a weekly day of rest required a certain discipline. Families worked hard to plan and prepare for the day when work would be laid aside. And unfortunately, religious curmudgeons sometimes made this special day feel like a day of repression, as though "day of rest" meant "day of no fun." But surely this was a corruption of the original intention—a misuse of the gift of Sunday rest.

In my experience, at least, such joyless legalism was never the norm for Sunday dinner. Sunday was different, yes, but different in a way that made things better for everyone. It was a day of rest, to be sure, but it was also a true day of celebration—a time to delight in the company of loved ones, to review and rebuild the unwritten customs of our past, and to enjoy together a bounty of wholesome foods. This includes the scrumptious traditional meals our parents, grandparents, and great-grandparents brought to this country, for food—along with language, religion, and art—is one of the essential pillars of any culture.

Throughout history, special meals have come to symbolize special times, and such meals mark our family lives as well: birthday dinners, reunion picnics, weddings, anniversaries. When other details of past events fade, the flavors of the food we shared together linger in the memory. And year after year, as holidays approach, we relish with anticipation the savory tastes and aromas we've come to associate with those annual festivities.

The Sunday table, too, has always been a center for family celebrations. Restful Sundays provide us with unhurried hours for enjoying our shared lives—exploring our heritage, remembering the sacrifices of those who made our lives possible, and giving thanks for God's kindness and blessings.

But the Sunday dinner offers even more than true rest and joyful celebration. It also provides something often overlooked in this casual age: the gift of encouragement and inspiration. It helps us remember that there is indeed something beyond and above our commonplace world.

When architects created the great cathedrals of Europe, they sought to inspire—and they succeeded. The grand arches draw our eyes up and away from everyday life to contemplate the very heights of heaven. They mark a space and a time that is special and set apart.

The Sunday table has the ability to lift us up as well, to remind us that there is more to life than just daily bread. That's why Sunday dinner has always been a time to break out our very best—to set our finest table, elegant or cheerful with beautiful linens and dishes, bright with flowers, and bountiful with platters of our favorite foods.

And what an inspiring transformation Sunday can bring! The everyday table, rushed with kids, piled with homework, where we read the morning paper, is transformed and set apart. A tablecloth covers the ordinary wood. The china may not be showpiece quality, but it gleams with meaning and memories. The centerpiece flowers give humble testimony to the beauty of creation. We dress in our nicest clothes, put on our company manners. And the meal itself—carefully planned, lovingly prepared, and gratefully shared—provides a vivid and delicious and, yes, inspirational picture of what life can be at its best.

Its Sunday best.

I was fortunate to enjoy such Sunday celebrations with my extended family when I was growing up. My mother, my two sisters, my brother, and I loved to spend Sunday afternoons at our grandparents' home. Cousins, aunts, and uncles gathered there as well, and guests were always welcome. Birthdays and special holidays such as Memorial Day, Easter, and Mother's Day became much-anticipated and long-remembered reunions.

My grandmother did most of the cooking, although we all pitched in to keep her Sunday workload light. Grandma was a pioneer, raised in the heart of Texas. Her mother's family was of sturdy Scots-Irish descent. Her father and uncle had walked the old war trails from the Eastern Cherokee Nation in Georgia to Texas and the Oklahoma territories. And it was in Oklahoma that Grandma met Grandpa at his tenth birthday party. His family had traveled there from Virginia, and the party took place as both families prepared their covered wagons for the long journey farther west.

Their families would be among the last of those that traveled the old trails toward California and Oregon. And although the two families took different routes west, my grandparents remembered each other. Remarkably, they found each other on the West Coast and eventually married. Grandpa went to work for the railroad, and their five children were born up and down the Union Pacific line, from Seattle to Los Angeles.

My grandparents were never rich. Like many Depression-era families, they learned to make do with what they had. They ate simple, well-balanced meals, freshly prepared with wholesome but inexpensive ingredients. But those meals must have had some merit: Both of my grandparents lived to nearly ninety years of age.

Our table was mostly Southern in influence: black-eyed peas and corn bread for good luck on New Year's Day, baked ham for Easter. But we also enjoyed many other American standards—New England boiled dinner, Yankee pot roast, and home-baked beans—found in classic volumes on American cookery by Mary Randolph, Mrs. T. J. Crowen, and Fannie Farmer.

For me, growing up with little never meant having less. The Sunday meal was always memorable.

When my wife and I began a family of our own twenty-five years ago, we wanted to build the same kinds of Sunday memories and traditions we had known as children. In our busy world we constantly looked for opportunities to enjoy meaningful family time. Above all else, we wanted one day each week to be set aside for nurturing our lives together. So Sunday became our family day, the day we would spend together. First, we would attend church as a family. Then later, if one child had a soccer game, for instance, we'd all go to the game. If such activities conflicted with our normal dinnertime, we'd bring a snack and plan for a family meal later in the day. Or we'd eat a light breakfast so our midday dinner could be enjoyed early.

To the best of our ability, we guarded our Sundays together—not out of some legalistic obsession or obligation, but simply because we wanted a day away from the worries of the world and the often frantic pace of everyday life. We wanted to carve out a day of retreat, a day of rest, one day a week to just enjoy each other.

On many Sundays, we would try to plan something special for the day—an activity that was both leisurely and family oriented. Sometimes we'd set off to explore a museum. Other times we'd head for the countryside. And like so many families, we enjoyed going out for an occasional Sunday brunch—a nice break from the labors of our own kitchen.

Most Sundays, however, we cooked our Sunday dinner. Cooking was part of the fun—something we enjoyed doing together—as was sitting down to real Sunday dinner with friends and family. The Sunday dinner table became the place where we could share thoughts as well as food and discuss the questions of the day, often with guests. It was the place where our children learned good manners, how to carry on meaningful conversations, to be gracious hosts—setting an inviting table and clearing as guests enjoyed after-dinner discussion—and to help in the kitchen, which equipped them with useful life skills.

Sunday by Sunday, we added treasured pages to the albums of our memories. And because Sunday dinner has always been special to us, I suppose it's no surprise that it even became a part of my professional life.

For more than thirty years, you see, I have been privileged to make a living as a professional chef. I have worked in some of the finest establishments in this country. But by far the most memorable segment of my career was my nearly twelve years as executive chef of the Blair House, the presidential guest house, located across Pennsylvania Avenue from the White House.

Since 1942, Blair House has catered to our nation's most important guests. During my tour of duty there, I had the honor of serving three presidents, as well as nearly every major world leader of the current generation—from Queen Elizabeth II and Prince Philip to Nelson Mandela, Mother Teresa, Boris Yeltsin, Margaret Thatcher, Prime Minister Benazir Bhutto of Pakistan, President Vaclav Havel of the Czech Republic, the emperor and empress of Japan, President François Mitterrand of France, and President Jiang Zemin of China.

While many of the meals we served during that time were exquisite formal banquets, many were the well-loved, familiar kinds of meals that reflect the bounty of our nation—the simple yet wonderful tastes that make up what we know as regional American foods.

And through those years, whenever I was asked about the food we created and the hospitality we offered at the Blair House, I had a ready reply:

"Just think of Sunday dinner."

It is my hope that this book will help you think of Sunday dinner in your own life. It is a full-hearted celebration of our American culture—our deep religious heritage, our unique regional cuisine, and our time-honored traditions of hospitality, welcome, and ease.

But *A Return to Sunday Dinner* is meant to be more than a beautiful book filled with tempting recipes. I hope it will inspire you to create your own special Sunday dinners for family and friends—and to do so with aplomb and ease.

Sunday dinner is meant to be special, after all—a true celebration—but it is also the highlight of a day of rest. Recognizing this, I chose and developed the recipes in this volume with an eye to simplicity of preparation. There is no meal in this book that cannot be created by a cook (or cooks) of moderate skill, from ingredients that are readily available in your local grocery. And the recipes can all be prepared either quickly or ahead of time. Everyone understands the need for meals that can be put in the oven to be ready when a ravenous family returns home from church.

Sunday dinner, I believe, can be both a touchstone to our past and a foundation on which to build memories. Whether or not Sunday dinner is part of your personal past, this weekly time of rest, celebration, and inspiration can be part of your life right now. This book is all the invitation you need.

It's Sunday, and dinner's ready.

Welcome to our table!

Our Sunday Best

SUNDAY BEST ROAST BEEF WITH PAN GRAVY
SOUR CREAM MASHED POTATOES
TANGY CHEESE BROCCOLI
GLAZED BABY CARROTS
SESAME CLOVERLEAF ROLLS
BITTERSWEET CHOCOLATE–BUTTERMILK CAKE

Remember that phrase "Sunday best"? When I was a child, I heard it at least once a week. Sunday was when we wore our nicest clothes and shoes, all pressed and mended and shined, and tried to remember our company manners. We set the table with our most beautiful linens and china and feasted on the most delectable foods we could afford. It wasn't a way of showing off, but a way of showing respect. We honored God with the highest quality of what we had to offer.

In the American culinary tradition, the Sunday roast represents that ideal. When meat was a luxury, when good-quality tender meat was expensive and hard to find, when having meat for dinner mostly meant a stew, meat loaf, or even Swiss steak, we saved the choicest cut of beef for the Sunday dinner table.

By definition, a roasted piece of meat is succulent, tender, and juicy, with a caramelized seasoned crust on the outside and a pink juicy middle. Until the late nineteenth century, large cuts of meat were roasted on a spit over hot coals or in an open-hearth kitchen, turned continually, and then basted with the drippings caught in a pan below the spit. Great care was needed to cook the meat properly and safely. The modern oven changed all that, but a tender, well-cooked roast is still a culinary triumph.

My own childhood memories often carry me back to my grandmother's table on roast-beef Sundays. Grandma didn't dish food onto plates in the kitchen like a diner. Everything came to the table in steaming bowls—mashed potatoes, hand-whipped and creamy; bright green broccoli dripping with golden butter; hot, soft rolls fresh from the oven and covered with a napkin—all set before us in silence. Last came the roast, crusty, rare, and dripping with juice, arranged on Grandma's best platter with thin slices laid around the edges and the remainder standing ready to be carved for seconds.

After dinner, when the table had been cleared, a tall, moist chocolate cake would be uncovered and cut with a silver cake service. Each plated slice was passed from hand to hand round the table, with all the children hoping the biggest piece would stop with them! Then came cups of good strong coffee for the adults and more cold milk for the kids (which was always poured from a pitcher).

This was Sunday dinner as I remember it, Sunday as it was meant to be—and still can be. Careful handiwork, loving preparation, mouthwatering food, and family and guests gathered around a beautifully set table. It's all quite simply the best: our Sunday best.

SUNDAY BEST ROAST BEEF
WITH PAN GRAVY
8 SERVINGS

A great Sunday roast comes in many forms: standing rib, eye of the top round, bottom round or—my favorite—a rump roast. (The rump is the tender tip of the round.) My mother always picked a larger-than-needed roast for dinner; then we'd enjoy great roast beef sandwiches and often a hearty stew from the leftover meat.

ROAST BEEF

1 4- to 5-pound boneless rump roast
2 tablespoons Worcestershire sauce
1 teaspoon granulated garlic
1 teaspoon onion powder
1 teaspoon paprika
1 tablespoon coarse-ground black pepper
2 teaspoons coarse salt

Adjust the rack to the bottom of the oven and preheat to 450°F.

PREPARE THE ROAST:

FIRST, blot any excess moisture from the roast using paper towels. Rub the Worcestershire sauce over the entire roast; allow the roast to sit for a few minutes, turning it several times so that the meat can absorb the Worcestershire.

SECOND, combine the granulated garlic, onion powder, paprika and coarse-ground pepper in a small bowl; sprinkle the seasoning mixture evenly over the roast, pressing it into the fat and meat just enough to stick. Allow the seasoned roast to stand at room temperature for 20 to 30 minutes before roasting.

THIRD, rub the roast with the coarse salt and place it fat side up in a shallow roasting pan. Roast for 15 minutes, then lower the oven temperature to 325°F. Continue to cook until the internal temperature reaches 5 to 10 degrees below the desired serving temperature, about 2 hours. (*Note:* Allow about 20 minutes per pound for medium-rare.) When the roast is done, carefully remove the pan from the oven and transfer the roast to a clean cutting board. Allow the roast to stand for 20 minutes before slicing.

PAN GRAVY

3 tablespoons all-purpose flour
2 cups beef broth
Salt and pepper to taste

MAKE THE GRAVY:

Use a spoon to skim all the fat from the liquid that remains in the roasting pan. Reserve about 4 tablespoons of fat in a small mixing bowl and cool until it is just barely warm, 4 to 5 minutes. Whisk the flour into the fat to form a *roux*. Scrape the drippings from the bottom of the pan, add in the beef broth and stir over medium heat until the broth begins to simmer. Whisk in the roux and bring to a boil, then simmer for 4 to 5 minutes. Add a little water, a tablespoon at a time, as needed to achieve the desired consistency. Season to taste with salt and pepper.

PRESENT THE ROAST:

Use a sharp carving knife to cut thin slices against the grain. Arrange the slices on a decorative platter and pour the irresistible juices left on the cutting board over the meat. Pass the gravy alongside in a gravy boat.

SOUR CREAM
MASHED POTATOES
8 SERVINGS

The key to truly great mashed potatoes is starting with starchy potatoes. In my opinion, the very best are White Rose or Yukon Gold. I find that russets are better for baking and that waxy potatoes, such as red-skins, are better for roasting.

MASHED POTATOES

8 medium potatoes
½ cup (1 stick) butter
⅔ cup whole milk
1 cup sour cream
1 tablespoon fresh snipped chives
Salt to taste

MAKE THE MASHED POTATOES:

FIRST, peel and quarter the potatoes. Cut each quarter in half and place in a large pot filled with enough cool salted water to cover them completely. Bring to a boil, reduce the heat to a robust simmer (*not* a rolling boil) and let the potatoes cook undisturbed until they are just beginning to fall apart, 20 to 25 minutes.

SECOND, drain off the water and return the pot to the stove. Let the potatoes cook for a minute, shaking the pot to evaporate the excess moisture. Add in the butter and continue to shake the pot until the butter melts completely and coats all of the potatoes (this will keep the potatoes from becoming sticky when they are mashed). Pour in the milk and heat until it begins to boil.

THIRD, remove the potatoes from heat. Use a potato masher or stiff wire whip to thoroughly mash the potatoes in an up-and-down motion. Add in the sour cream and whip for another minute or so until they are smooth. (*Note:* Be careful not to whip too hard or for too long, because over-blending will make the potatoes sticky, not fluffy.) Fold in the chives and season to taste with salt.

The pleasantest

hours of our life

are all connected

by a more or less

tangible link,

with some

memory of

the table.

CHARLES PIERRE MONSELET

TANGY CHEESE BROCCOLI

8 SERVINGS

Broccoli is such a wonderful, good-for-you vegetable—and it is available year-round! When grocery shopping, look for a head of broccoli with a tight, firm flower. Steaming broccoli will give it vibrant color as well as help it to retain its nutrients and all of its wonderful flavor. It is especially good when topped with this easy cheese topping.

BROCCOLI

2 pounds fresh broccoli
2 tablespoons butter
Pinch of salt

PREPARE THE BROCCOLI:

~ **FIRST,** trim about 3 to 4 inches of the heavy stalk from the bottom of each broccoli flower with a sharp paring knife; then split each stalk lengthwise through its stem into 3 or 4 pieces. Avoid cutting through the small tender buds when possible; keeping the florets whole and the large stems thin will help the broccoli cook evenly.

~ **SECOND,** place the broccoli in a shallow saucepan—make sure it is large enough that there are no more than two layers of broccoli. Pour in just enough water to cover the bottom of the pan by ½ inch. Season with the butter and a pinch of salt.

~ **THIRD,** bring the water to a full boil over medium-high heat. Place a tight-fitting lid over the pan and steam the broccoli until just tender, 5 to 6 minutes.

TOPPING

4 slices American cheese
1 3-ounce package cream cheese
1 cup grated cheddar cheese
3 tablespoons whole milk
4 to 5 drops Tabasco sauce

PREPARE THE TOPPING:

~ **FIRST,** use a sharp paring knife to dice the American cheese and cube the cream cheese; combine with the grated cheddar in the bowl of a food processor fitted with a steel blade. Add in the milk and a few drops of Tabasco sauce. Blend until it becomes a smooth sauce, 2 to 3 minutes. (*Note:* The topping can then be transferred to a glass dish, sealed with plastic wrap and refrigerated for up to 2 days; return to room temperature before heating.)

~ **SECOND,** melt the cheese topping in the microwave for about 30 seconds; or melt over low heat in a small saucepan, stirring constantly, for 3 to 4 minutes.

SERVE THE BROCCOLI:

~ Drain the liquid from the saucepan and arrange the steamed broccoli in a serving bowl; pour the melted cheese sauce over and serve immediately.

GLAZED BABY CARROTS
8 SERVINGS

Tiny carrots are sweet all by themselves. The addition of butter, honey and orange juice brings out their naturally sweet flavor even more, making the simple sublime.

CARROTS

4 cups peeled baby carrots
¼ cup (½ stick) butter
¼ cup honey
1 cup freshly squeezed orange juice

PREPARE THE CARROTS:

FIRST, place the carrots into a skillet of boiling salted water and simmer until they are tender on the outside and still crunchy in the middle (al dente), 4 to 6 minutes. Drain off the water.

SECOND, add the butter to the drained carrots and continue cooking over medium heat just long enough to melt the butter. Toss the carrots in the melted butter, then add in the honey and orange juice; blend together until the liquid begins bubbling. Simmer for 6 to 8 minutes, tossing the carrots from time to time, until the liquid is reduced to a glistening glaze.

SESAME CLOVERLEAF ROLLS
2 DOZEN ROLLS

With their golden crusts and light, airy centers, cloverleaf rolls are always a favorite—and they are so easy to make. I like them plain as well as sprinkled with sesame seeds.

ROLLS

1 package (2¼ teaspoons) active dry yeast
¼ cup warm water, about 110°F
1 cup whole milk
2 tablespoons granulated sugar
½ cup (1 stick) butter
2 large eggs, room temperature
1 large egg yolk, room temperature
3½ cups all-purpose flour
1 teaspoon salt
1 large egg white, room temperature, well beaten
2 tablespoons sesame seeds

MAKE THE ROLLS:

FIRST, sprinkle the yeast over the water and let stand for 1 minute, then stir until the yeast is dissolved.

SECOND, scald the milk with the sugar by heating it in a small saucepan to the point of boiling. Remove it from heat and swirl in the butter until it melts completely. Cool in the pan until lukewarm.

THIRD, lightly beat the 2 eggs and the egg yolk together; combine with the dissolved yeast and the lukewarm milk. Then stir in 2 cups of the flour.

Continue stirring until the batter is smooth and elastic, about 120 strokes. Scrape down the sides of the bowl with a rubber spatula. Cover the bowl with a clean tea towel and set in a draft-free place until the dough is bubbly and has doubled in volume, about 1 hour.

FOURTH, whisk the salt into the remaining 1½ cups of flour. Use an electric mixer fitted with a dough hook to slowly incorporate the flour mixture into the bubbly dough on low speed. Scrape down the sides of the bowl with a rubber spatula. Increase the mixer speed to medium and add in a little extra flour as necessary, a tablespoon at a time, until the dough begins to pull away from the sides of the bowl. Reduce the mixer speed to low and knead for 5 minutes; the dough should attain a smooth, soft, silky texture. Dust the dough with a little flour to keep it from sticking to your hands and form it into a ball. Place in a lightly oiled bowl and cover with plastic wrap. Refrigerate for at least 30 minutes and up to 4 hours.

BAKE THE ROLLS:

Divide the dough into 6 equal pieces and roll the pieces between your hands into 12-inch ropes. Divide each rope into 12 equal pieces and roll the pieces into little balls. Place 3 balls into each of 24 lightly greased muffin cups. Use a pastry brush to glaze the tops of the rolls with the beaten egg white, and then sprinkle with the sesame seeds. Cover the rolls with a clean tea towel, set in a draft-free place and let them rise until doubled in size, about 1 hour. Bake at 400°F for 12 to 15 minutes. Brush the tops with melted butter while the rolls are still hot.

BITTERSWEET CHOCOLATE–
BUTTERMILK CAKE
12 SERVINGS

Without a doubt, this chocolate cake is Sunday dinner dessert at its best! Nothing could be more truly American than moist, dense layers of cake and oh-so-satisfying chocolate-fudge frosting.

Easy time-saving

AND DO-AHEAD TIPS:

FRIDAY EVENING

Bake the cake layers, cool, cover tightly with plastic wrap and refrigerate. Prepare the cheese topping for the broccoli and refrigerate.

SATURDAY

Prepare the cake frosting and cool; assemble the cake. Trim and portion the broccoli, transfer to a well-sealed container and refrigerate.

SUNDAY MORNING

Prepare the dough for the rolls and refrigerate. Peel and cut the potatoes; place in a pot and cover with cold water. Remove the roast from the refrigerator and bring to room temperature before seasoning.

CHOCOLATE CAKE

2 cups cake flour
¼ cup cocoa powder
1 teaspoon baking soda
½ teaspoon salt
4 ounces unsweetened chocolate
1 cup shortening
2 cups granulated sugar
2 teaspoons pure vanilla extract
4 large eggs, room temperature
1 cup buttermilk

~ Adjust the baking rack to the middle of the oven and preheat to 350°F.

MAKE THE CAKE LAYERS:

~ **FIRST,** grease and lightly flour two 9-inch round cake pans with 2-inch sides. Sift together the cake flour, cocoa powder, baking soda and salt; set aside.

~ **SECOND,** melt the unsweetened chocolate in a small dish in the microwave or over medium heat in a small pan on the stove; stir until smooth, then cool to room temperature.

~ **THIRD,** combine the shortening and sugar in the bowl of a mixer fitted with a paddle; cream together on high speed until light and fluffy, 6 to 8 minutes. Turn the mixer off and scrape down the sides of the bowl with a rubber spatula, then add in the vanilla and the melted, cooled chocolate. Mix at medium speed until the chocolate is completely incorporated, then lower the mixer speed to medium-low. Add in the eggs one at a time, mixing well after each addition.

~ **FOURTH,** turn the mixer speed down to low. Add in the sifted dry ingredients in 4 batches alternately with the buttermilk, beating slowly but thoroughly after each addition. When the ingredients are fully incorporated, increase the speed to medium and beat for 1 minute.

~ **FIFTH,** divide the batter evenly between the prepared pans and bake for 30 to 35 minutes. The cakes are done when they begin to pull away from the edges of the pan and spring back when pressed gently in the center.

~ **SIXTH,** allow the layers to cool in the pans for 10 minutes on wire racks; then carefully run a thin sharp knife around the inside edge of each pan to loosen. Turn the cake layers out onto a cooling rack.

FROSTING

4 ounces bittersweet chocolate
4 ounces unsweetened chocolate
1½ cups (3 sticks) unsalted butter, chilled
¼ cup light corn syrup
2 cups heavy cream
1½ cups granulated sugar
2 teaspoons pure vanilla extract

PREPARE THE FROSTING:

~ **FIRST,** chop the bittersweet chocolate and unsweetened chocolate into tiny pieces and slice the cold butter into 1-inch pats. Combine the butter and chocolate in the bowl of a food processor fitted with a steel blade. (*Note:* It's important that the butter be cold, so that the chocolate and butter will melt at the same rate and blend smoothly with the scalded cream.)

~ **SECOND,** combine the corn syrup, cream, sugar and vanilla in a large saucepan. Whisk constantly over medium-high heat until the sugar fully dissolves and the mixture comes to a boil. Continue cooking for 2 more minutes, stirring to keep the syrupy mixture from boiling over the edge of the pan; then remove from heat and swirl gently until the bubbling subsides.

~ **THIRD,** immediately pour the hot cream mixture over the chocolate and butter. Quickly secure the processor lid and blend until the chocolate and butter are completely melted and have blended thoroughly with the cream, about 1 minute. (*Note:* If you don't have a food processor, place the chocolate and butter in a mixing bowl, pour in the scalded cream mixture and whisk vigorously for 3 to 4 minutes.)

~ **FOURTH,** pour the frosting into a glass dish and press a sheet of plastic wrap directly onto the surface. Let the frosting rest at room temperature for approximately 2 hours (do not refrigerate). The chocolate and butter will slowly bind with the cream to form a smooth, easy-to-spread, rich chocolate frosting that is thick enough to hold soft peaks.

ASSEMBLE THE CAKE:

Place 1 layer of the cake on a serving platter or cake stand. Use an icing spatula or table knife to spread about ⅓ of the frosting evenly on the cake. Place the second layer over the first and cover the top and sides with the remaining frosting.

In the quiet, unhurried atmosphere, wholesome and inspiring conversation can linger on through dessert and well into our second cup of coffee.

RC

From Hearth and Home

SAGE-RUBBED ROAST PORK LOIN WITH APPLE CIDER GLAZE
WHITE CHEDDAR POTATO BAKE
STONE-GROUND CORN MUFFINS
HONEY-HAZELNUT ACORN SQUASH
GARDEN PEA AND CABBAGE SALAD
FARMHOUSE RHUBARB LATTICE PIE

Picture a Sunday after church. We gather together with family and friends around the amber glow of an inviting hearth, wrapping ourselves in the toasty warmth of the coals and in the comfort of God's unchanging love. We hold one another in His gentle care and luxuriate in familiar sights and sounds: children running and laughing, bustling sounds from the kitchen, the creak of a rocking chair, the sound of a story told from days gone by. And floating through it all are the warm, enticing aromas of an unforgettable Sunday dinner.

Each of us has a vision of what that perfect time should be. Each of us can make our own Sunday moments just as warm, inviting, and bright.

Home, in other words, is where *your* heart is.

Perhaps it is the ambience of the hearth that sparks such reflections. The soft flames dancing bright from a crackling fire. The deep hues of brick or stone, held tight for the ages with mortar. Family pictures and treasured mementos lined up on a hand-carved mantle. The smooth warmth of the hearth itself.

The hearth was once the center of every home; it was the source of heat, the place where meals were cooked. While most of us now have furnaces and kitchens, people still gravitate toward the dancing warmth of a fireside. Here is a place for quiet contemplation, a place to cozy up with a favorite quilt, to enjoy a book or read the Sunday paper or simply sit and talk. Even in homes without fireplaces, Americans still gather around the hearth of friendship and family to cherish God's blessings—the Lord's very presence is the hearthstone of the home.

The flavors of hearth and home are found throughout our land; they are as varied as our heritage. Few capture those flavors quite so well, though, as the foods rooted in Indiana and in the Ohio River Valley, where the influences of the Shaker communities have been passed down for us to enjoy.

Shaker communities once flourished from Maine to Kentucky. These set-apart religious communities were committed to excellence in all that they set out to do—from their elegantly simple handmade furniture and implements to their renowned apple cider. The Shakers were farmers, and theirs was a world rich with the simple tastes of home-made goodness: bread-and-butter pickles, green-tomato relish, apple butter, abundant fruit pies, maple syrup, and fresh herbs for seasoning. Who doesn't love the roasted caramel flavor of a moist and juicy cider-basted pork loin, creamy cheddar potatoes, baked squash, and corn muffins longing to be spread with butter, honey, or homemade jam? Such simple but lively flavors are the ones our taste buds and our hearts most long for, all flavored with the memories of hearth and home—Sunday dinner as it was meant to be.

Easy time saving
AND DO AHEAD TIPS:

FRIDAY EVENING
Prepare the pastry dough, hazelnut butter and apple cider glaze; refrigerate each separately.

SATURDAY
Prepare the vegetables and the dressing for the salad and refrigerate. Season the pork roast; wrap it in plastic and refrigerate. Bake the rhubarb pie and store at room temperature.

SUNDAY MORNING
Prepare the acorn squash and the potato casserole for baking. Butter the muffin cups. Prepare the corn muffin batter.

SAGE-RUBBED ROAST PORK LOIN
WITH APPLE CIDER GLAZE
8 SERVINGS

The sweet cider glaze is an excellent complement to this pork loin roast. The flavor of the crisp apples, along with a hint of spice and the earthy aroma of sage, is bound to create a memorable feast.

NOTE: *For a truly elegant presentation, have your butcher prepare a roast from the rib end of the loin. Be sure to have the roast tied securely with twine and "Frenched" by trimming the ends 1 inch down from the tips.*

PORK LOIN

½ tablespoon mustard seeds
1 tablespoon peppercorns
2 tablespoons whole-grain mustard
¼ cup fresh chopped sage
1 5- to 6-pound bone-in pork loin roast
1 tablespoon vegetable oil
1 tablespoon coarse salt

CIDER GLAZE

2 sweet-tart apples
1 small sweet onion
2 cups apple cider
¼ cup dark corn syrup
1 tablespoon prepared mustard
½ cup packed brown sugar
1 tablespoon cider vinegar
Pinch of ground cloves

PREPARE THE PORK LOIN:
~ Crush the mustard seeds and peppercorns using a mortar and pestle or the bottom of a heavy skillet. Blend into a paste with the mustard and sage. Rub the roast with the vegetable oil and then season the pork loin by rubbing it all over with the mustard paste. Cover the seasoned roast with plastic wrap and refrigerate overnight or for up to 24 hours.

MAKE THE CIDER GLAZE:
~ FIRST, core and slice the apples; peel and thinly slice the onion. In a heavy-bottomed saucepan whisk together the apple cider, corn syrup, mustard, brown sugar, cider vinegar and pinch of ground cloves. Place the saucepan over a burner set to medium heat. Add in the apple and onion slices.

~ SECOND, bring the mixture to a boil and reduce the heat to medium-low. Simmer the sauce until the apples are fully cooked, about 25 minutes; then strain the mixture through a sieve into a small bowl. Press firmly on the solids with a rubber spatula to squeeze out all the savory juices and pulp from the apple and onion slices. Discard the bits of apple peel and onion that remain in the sieve.

COOK THE PORK LOIN:

~ FIRST, remove the seasoned roast from the refrigerator and allow it to rest at room temperature for about 1 hour. Cover the Frenched rib bone ends with foil to keep them from charring.

~ SECOND, position one oven rack near the bottom of the oven and the second rack just above the middle, leaving enough room for the roast to easily fit on the bottom rack. Preheat the oven to 425°F. Season the pork loin with the coarse salt. Place the roast, with the ribs pointing upward, in a shallow roasting pan. Carefully slide the pan into the oven, then lower the heat to 325°F and allow the pork to cook until the internal temperature registers about 130°F on a meat thermometer, 2 to 2½ hours.

~ THIRD, increase the oven temperature to 350°F and baste the roast with a generous amount of cider glaze, using a pastry brush to apply the glaze over the roast's entire surface. (*Note:* At this time you can place the squash and the potatoes on the upper rack of the oven.) Repeat this glazing process two or three times while continuing to roast the meat for an additional 25 to 30 minutes.

~ FOURTH, when the roast is fully cooked to an internal temperature of about 150°F, take it out of the oven. Carefully remove the roast from the pan and allow the meat to rest on a clean cutting board for 20 to 25 minutes. The temperature will rise by another 5 to 10 degrees, giving you a medium serving temperature of 160°F.

~ FIFTH, place the roasting pan on top of a burner that is set to medium heat. Pour about ¼ cup of warm water into the roasting pan and use a whisk to scrape the bits of meat from the bottom. Whisk in any remaining cider glaze and blend it with the pan juices. Simmer for 2 to 3 minutes to reduce the liquid and fully incorporate the rich flavors.

PRESENT THE ROAST:

~ After all your effort, you'll want to present your beautiful roast to your guests before carving. Remove the foil from the rib bone ends and the twine from the roast. Transfer the roast, ribs pointing up, to a platter or decorative cutting board for all to admire.

CARVE THE ROAST:

~ Hold the rib closest to you to secure the roast and carefully slice between each bone to cut each portion. The bones will have a slight curve to them, so use them as your guide rather than trying to cut straight down. Pass the pan juices alongside in a gravy boat.

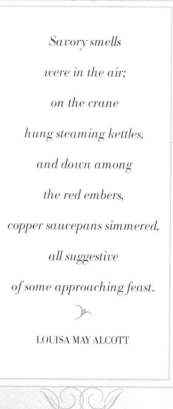

Savory smells

were in the air;

on the crane

hung steaming kettles,

and down among

the red embers,

copper saucepans simmered,

all suggestive

of some approaching feast.

LOUISA MAY ALCOTT

WHITE CHEDDAR POTATO BAKE
8 SERVINGS

Using sharp cheddar from Oregon or aged cheddar from Vermont makes these potatoes particularly flavorful. This dish is also a great way to use up any leftover mashed potatoes.

POTATO BAKE

8 medium potatoes
½ cup (1 stick) butter
½ cup whole milk
1 large egg
Salt and pepper to taste
2 cups grated cheddar cheese

PREPARE THE POTATO BAKE:

FIRST, peel the potatoes and quarter them. Cut each quarter in half and place the potatoes in a large pot filled with enough cool salted water to cover them completely. Bring to a boil, reduce the heat to a robust simmer (*not* a rolling boil) and let the potatoes cook undisturbed until they are just beginning to fall apart, 20 to 25 minutes. Drain the water from the potatoes.

SECOND, preheat the oven to 350°F. Return the pot to the stove and let the potatoes cook for 1 minute, shaking the pan to evaporate the excess moisture. Add in the butter and continue to shake the pan until the butter melts completely and coats all the potatoes (this will keep them from becoming sticky when they are mashed). Pour in the milk and heat until it begins to boil.

THIRD, remove the potatoes from heat. Use a potato masher or stiff wire whip to thoroughly mash the potatoes in an up-and-down motion. Beat in the egg with a wooden spoon, then season with a little salt and pepper. Fold in 1½ cups of the grated cheddar cheese.

FOURTH, butter a 1½-quart ovenproof baking dish. Use a rubber spatula to spread the potato mixture evenly in the dish. Bake for 20 to 25 minutes.

FIFTH, sprinkle the remaining ½ cup of cheese over the potatoes. Increase the oven temperature to 400°F and bake for an additional 15 minutes.

If you call the Sabbath a delight and the LORD's holy day honorable… then you will find your joy in the LORD.

ISAIAH

STONE-GROUND CORN MUFFINS
1 DOZEN MUFFINS

Where breakfast muffins tend to be sweet, these are more savory—a bit like corn bread. And while golden squares of corn bread are a perennial favorite, corn muffins give you that toasted crunch on every side.

CORN MUFFINS

½ cup shortening
¼ cup granulated sugar
2 large eggs, room temperature
1 cup all-purpose flour
1 tablespoon baking powder
½ teaspoon salt
1½ cups stone-ground cornmeal
1 cup whole milk

~ Preheat the oven to 400°F.

MAKE THE MUFFINS:

~ **FIRST,** butter 12 standard muffin cups (each about ½-cup capacity).

~ **SECOND,** thoroughly cream the shortening and sugar on high speed using an electric mixer fitted with a paddle. Turn the motor down to medium speed and add in the eggs one at a time, beating well to incorporate after each addition.

~ **THIRD,** sift the flour, baking powder and salt into a separate bowl. Add in ¾ cup of the cornmeal and whisk thoroughly to combine.

~ **FOURTH,** beat together half of the flour mixture with the milk in a separate bowl; then blend at low speed into the shortening mixture.

~ **FIFTH,** scrape down the sides of the bowl with a rubber spatula and gently fold in the remaining flour mixture. *(Note:* Do not overmix, or the muffins will be tough.) Then fold in the remaining ¾ cup cornmeal.

~ **SIXTH,** fill the muffin cups ¾ full. Bake until the tops are golden and beginning to crack, 15 to 18 minutes. Cool the muffins in their tin for 5 minutes, then turn out onto a cooling rack.

HONEY-HAZELNUT ACORN SQUASH
8 SERVINGS

Baked squash is one of the many dishes the American Indians introduced to European settlers. In turn, Europeans introduced honey to America. I love the nutty aroma that is brought out when squash is roasted. It is even more wonderful with the addition of hazelnuts, brown sugar, honey and nutmeg.

BAKED SQUASH

2 medium acorn squash
1 tablespoon vegetable oil
½ cup hazelnuts
½ cup (1 stick) butter
¼ cup packed brown sugar
¼ cup honey
Pinch of allspice

~ Preheat the oven to 350°F.

PREPARE THE SQUASH:

~ **FIRST,** use a sharp knife to cut each of the squash into quarters. Remove the seeds and thoroughly clean out any membrane. Rub each of the quarters with a little vegetable oil.

~ **SECOND,** place the squash quarters, cut side down, in an oven proof baking dish. Bake until the squash are tender when a knife is inserted, about 30 minutes.

~ **THIRD,** coarsely chop the hazelnuts in a food processor fitted with a steel blade. Add the butter and brown sugar and pulse to blend.

~ **FOURTH,** when the squash are tender, carefully turn over so the rind sides are down, then spoon an equal amount of the hazelnut butter into the centers. Turn the oven up to 400°F. Drizzle the squash with the honey and dust with a pinch of allspice, then bake for an additional 15 minutes.

GARDEN PEA AND CABBAGE SALAD
8 SERVINGS

I doubt there is a better way to enjoy the sweet flavor of peas than when they are complemented by cabbage, green onions and sour cream dressing.

PEA AND CABBAGE SALAD

2 cups fresh blanched peas or frozen peas, thawed
4 cups shredded green or Savoy cabbage
½ cup diced celery
¼ cup chopped scallions
½ teaspoon salt

DRESSING

1 cup sour cream
½ cup mayonnaise
2 teaspoons Dijon mustard
1 teaspoon white wine or cider vinegar

MAKE THE SALAD:

~ **FIRST,** combine the peas, cabbage, celery and scallions in a decorative salad bowl. Sprinkle the salt over the vegetables and toss together well.

~ **SECOND,** use a stiff wire whisk to blend the sour cream with the mayonnaise, mustard and vinegar in a stainless mixing bowl. Just before serving, use a rubber spatula to gently fold the dressing into the vegetables.

FARMHOUSE RHUBARB LATTICE PIE

8 SERVINGS

Rhubarb arrives in early spring and in cooler climates lasts throughout the summer growing season and into early fall. People often enjoy rhubarb combined with either strawberries during the summer or apples in autumn. Both options are wonderful; you can substitute an equal quantity of sliced strawberries or apples for 1 to 2 cups of the rhubarb and reduce the sugar just a bit. I think you'll agree, though, that this homey pie is just fine as it is!

PIE CRUST

2¼ cups all-purpose flour
1 teaspoon salt
¾ cup shortening
6 to 7 tablespoons cold water

MAKE THE PIE CRUST:

~ **FIRST,** whisk the flour and salt together in a mixing bowl. Cut in the shortening with a pastry cutter until the mixture reaches the consistency of coarse crumbly meal.

~ **SECOND,** turn the mixture out onto a clean dry surface and knead in just enough of the cold water for the dough to come together in a pliable, tender ball. Divide the dough into two equal portions and roll into balls. Flatten each ball into a disk by gently pressing it between your hands. Wrap each disk in plastic wrap and chill for at least 30 minutes and up to 1 week.

RHUBARB FILLING

5 cups sliced rhubarb (about 6 medium stalks)
6 rounded tablespoons all-purpose flour
1½ cups granulated sugar
⅛ teaspoon salt

MAKE THE FILLING:

~ Trim away any dry or woody ends from the rhubarb stalks and slice enough of the rhubarb into ¾-inch-thick slices to yield 5 cups. Place the rhubarb slices into a stainless mixing bowl and toss together with the flour, sugar and salt. Allow the mixture to stand at room temperature for 20 to 25 minutes.

STREUSEL TOPPING

2 tablespoons unsalted butter
1 tablespoon all-purpose flour
¼ cup packed brown sugar

MAKE THE STREUSEL TOPPING:

~ Cut the butter, flour and sugar together with a pastry cutter until the mixture is the consistency of coarse crumbly meal. Set aside.

ASSEMBLE THE PIE:

~ FIRST, when the pie dough has chilled for at least 30 minutes, roll out the bottom crust on a clean, lightly floured surface to a circumference of 10 inches and a thickness of ¼ inch. Line the inside of a 10-inch pie plate with this crust. Shape the second piece of dough into a square. Roll it out in a 12-inch square and cut into 18 ¾-inch-wide strips.

~ SECOND, preheat the oven to 400°F. Toss the rhubarb mixture together again, so that the juices from the fruit are fully combined with the sugar and flour. Spoon the filling into the crust and sprinkle the streusel over the top. Lay the strips of dough alternately 1 inch apart, beginning in the middle of the pie circle. Fold back the strips as you weave them over and under to create a lattice pattern. Trim and crimp the crust edges.

~ THIRD, sprinkle the top of the crust with a little sugar and bake until the crust is golden and the filling is bubbling through the lattice top, 45 to 50 minutes.

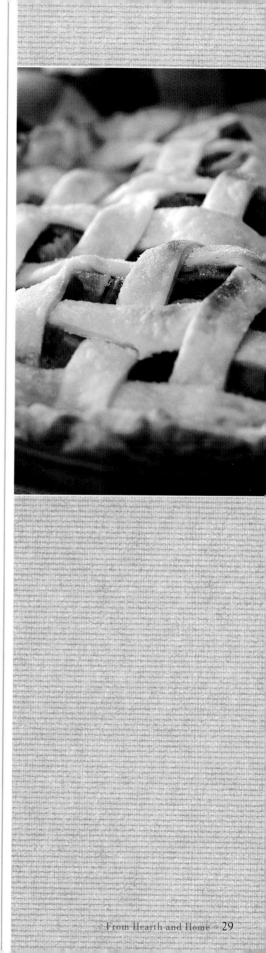

Savoring Simplicity

> SAVORY CHICKEN AND DUMPLINGS
> SWEET CORN AND LIMA BEAN SUCCOTASH
> ICED GREEN ONIONS AND RADISHES
>   *with* CELERY SEED DRESSING
> BUTTERMILK-DILL DINNER ROLLS
> COCONUT DREAM CHIFFON CAKE

Often it is the simple things in life we savor most: a quiet walk, a beautiful sunset, a good book by a crackling fire, a gentle summer rain. The memory of one special dish, understated, completely sublime, and unpretentious in its making and presentation, is another. Sunday dinner can evoke those same feelings. And chicken and dumplings must certainly be among the simplest and most savory of Sunday dinners.

Chicken and dumplings can be found in almost every style of regional American cookery: from the heart of the South to the heart of New Jersey; from the Louisiana Bayou to the Texas panhandle; across the Ozarks and the high Western plains; around Memphis and Chicago; from the great northern lakes to the great Northwest woods. Wherever Americans gather to say grace, the homey appeal of this simple stew makes it a Sunday dinner favorite. Indeed, it would be difficult to find a nineteenth- or early-twentieth-century family cookbook in which chicken and dumplings did not appear.

The exact origin of chicken and dumplings is uncertain. Stewed poultry, or fricassee, as well as light and melting dumplings are hallmarks of central European cookery such as that found in the Czech Republic, Hungary, Poland, and Ukrainia. The word *dumpling* itself, probably a variation of *lump,* is English. And African Americans, especially those whose ancestry is rooted in the Ivory Coast and Congo, where the family pot simmered all day, may well have contributed this classic to Southern cuisine. Then there were the Swiss, the Germans, and the Irish—almost everyone, it seems, brought some variation of chicken and dumplings to the American Sunday table.

Each family recipe, in fact, is unique. In most recipes the broth is thickened with just flour or cornstarch, but other recipes call for egg yolks and cream, which is a rich and wonderful variation. Dumplings can be made with broth, milk, or buttermilk, bound with eggs, lightened with baking powder, and "cut in" with chicken fat, butter, or shortening. They can be rolled and cut like wide noodles, dropped like biscuits, pinched from soft dough, shaped into little ovals, or cut into thick squares called slick dumplings. They can be cooked separately after the chicken has been removed from the broth, steamed on top of the chicken, or baked atop the stew like a cobbler crust. When finished, the dish can be served like a casserole, spooned over rice, or presented in bowls with fat juicy pieces of chicken sitting beneath the savory dumplings and sauce.

So which of these is the authentic, all-American chicken and dumplings? All of them! No wonder this has been a Sunday dinner favorite throughout the country!

Savory Chicken and Dumplings

Serves 8

Chicken:
2 large onions, thinly sliced
2 cups peeled and finely sliced
1 carrot, thinly sliced
1 rib celery with leaves, thinly sliced
1 small onion, quartered
thyme
sage

[...] onion, thyme and sage; bring
reduce heat to low; cover
and simmer until the c[...]
About 1 hour.

Dumplings:
2 cups all-purpose flour
1 tablespoon baking po[...]
1/2 teaspoon white pep[...]
1/2 teaspoon dry mi[...]
1 teaspoon salt
2 large eggs, well [...]

SAVORY CHICKEN AND DUMPLINGS
8 SERVINGS

On the nineteenth-century farm, chickens were kept for laying eggs; when they became too old and were too tough for frying or baking, they went into the pot for a soup or stew. While stewing a chicken may no longer be necessary to create a tender dish, the rich flavor of a slowly stewed bird is hard to beat. I prefer using only thighs for this dish. The key to light, wonderful dumplings is a tight-fitting lid for the pot. Drop the dumplings in the pot and then cover until they are done. Resist the temptation to have a look inside while they're cooking—it's a test of faith!

CHICKEN

8 large chicken thighs
2 cups chicken broth
1 carrot, peeled and thinly sliced
2 ribs celery with leaves, thinly sliced
1 small onion, quartered
1 sprig of thyme
Pinch of rubbed sage

STEW THE CHICKEN:

Thoroughly rinse the chicken thighs under cold running water; then pat dry. Place the chicken in a single layer, skin side up, in the bottom of a large casserole or Dutch oven. Pour in the chicken broth, as well as enough cold water to just cover the chicken, about 4 cups. Add in the carrot, celery, onion, thyme and sage; bring to a boil, reduce the heat to low, cover the casserole and simmer until the chicken is tender and nearly falling from the bones, about 1 hour.

DUMPLINGS

2 cups all-purpose flour
1 tablespoon baking powder
½ teaspoon dry rubbed sage
1 teaspoon salt
½ teaspoon white pepper
2 large eggs, room temperature
2 tablespoons rendered chicken fat or shortening
⅔ cup whole milk
6 cups cooking liquid from the chicken
plus additional chicken broth, if needed

MAKE THE DUMPLINGS:

FIRST, whisk together the flour, baking powder, sage, salt and white pepper in a mixing bowl.

~ **SECOND,** combine the eggs with the chicken fat or shortening in a separate bowl; whisk together until the shortening is broken into little bits and has partially blended with the eggs. Whisk in the milk, leaving the little bits of shortening floating on the surface.

~ **THIRD,** use a fork to blend the dry ingredients into the egg mixture, ½ cup at a time. Once the mixture is too stiff to blend with the fork, knead with the tips of your fingers just enough to incorporate the remaining flour. The dough will be fairly light, moist and sticky. Wrap the dough in plastic and refrigerate for at least 30 minutes and up to 4 hours.

ASSEMBLE THE CHICKEN AND DUMPLINGS:

~ **FIRST,** dust the dough with a little flour, divide into 2 pieces and roll each piece on a lightly floured work surface into a 2-inch-round log; use a sharp knife to slice each log into 8 biscuit-size pieces.

~ **SECOND,** remove the tender chicken thighs from the broth with a slotted spoon, transfer to a warm serving platter and tent with foil to keep warm. Strain the broth through a fine sieve and add in enough extra chicken broth to measure 6 cups. Return to high heat until the broth begins to bubble vigorously; then place the dumplings directly into the stock. Gently lift the dumplings with a fork to make sure they do not stick to the bottom. Reduce the heat to medium-low, cover with a tight-fitting lid and cook undisturbed for 12 to 15 minutes. The dumplings will soak up a little more than half the liquid and double in size as they cook.

GRAVY

3 cups cooking liquid from the chicken
plus additional chicken broth, if needed
1 chicken bouillon cube
¼ cup all-purpose flour
1 cup half-and-half
Salt and white pepper to taste

MAKE THE GRAVY:

~ **FIRST,** transfer the dumplings to the warm serving platter alongside the chicken. Strain the liquid and add in enough chicken broth to measure 3 cups. Return the liquid to the pot and increase the heat to medium. Add the bouillon cube to the simmering broth.

~ **SECOND,** whisk together the flour and half-and-half in a small bowl until completely smooth, then slowly add to the simmering broth, stirring constantly; continue stirring until the gravy thickens, about 3 minutes. Adjust the seasoning to taste with salt and white pepper. Pour over the chicken and dumplings and serve immediately, passing any extra gravy in a gravy boat.

SWEET CORN AND LIMA BEAN SUCCOTASH
8 SERVINGS

Succotash is a dish of American Indian origin that became a favorite in early colonial cookery. It was originally served as a main dish—corn and lima beans cooked with wild game. Puritans had no taste for game, which in England was reserved for royalty, so they began using salt pork and chicken. In the South and eventually the Midwest, succotash became a vegetable dish like this one. Its variations are still passionately debated in New England, where an annual Succotash Festival is held.

SUCCOTASH

¼ cup (½ stick) butter
½ cup thinly sliced onion
2 cups fresh blanched lima beans or frozen lima beans, thawed
2 cups fresh steamed corn or frozen corn, thawed
1 teaspoon granulated sugar
1 cup half-and-half
Salt and white pepper to taste

MAKE THE SUCCOTASH:

FIRST, melt the butter in a large skillet over medium heat. Add in the sliced onion and sauté until translucent, 2 to 3 minutes; add in the lima beans and the corn. Sauté for 2 more minutes, being careful not to let the butter brown. Season with the sugar.

SECOND, pour in the half-and-half and bring to a simmer; cook until the vegetables have absorbed most of the liquid, the dish is slightly thickened and the vegetables are tender, about 10 minutes. Season to taste with salt and white pepper.

My great-grandmother, Caroline Yoder, owned a farm in northern Indiana, in the heart of Amish/Mennonite country and right in the middle of some of the most fertile farmland in America. She was Old Order Mennonite and as a child had emigrated with her parents from Germany. My deceased great-grandfather, Jacob Yoder, was Amish.

Because of my parents' troubled marriage, I lived nearby with my grandparents. Every Sunday after church the three of us would make the short drive to my great-grandmother's farm, arriving with the rest of the extended family. My grandfather was one of nine children, which meant a lot of people for Sunday dinner!

My heart would pound with excitement when we turned the last corner of the country dirt roads and the farmhouse came into view. I knew that my Mennonite cousins, with their thick yellow braids and starched white caps, would be waiting for me, eager to explore the meadows and fields. We particularly loved to slide down the bales of hay that were piled high in the barn.

In the summertime, long tables would be set up on the lawn and covered with delicious dishes, many of them prepared with homegrown meat, fruits, and vegetables. And oh, the glorious desserts—all kinds of fruit pies, assorted cakes, and gooey baked goods. My favorite dessert was big-pearl tapioca pudding with fluffy meringue topping. Would Aunt Edna remember to prepare it? I always headed straight for it as soon as I spotted it—after grace was said, of course!

I was lonely—the only child of soon-to-be-divorced parents, desperately needing a place to belong. My memories of those Sunday afternoons, spent with simple people who expressed their faith and hospitality through food, have nourished me all my life. The fellowship of their table clearly said to me: "Welcome, my child...you are home."

SANDRA YODER SMALLMAN

ICED GREEN ONIONS AND RADISHES WITH CELERY SEED DRESSING

8 SERVINGS

The relish tray was once a standard addition to the American table, even in formal circles at the finest white-tablecloth restaurants—I miss that. I think it's time that custom made a comeback. You may want to include the carrots, celery sticks and sweet pickles, but the crisp, spicy crunch of radishes and green onions alone are a wonderful contrast to this simple menu.

RELISH TRAY

2 bunches green onions
2 bunches radishes
Baby carrots
Celery sticks
Sweet pickles

PREPARE THE VEGETABLES:

~ Snip the root ends from the green onions and trim any wilted green tops. Trim the root ends from the radishes and trim the green tops. Place all the raw vegetables (including baby carrots and celery sticks) in a bowl of ice water for 1 hour before dinner so they will be icy cold and crunchy.

DRESSING

½ cup minced sweet onion
¼ cup granulated sugar
¼ cup cider vinegar
½ teaspoon celery seeds
1 teaspoon dry mustard
¼ teaspoon salt
⅓ cup vegetable oil

MAKE THE DRESSING:

~ Combine the onion, sugar and vinegar in a saucepan. Stir over medium-high heat until the sugar is dissolved and the onion is soft, about 2 minutes. Whisk in the celery seeds, mustard and salt. Purée the mixture in a blender; slowly pour in the oil and continue to purée until the dressing is smooth. Pour into a small, decorative serving bowl, cover with plastic wrap and chill until ready to serve.

SERVE THE RELISH TRAY:

~ Drain the ice water from the raw vegetables and shake off any excess water. Arrange the vegetables on a decorative platter with an accompanying smaller dish of dressing and a small ladle, so that each person can spoon the dressing over their selection. (*Note:* It's nice to have 2 or more relish trays within easy reach on each end of the table, to avoid passing all the way to the other end.)

BUTTERMILK-DILL DINNER ROLLS
20 ROLLS

Fresh rolls are always a treat, especially for Sunday dinner. These simple pull-apart rolls, with their tang of buttermilk and dill, will become a family favorite. Their soft texture is also perfect for sopping up all the savory chicken and dumpling gravy!

DINNER ROLLS

1 package (2¼ teaspoons) active dry yeast
¼ cup whole milk, warm (about 110°F)
1 cup buttermilk
⅓ cup granulated sugar
⅓ cup shortening
2 large eggs, room temperature, lightly beaten
3½ cups all-purpose flour
2 teaspoons salt
1 tablespoon fresh chopped dill

MAKE THE ROLLS:

- **FIRST,** sprinkle the yeast over the warm milk and let stand for 1 minute; then stir until the yeast is dissolved.

- **SECOND,** scald the buttermilk with the sugar in a small saucepan or in a glass dish in the microwave until it just begins to boil. Remove the pan from heat and swirl in the shortening until it melts. Cool to lukewarm.

- **THIRD,** combine the dissolved yeast with the lukewarm buttermilk in a mixing bowl. Whisk in the beaten eggs, then add in 2½ cups of the flour and stir with a wooden spoon until the mixture reaches the consistency of a thick batter. Continue stirring for about 120 strokes. Scrape down the sides of the bowl with a rubber spatula. Cover with a clean tea towel and set in a draft-free place until it is bubbly and has doubled in volume, about 1 hour.

- **FOURTH,** combine the remaining 1 cup of flour with the salt and dill. Use an electric mixer fitted with a dough hook to slowly add the flour to the bubbly dough. Beat on low speed until a soft dough forms and pulls away from the edges of the bowl, adding in extra flour if needed. Continue to knead the dough on low speed for about 5 minutes. Cover the bowl with plastic wrap and refrigerate for at least 30 minutes and up to 4 hours.

- **FIFTH,** divide the dough into 20 equal pieces and roll the pieces into balls. Place the balls about ¾-inch apart in a lightly greased 9x13-inch baking pan. Cover with a clean tea towel and set in a draft-free place; let the rolls rise until they have doubled in size, about 1 hour. Bake at 350°F for 20 to 25 minutes. Brush the tops with melted butter.

Easy time-saving
AND DO-AHEAD TIPS:

SATURDAY
Bake and frost the chiffon cake. Prepare the celery seed dressing and refrigerate. Prepare the vegetables for the relish tray and refrigerate in well-sealed containers.

SUNDAY MORNING
Prepare the buttermilk roll dough and the dumpling dough; refrigerate.

COCONUT DREAM CHIFFON CAKE
12 SERVINGS

Chiffon cakes are light, moist, and laden with fresh butter and eggs. Certainly they are a treat from the past. New desserts may come and go, but we keep returning to savor the simple, elegant creations that we fondly remember and always enjoy. The ice cream man in my neighborhood sold some wonderful treats. One of my favorites was orange sherbet with a coconut ice cream center covered with flaked coconut. Surely it is the inspiration for this American classic.

CAKE

2¼ cups cake flour
1 tablespoon baking powder
½ teaspoon salt
8 large egg yolks, room temperature (reserve whites)
¾ cup superfine sugar
6 tablespoons vegetable oil
1 tablespoon orange zest
6 large egg whites, room temperature
½ teaspoon cream of tartar
⅔ cup superfine sugar
¾ cup freshly squeezed orange juice
1 teaspoon pure coconut extract

MAKE THE CAKE:

~ **FIRST,** sift the cake flour, baking powder and salt into a mixing bowl.

~ **SECOND,** beat the egg yolks at medium speed until they are light and lemon colored, 2 to 3 minutes. Gradually add in ¾ cup superfine sugar and beat until thick and pale yellow, 3 to 4 minutes. Turn the mixer speed down to low and pour in the vegetable oil in a slow steady stream until fully emulsified. Then fold in the orange zest.

~ **THIRD,** combine 6 egg whites with the cream of tartar in a separate bowl; using clean dry beaters, mix at medium-high until soft peaks begin to form. Then gradually add in ⅔ cup superfine sugar. Increase the mixer speed to high and continue beating until firm peaks form, 3 to 4 minutes.

~ **FOURTH,** blend the flour mixture into the egg yolk mixture in 3 batches alternately with the orange juice. Fold in the coconut extract and scrape down the sides of the bowl. Use a rubber spatula to gently fold in half of the beaten egg whites; when they are fully incorporated into the batter, gently fold in the remaining whites.

~ **FIFTH,** pour the batter into an ungreased 10-inch tube or angel food cake pan and bake in the middle of a 325°F oven for 60 to 70 minutes. When the cake is done it will spring back when the top is gently pressed. Invert the pan onto a cooling rack. When the cake is cool, carefully run a thin knife around the edges of the pan and center tube to loosen. Gently push the cake from the bottom to remove it from the pan and then carefully remove the bottom, again by running a sharp thin knife around the edges.

FROSTING

2 large egg whites, room temperature
1¼ cups granulated sugar
2 tablespoons light corn syrup
⅛ teaspoon cream of tartar
¼ cup freshly squeezed orange juice
1 teaspoon orange zest
1 teaspoon pure coconut extract
1 cup flaked sweetened coconut

PREPARE THE FROSTING:

~ **FIRST,** combine 2 egg whites with the sugar, corn syrup, cream of tartar, orange juice and orange zest in a stainless mixing bowl or in the top of a double boiler. Dissolve the sugar by beating for about 1 minute with a handheld electric mixer running on high speed.

~ **SECOND,** place over a pan of rapidly boiling water and continue to beat until soft peaks form, 5 to 8 minutes.

~ **THIRD,** remove the bowl from the boiling water. Add in the coconut extract and continue beating until the frosting reaches spreading consistency, 2 to 3 minutes.

~ **FOURTH,** frost the top, center and sides of the cooled cake, creating soft peaks with the tip of an icing spatula or butter knife. Sprinkle with the flaked sweetened coconut.

A Quiet Sunday with Friends

> SLOW-COOKED BEEF BRISKET
> *with* MUSHROOMS, RED BEETS AND PEARL ONIONS
> PENNSYLVANIA DUTCH EGG SPAETZLE
> AMISH POTATO ROLLS
> BUTTERED BRUSSELS SPROUTS WITH PARSLEY AND CHIVES
> BAKED APPLES WITH WALNUTS AND CREAM

For a beautiful look at the simple life, why not try a quiet Sunday ride through Lancaster County in southeast Pennsylvania? Life here moves at a slower pace than you might be accustomed to. The clip-clop of horses' hooves echoes along the country roads, across covered wooden bridges spanning quiet streams, and past rolling green hills and tidy farms, where windmills turn faithfully in the gentle breeze. The buggies are horse drawn, mule teams plow the fields, and the dress is simple for those who call themselves the "plain people." These are the Amish and Mennonites who first came to this area centuries ago to take advantage of William Penn's "holy experiment."

Penn, an English Quaker, established Pennsylvania in 1682, when he received the lands from the English crown in payment for a debt. Imprisoned numerous times for his religious beliefs, Penn determined to use his newly acquired property to create something new: a society built on pacifism, equality for all peoples, and religious tolerance. He and his Quaker followers, who called themselves Friends, named their capital Philadelphia, meaning "city of brotherly love," and established a charter offering an almost unprecedented freedom of belief.

This religious freedom quickly attracted a variety of persecuted religious groups from all over Europe but especially Germany and Switzerland. The German-speaking settlers became known as the Pennsylvania Dutch—a misunderstanding of *Deutsch*, their word for *German*—and included colonies of Amish and Mennonites, whose beliefs stressed simple or "plain" living. Unadorned clothing, avoidance of modern conveniences, strict pacifism, and a close community life characterized these settlements. Like the Quakers, they conducted worship services in homes or in simple meeting houses—a gathering of friends, followed by a Sabbath Day dinner—traditions that continue to the present day.

We, too, humbly gather in churches around the country to worship freely, grateful for those who walked the road before us. We, too, call ourselves friends. What better way to extend that friendship than by breaking bread around a common table in mutual celebration of the Lord's bounty?

Bounty is indeed the word to describe the culinary riches the Commonwealth of Pennsylvania offers. In cities and small towns and at rural crossroads, farmer's markets offer crisp, tart, juicy apples, dairy-rich cream and butter, fresh-from-the-garden vegetables, and mushrooms in abundance. (Pennsylvania is the world's largest mushroom producer.) Cooking styles such as slow-cooked meats simmered in a traditional black vinegar sauce, rich egg noodles or dumpling-like spaetzle, and delicious fruit-based desserts still reflect the old-world traditions of the people who settled here.

From the simple abundance and rich history of this peaceful region comes a hearty and satisfying menu overflowing with abundant old-world flavor. This is a meal that bids us to the Sunday table for a quiet peaceful dinner with friends.

Easy time saving
AND DO-AHEAD TIPS:

SATURDAY

Peel the onions and beets and refrigerate them in well-sealed containers. Prepare the spaetzle, cool in cold water, drain and refrigerate in a well-sealed container. Cook and mash the potatoes for the rolls, and reserve ½ cup of potato water; refrigerate the mashed potatoes and reserved potato water.

SUNDAY MORNING

Prepare the potato roll dough; refrigerate before shaping into rolls. Wash and cut the mushrooms and refrigerate in a well-sealed container. Braise the roast and bring it to a slow simmer. Prepare the apples for cooking and refrigerate.

SLOW-COOKED BEEF BRISKET WITH MUSHROOMS, RED BEETS AND PEARL ONIONS

8 SERVINGS

Braised brisket is slow-cooked, just like any great pot roast. I prefer to use a nice variety of mushrooms as an accompaniment—especially meaty portabello and shiitake mushrooms. For the dark vinegar I use balsamic, which is readily available throughout the country. The inclusion of red beets and onions creates a dark-hued gravy with a remarkably earthy flavor.

BEEF BRISKET

1 4- to 5-pound beef brisket, excess fat trimmed, about 2 inches thick
Salt and pepper
Vegetable oil to season the pan
½ cup balsamic vinegar
2 cups beef broth
½ cup dark raisins
2 sprigs fresh thyme
16 ounces (1 dry pint) red pearl onions
4 large red beets
2 pounds assorted mushrooms
Pinch of salt

MAKE THE BRISKET:

FIRST, season the meat by rubbing it with salt and pepper.

SECOND, pour in just enough oil to coat the bottom of a Dutch oven or heavy casserole fitted with a lid. Heat the oil over medium-high heat until it just begins to smoke. Reduce the heat slightly and brown the meat on all sides, beginning with the leanest side, turning it every minute or so for about 10 minutes.

THIRD, when the meat is browned on all sides, place it in the center of the pan with the fat side up, then pour in the vinegar. Fit the lid onto the pan and simmer for 5 minutes, then reduce the temperature of the burner to low. Pour in the beef broth and enough water to cover the roast a little less than halfway, and add in the raisins and the thyme sprigs. Then replace the lid and allow the roast to simmer slowly over low heat on the stovetop or in a 300°F oven for about 2 hours.

PREPARE THE VEGETABLES:

~ FIRST, put the onions in a medium bowl and cover them with boiling water (this will make them easy to peel). Steep for 5 minutes, then drain well; trim off the root ends with a paring knife and peel away the skin, leaving the onions whole. Peel the beets, leaving about an inch of the tops, if desired; cut the beets into quarters. Clean the mushrooms under cool running water to remove any soil, then remove and discard any woody stems. Cut the mushrooms into halves, quarters or thick slices.

~ SECOND, when the roast has simmered for about 2 hours, place it over medium heat. Add the beets to the liquid surrounding the roast and simmer for 15 minutes. Add in a little more water, if needed; then add in the onions and the mushrooms so they cover both the roast and the beets. Season them with a pinch of salt. Replace the lid and return the casserole dish to the oven or place over low heat on the stovetop and cook for 45 minutes.

~ THIRD, when the brisket is done cooking, the meat should be tender, just falling away from the fat, but still firm enough to slice easily. Transfer the roast to a clean cutting board and allow it to rest for 15 minutes. Use a slotted spoon to transfer the beets, mushrooms, onions and raisins from the Dutch oven to a bowl. Remove and discard thyme sprigs. Return the Dutch oven to low heat on the stovetop.

GRAVY
3 tablespoons all-purpose flour
¼ cup water
Salt and pepper to taste

MAKE THE GRAVY:

~ In a small bowl blend the 3 tablespoons of flour with ¼ cup of water and use a stiff wire whisk to form a smooth paste. Turn the burner heat to medium-high. When the liquid remaining in the Dutch oven begins to simmer, add in about half of the paste as you whisk constantly. Add more paste, a little at a time, until the gravy has thickened. Turn the heat to low and allow the gravy to simmer for 5 minutes, then season to taste with salt and pepper.

PRESENT THE BRISKIT:

~ Place the brisket on a platter and artfully arrange the beets, mushrooms and onions around it; lace the platter with some of the gravy. Pass the extra gravy separately in a gravy boat.

PENNSYLVANIA DUTCH
EGG SPAETZLE
8 SERVINGS

Spaetzle are little dumplings made from fresh egg pasta, and they are traditionally served with pot roast, brisket or short ribs. They are easy to prepare and quite delicious. The trick is to make the batter an hour ahead and have ready a pot of boiling water that is large enough to keep the little bits of batter from sticking to one another as they cook.

EGG SPAETZLE

4 large eggs, room temperature, lightly beaten
2 cups whole milk
Pinch of nutmeg
1 teaspoon salt
Pinch of ground pepper
4 cups all-purpose flour
½ cup (1 stick) butter

MAKE THE SPAETZLE:

~ **FIRST,** beat the eggs into the milk using a stiff wire whisk, then add in the nutmeg, salt and pepper; use a wooden spoon to mix in the flour, 1 cup at a time, beating well after each addition until the mixture is smooth and elastic; *or* combine the first 6 ingredients in a food processor fitted with a steel blade and pulse for 30 seconds. The mixture should now be the consistency of thick, slightly elastic pancake batter. Let the spaetzle batter stand at room temperature for 1 hour.

~ **MEANWHILE,** bring a large pot of cool salted water to a boil.

~ **SECOND,** suspend a large-holed colander or spaetzle sieve about 6 inches over the top of the boiling water. Try a test batch by first putting a couple of tablespoons of the spaetzle batter through the colander into the boiling water—if it runs quickly through the colander, add a little flour, a tablespoon at a time, to thicken the batter; if you have to press down hard to push the batter through the holes, add a little milk.

~ **THIRD,** working in 4 separate batches, pour the dough into the colander, pressing it through the holes with a rubber spatula (the droplets will form little "dumplings"). When the first little dumplings begin to float, stir the water gently to keep them from sticking together. Cook the spaetzle until tender, 4 to 5 minutes.

~ **FOURTH,** carefully remove the spaetzle from the boiling water using a large slotted spoon or small strainer; submerge immediately in a bowl of cold water. When all of the spaetzle have cooled, drain thoroughly and transfer to a glass or stainless bowl. The spaetzle can be prepared a day ahead up to this point—toss them in a little vegetable oil, cover tightly with plastic wrap and refrigerate.

~ **FIFTH,** transfer the spaetzle to a colander and run under hot water for a minute, then shake off the excess water. Heat a nonstick skillet over medium-high heat. Cut the butter into pats and quickly add them to the hot skillet so that they melt all at once. Add the cooked spaetzle to the melted butter and toss continually with a wooden spoon to keep them from sticking to the bottom of the skillet; sauté for 1 minute so that the spaetzle can absorb the butter. Serve immediately.

AMISH POTATO ROLLS

2 DOZEN ROLLS

Potato breads are soft and densely textured (and a great way to use up leftover mashed potatoes). The ever-efficient Germans often used potato water to make natural yeast starters for bread. Incidentally, a variation of these rolls can be found accompanying another German-influenced American dish—the hamburger.

POTATO ROLLS

2 medium potatoes, scrubbed and peeled
½ cup reserved warm potato water (about 110°F)
2 tablespoons granulated sugar
1 package (2¼ teaspoons) active dry yeast
¼ cup (½ stick) unsalted butter
⅔ cup whole milk
1 teaspoon salt
1 large egg, room temperature, lightly beaten
4½ cups all-purpose flour, sifted

MAKE THE POTATO ROLLS:

FIRST, cook the potatoes in boiling salted water until they are tender when pierced with a fork. Drain them completely, reserving ½ cup of the potato water; cool the potato water to lukewarm. Mash the potatoes and measure out 1 cup for making the rolls. Cool the mashed potatoes to room temperature.

SECOND, dissolve the sugar in the lukewarm potato water and sprinkle the yeast over the surface. Let the yeast mixture stand until it becomes foamy, about 5 minutes; then stir to dissolve.

THIRD, combine the butter, milk and salt in a small heavy-bottomed saucepan and heat until the butter is just melted. Remove from heat and use a wooden spoon to mix in the 1 cup of reserved mashed potatoes; add in the lightly beaten egg, then the dissolved yeast.

FOURTH, transfer the dough to the bowl of a mixer fitted with a dough hook. Slowly add in 4 cups of the sifted flour, 1 cup at a time; scrape down the sides of the bowl after each addition. Knead on low speed until the dough is smooth and elastic, 4 to 5 minutes. Then cover the bowl with a clean tea towel and set it in a draft-free place until it has doubled in size, about 1 hour.

FIFTH, punch the dough down. Knead in the remaining ½ cup flour, as needed. The dough should be soft and slightly sticky, but firm enough to just hold its shape. Cover the bowl with a clean tea towel and allow it to rise in a draft-free place for another 30 minutes. (*Note:* At this point you can refrigerate the dough for up to 2 hours before shaping the rolls.)

SIXTH, place the dough on a clean cutting board that has been dusted with a little flour and divide into 2 dozen equal pieces. Dust each piece with a little more flour and roll into a ball.

SEVENTH, place the balls about 1 inch apart on a well-greased baking sheet. Cover the pan with a clean tea towel and let the rolls rise for another 15 to 20 minutes (or for about 40 minutes if the dough was refrigerated). Use a pastry brush to lightly brush the tops of the rolls with a little milk, then bake them in a 400°F oven for 10 to 12 minutes.

BUTTERED BRUSSELS SPROUTS
WITH PARSLEY AND CHIVES
8 SERVINGS

Tender baby brussels sprouts are the best choice when available, so look for nice small ones that are bright green. Their wonderful flavor is enhanced by sweet creamery butter, fresh parsley and zesty chives.

SPROUTS

2 pounds brussels sprouts, trimmed and halved
6 tablespoons (¾ stick) butter
Salt to taste
1 tablespoon fresh snipped chives
½ tablespoon fresh chopped parsley

MAKE THE BRUSSELS SPROUTS:

~ **FIRST,** bring a large pot of salted water to a full boil. Drop the brussels sprouts into the water and cook them until they are bright green and tender, about 8 minutes. Drain the brussels sprouts thoroughly.

~ **SECOND,** melt the butter in a small skillet over low heat; when the butter begins to bubble, add in the brussels sprouts and season to taste with salt. Cover the skillet with a tight-fitting lid and steam the sprouts in the butter for 3 to 4 minutes. Just before serving, toss in the chives and parsley.

There is no better

time or place

to build friendships

than around the joy-filled,

warm, and inviting table

we set for friends

on Sunday.

RC

BAKED APPLES WITH WALNUTS AND CREAM
8 SERVINGS

This is one of my very favorite childhood desserts—simply wonderful. It is best to use a crisp, sweet-tart variety of apple, such as the Cox Pippin, McIntosh, Winesap or Jonathan (Granny Smith are generally too tart). Combined with fresh cream, the cinnamon-apple syrup imbues the flavor of warm caramel.

BAKED APPLES

8 medium sweet-tart apples
1 cup chopped walnuts
1 cup packed dark brown sugar
½ teaspoon allspice
1 teaspoon cinnamon
½ cup (1 stick) unsalted butter
⅔ cup apple cider, room temperature
1 quart heavy cream

~ Preheat the oven to 350°F.

MAKE THE BAKED APPLES:

~ **FIRST,** wash, dry and core the apples.

~ **SECOND,** combine the chopped walnuts, brown sugar, allspice and cinnamon in a small bowl. Fill the center of each apple with an equal amount of this mixture and place it into a deep baking pan. The pan should be large enough to ensure that the apples do not touch one another.

~ **THIRD,** dot the top of each apple with 1 tablespoon of butter, pour the apple cider into the pan and sprinkle any remaining filling over the top of the apples. Bake them for 45 to 50 minutes. The apples are done when the skin is just beginning to split around the top and they are easily pierced with a fork.

~ **FOURTH,** remove the apples from the oven and baste them with the natural syrup. Just before serving, use a large spoon to transfer each apple to a wide serving bowl. Pour some of the remaining syrup from the bottom of the pan and ½ cup heavy cream over each apple. Serve immediately.

I know the look of

an apple that is

roasting and sizzling

on the hearth

on a winter's evening,

and I know the comfort

that comes of eating it hot,

along with some sugar

and a drench of cream…

I know how the nuts

taken in conjunction with

winter apples,

cider and dougnuts,

make old people's tales

and old jokes

sound fresh

and crisp

and enchanting!

MARK TWAIN

Sweet Comfort and Soul

BONELESS SMOTHERED PORK CHOPS
BRAISED COUNTRY GREENS
TWICE-BAKED SWEET POTATO CASSEROLE
SUNDAY COMFORT MACARONI AND CHEESE
BANANA BLACK-BOTTOM CREAM PIE

The soul of Sunday dinner is found in the sweet comfort of fellowship. Sunday is a day to rejoice, a day to worship God, a day for folks to gather together after church. For Americans of African heritage, Sunday dinner is a tradition for both family and extended family. Just as church became a place of refuge from oppression and a center for struggle against slavery and social injustice, Sunday became a day for strengthening community ties and faith, as families gathered to praise and worship God.

By the later years of the eighteenth century, a large native-born population of African Americans began to emerge. With that came the desire to establish churches that met the unique needs of slaves and former slaves. In 1787, two freed slaves in Pennsylvania, Richard Allen and Absalom Jones, began a benevolent organization called the Free African Society. In 1794 Reverend Allen, responding to the "unkind treatment" of his fellow blacks in their Methodist Church, founded what would eventually become the African Methodist Episcopal Church. The AME and other African American churches became important centers of community and culture, offering education and hope along with spiritual comfort and release.

The joyous hand clapping and jubilant heart-and-soul celebration that are the hallmarks of the gospel choir have changed our American ways of worship and touched every aspect of American music. The African American influence on our cuisine has been equally profound. Cooking, usually a slave's job, became a creative outlet and an art form, passed from generation to generation. Until the last half of the twentieth century, in fact, most of the nation's finest cooks and chefs were of African descent—from the finest hotels and restaurants in Boston and Chicago to the social world of Philadelphia and Washington, D.C.—including the White House, Senate dining rooms, and Blair House.

"Soul food," a term coined in the 1960s to refer to African American home-style cooking, began as a slave's diet—a mix of African ingredients and cooking styles, indigenous foods and scraps and rations allotted from the plantation. It then became more sophisticated as African cooks moved into plantation kitchens. Corn and sweet potatoes, first introduced to African soil in the sixteenth century by Portuguese traders, returned to our shores along with vegetables such as okra, black-eyed peas, yams, and the exotic fruits found in the Caribbean. Add to that the regional influences of West Indian, Caribbean, and French cooking and you have a cuisine that is the essence of comfort: It is perfect fare for a soul-satisfying Sunday.

BONELESS SMOTHERED PORK CHOPS

8 SERVINGS

These delicious, tender pork chops are first coated with seasoned bread crumbs and a tang of mustard, then lightly fried and finally baked in the oven for a crusty outside and juicy center. The lard adds a wonderful, unmatched flavor—with fewer calories than olive oil!

NOTE: *Be sure to select center-cut pork loin chops that are cut 1 to 1½ inches thick and weigh 6 to 8 ounces each.*

PORK CHOPS

½ cup all-purpose flour
1 teaspoon salt
½ teaspoon pepper
2 large eggs
¼ cup prepared mustard
1 cup fresh bread crumbs
2 tablespoons fresh chopped parsley
8 boneless center-cut pork loin chops
¼ cup lard or vegetable shortening

~ Preheat the oven to 350°F.

MAKE THE PORK CHOPS:

~ **FIRST,** place the flour in a pie dish or on a large plate and season with the salt and pepper. Whisk the eggs into the mustard in a medium shallow bowl. Combine the bread crumbs with the parsley in a second pie dish or on another large plate.

~ **SECOND,** dredge the pork chops in the seasoned flour, shaking off any excess. Dip the chops next into the egg mixture, then coat both sides with the bread crumbs. Transfer the chops to a clean platter as you work.

~ **THIRD,** melt the lard in a large ovenproof skillet over medium-high heat. The lard is hot enough if a pinch of flour sizzles when sprinkled in the pan. Place the breaded chops in the skillet and fry them until golden, turning once, about 2 minutes per side. When the chops are done, transfer the uncovered skillet to the oven. Bake until the chops are crisp on the outside and moist and juicy in the middle, about 20 minutes; then remove the skillet from the oven and transfer the chops to a large serving platter. Tent the platter with foil to keep them warm.

GRAVY

¼ cup diced smoked bacon
2 cups thinly sliced onion
3 tablespoon all-purpose flour
2 tablespoons prepared mustard
2 cups chicken broth
Tabasco sauce
Salt and pepper to taste

MAKE THE GRAVY:

~ **FIRST,** add the bacon to the skillet that the chops were in and cook over medium-high heat just long enough to render the fat, about 2 minutes. Add in the onion slices and continue cooking for 2 to 3 minutes more. As the bacon and onion cook, scrape the bottom of the skillet with a wire whisk to loosen any browned bits that might be sticking to the bottom of the pan.

~ **SECOND,** add in the flour and mustard to the pan and whisk into a paste. Pour in the chicken broth, whisking to blend, then reduce the heat to medium-low and simmer until the gravy thickens, about 4 minutes. Add a dash of Tabasco sauce and season to taste with salt and pepper.

PRESENT THE CHOPS:

~ Pour the gravy over the chops just before serving. If desired, garnish with fresh parsley sprigs.

BRAISED COUNTRY GREENS
8 SERVINGS

Collard greens, mustard greens and turnip greens each have a spicy snap. The secret to cooking greens is to cook them just enough to become tender yet still retain a bit of crunch. It is a good idea to keep the seasonings simple so that the natural flavor of the greens is enhanced, not overwhelmed. I like to season the greens with salted country ham. Although 3 pounds may seem like a lot of greens, they quickly cook down.

GREENS

3 pounds fresh assorted greens
4 ounces country ham or bacon
1 tablespoon cider vinegar
1 cup chopped green onions
Salt, pepper and cayenne to taste

PREPARE THE GREENS:

- **FIRST,** wash the greens thoroughly in several changes of cool running water, removing any wilted or brown leaves. Dry the leaves and wash again, this time leaving the leaves wet—what water remains on the leaves is enough to steam them. Set aside.

- **SECOND,** dice the ham or bacon, including all the bits of fat, and sauté in a heavy-bottomed skillet over medium heat just long enough to render the fat, about 2 minutes. Add the collard greens to the pan first, as they take just a little longer to cook; let them cook down for 2 to 3 minutes, then add in the other greens. Cover the skillet with a tight-fitting lid and wilt the greens over medium heat, tossing from time to time with the ham or bacon, for about 15 minutes.

- **THIRD,** add in the vinegar and the green onions. Cook for 1 minute or so and then taste to test the seasoning. (Remember, country ham is quite salty.) Season to taste with salt, pepper and cayenne; continue to toss over heat until tender, 1 to 2 minutes more. Serve immediately.

TWICE-BAKED SWEET POTATO CASSEROLE
8 SERVINGS

This wonderful side dish is a perfect complement to pork. Baking sweet potatoes gives them a nutty, toasted flavor. And baking them twice, especially if you add in a little brown sugar, vanilla and allspice, makes them even better.

SWEET POTATO CASSEROLE

3 pounds sweet potatoes
½ cup (1 stick) butter, softened
¼ cup heavy cream
2 large eggs
¼ cup packed light brown sugar
1 teaspoon pure vanilla extract
¼ teaspoon allspice
Pinch of mace
Salt and pepper to taste

Preheat the oven to 375°F.

MAKE THE CASSEROLE:

FIRST, scrub the sweet potatoes and prick their skins with a fork. Bake uncovered on a baking sheet until they are soft, about 1 hour. Allow the potatoes to cool, then peel away the skin using a sharp paring knife. Place the peeled potatoes in a mixing bowl and blend until smooth with a potato masher or stiff wire whisk.

SECOND, add the butter, cream, eggs, brown sugar and vanilla to the mashed sweet potatoes and use a stiff wire whisk to whip together thoroughly. Add in the allspice and mace, then season to taste with salt and pepper.

TOPPING

¼ cup (½ stick) unsalted butter
¼ cup packed light brown sugar
¼ cup chopped pecans

ASSEMBLE THE CASSEROLE:

Spoon the sweet potato mixture into a buttered baking dish, dot with pats of butter and sprinkle with the brown sugar and chopped pecans. Bake for 30 to 40 minutes. The sweet potatoes will puff up slightly and the topping will be bubbly and golden when the casserole is done.

SUNDAY COMFORT MACARONI AND CHEESE
8 SERVINGS

Thomas Jefferson is credited with bringing pasta to the American table. Macaroni, which he served to guests at the White House, was a favorite. No doubt it was his slave-born and celebrated chef, James Hemings, who created most of the wonderful dishes for which Monticello was known. After learning French cuisine on his travels with then–French ambassador Jefferson, Hemings became one of the foremost influences in American cookery.

Food, like a loving touch

or a glimpse of divine power,

has the ability to comfort.

NORMAN KOLPAS

MACARONI AND CHEESE

1 pound elbow macaroni
¼ cup (½ stick) butter
4 cups whole milk
16 slices American cheese
2 cups grated cheddar cheese
Tabasco sauce
Salt and pepper to taste

MAKE THE MACARONI AND CHEESE:

FIRST, cook the macaroni in a large pot of boiling salted water until tender but firm (al dente), about 5 to 6 minutes; then drain through a colander. Do not rinse.

SECOND, add the macaroni back into the pot with the butter and stir until the butter melts and coats the macaroni. Pour in the milk and bring the mixture to a boil over medium heat; cook for 2 more minutes. Break the cheese slices into pieces, add in all the pieces at once and stir until the cheese is completely melted. The starch from the pasta will combine with the butter, milk and cheese to form a rich, creamy sauce.

THIRD, stir in the grated cheddar cheese, add a dash of Tabasco and season to taste with salt and pepper. If the cheese sauce is too thick for your liking, add extra milk, a tablespoon at a time, until it reaches the desired conistency. Transfer to a decorative bowl and serve immediately.

It is hard to overstate the importance of eating together for a black family. I grew up in the projects of Richmond, Virginia, without the variety of foods and elegant table settings my family today is so fortunate to enjoy. But my memories of smells, tastes, and conversations are still vivid as I think back to gathering around the Sunday dinner table.

I was blessed to have a wonderful mother who, despite very difficult circumstances, taught us the value of family and the virtue of unconditional love. What we lacked in prestige, we made up for in cohesiveness—a tribute to our mama and the protective loyalty of our family.

Our family was our closest form of government, and our Sunday dinners served as our assembly meetings. Like British parliament sessions, these dinners were not always tranquil and serene. But they were an essential part of our upbringing, serving to discipline and encourage us and to enrich our lives through difficult times.

As one of the younger children, I often did little more than observe at these weekly rituals, venturing to add only a few words to the ongoing banter, debate, or discussion. Later in life I would cherish those childhood memories and yearn to reconstruct that atmosphere and those special times with family and friends.

There is an African saying: "To go back to tradition is the first step forward." So to go forward as a family, my husband, Charles, and I have worked to rediscover some traditions from our families and our community as well as establishing traditions of our own. Some of our favorite traditions include family prayer, red pajamas on Christmas Day, and Saturday morning doughnuts. And then there's Sunday dinner, which often becomes as lively as those dinners when I was growing up. Charles and I wanted to make sure we had the opportunity to explain our ideas, concepts, and values directly to our children. No subject was off-limits, so we heard and explained many things—some of them best left to your imagination.

While our Sunday dinners may not always have looked like a scene from *Ozzie and Harriet,* the lessons and love garnered around the table and in the kitchen have served me all my life. We have melded good manners, great food, and beautiful tableware with the high-spirited debate and high drama of a parliamentary hearing—and we truly love it!

KAY COLES JAMES

This sensational pie is the perfect combination of bananas, dark chocolate, sweet vanilla, rum custard and cream. You'll love the ease of making the Oreo cookie crust, which uses the whole cookie—filling and all! Make this wonderful pie a day ahead so that the flavors can infuse and intensify.

OREO COOKIE CRUST

2½ dozen Oreo cookies
5 tablespoons unsalted butter, melted

~ Preheat the oven to 400°F.

MAKE THE CRUST:

~ Place the cookies (including the cream filling) in the bowl of a food processor fitted with a steel blade; blend just long enough to achieve fine crumbs. Add in the melted butter and pulse until completely combined. Press the mixture into the bottom and up the sides of a 2-inch-deep pie pan. Bake the crust for 10 minutes, then remove from the oven and cool.

FILLING

1 tablespoon rum flavoring	3 cups half-and-half
2 teaspoons pure vanilla extract	4 large egg yolks, room temperature
1 teaspoon unflavored gelatin	¼ cup (½ stick) unsalted butter
6 ounces semisweet or bittersweet chocolate	3 ripe medium bananas
⅔ cup granulated sugar	1 pint heavy cream
3 tablespoons cornstarch	⅓ cup granulated sugar
¼ teaspoon salt	2 ounces semisweet or bittersweet chocolate, grated

PREPARE THE FILLING:

~ **FIRST,** combine the rum flavoring and vanilla in a small bowl. Sprinkle the gelatin over and let the mixture stand for 10 minutes; then whisk together until smooth.

~ **SECOND,** finely chop the 6 ounces of chocolate and transfer to a separate larger bowl.

~ **THIRD,** whisk together ⅔ cup sugar, cornstarch and salt in a heavy-bottomed saucepan and gradually add in the half-and-half and egg yolks, whisking lightly until smooth. Cook the mixture over medium-high heat, stirring constantly, until the custard is smooth, thick and bubbling, 6 to 8 minutes.

~ **FOURTH,** quickly add 1¼ cups of the hot custard into the chopped chocolate. Stir until the chocolate melts and the mixture is completely smooth. Immediately pour the chocolate filling into the baked crust and transfer to the freezer or refrigerator to cool, 5 to 10 minutes.

~ **MEANWHILE,** add 1 cup of the remaining hot custard to the dissolved gelatin and stir so that the gelatin is evenly blended; then pour it back into the remaining custard and whisk together. Let the rum custard cool for about 5 minutes. Cut the butter into pats and whisk them into the custard until the butter is completely blended.

~ **FIFTH,** cut the bananas into ½-inch-thick slices and toss the slices in a little rum or rum flavoring to prevent them from discoloring. Layer the slices of banana over the cooled chocolate custard in the cookie crust, then spoon the rum custard over the bananas and smooth the surface with a rubber spatula. Cut a 9-inch circle from a sheet of waxed paper, lightly coat it with butter and place it directly on top of the custard to keep a skin from forming. Chill in the refrigerator until set, about 4 hours; then, without removing the waxed paper, cover the pie with plastic wrap and return to the refrigerator.

PRESENT THE PIE:

~ **FIRST,** pour the cream into the chilled bowl of a mixer and add ⅓ cup sugar; mix with a chilled balloon whisk at medium speed until the sugar has dissolved, 3 to 4 minutes. Then whip on high until stiff peaks hold, about 2 more minutes.

~ **SECOND,** carefully remove the waxed paper from the top of the pie. Mound the whipped cream over the custard with a rubber spatula, or use a pastry bag to pipe large rosettes of whipped cream over the entire surface of the pie. Sprinkle with the grated chocolate just before serving; if desired, garnish each portion with additional banana slices.

When You're Family

> > > | CANNELLINI BEAN AND CLAM SOUP
> > > MARINATED ARTICHOKE AND FENNEL SALAD
> > > ONION FOCACCIA
> > > BAKED SEMOLINA GNOCCHI
> > > FAMILY-STYLE ROLLED VEAL SHOULDER ROAST
> > > FRESH PEPPERONATA
> > > CHOCOLATE APRICOT AMARETTI CHEESECAKE

When you're family, there's always a place at the table. When you're family, you're welcome to stay the night. When you're family, you don't need a reservation (although it's nice if you phone ahead!). For Americans of Italian heritage, Sunday has long been a treasured family day, begun in the warmth and bustle of the kitchen in the morning, continued around the great table after church, with good food and lively conversation lingering on until the evening.

The largest influx of Italians arrived in the East between 1880 and the 1920s, but many others came to California during the Gold Rush and afterward. They came mostly alone, without their families, crowded into steerage. Often families would scrape together enough money for one ticket, hoping the chosen one would prosper and help the rest as well.

And it happened. These Italians settled in the foothills beneath the Sierra Nevadas and along the Pacific coast from San Francisco to Monterey. They raised veal and planted grapes, olives, almonds, artichokes, figs, tomatoes, and peppers, transforming the valleys into a lush agricultural oasis. They built businesses: restaurants, produce companies, fisheries, and wineries. And in the Spanish Californian culture they found a compatible community of faith—with parish churches and mission schools—and a place to raise their families.

Many of San Francisco's earliest settlers came from northern Italy, from Liguria to Veneto. They brought to the city a love of opera, that famous sourdough bread, and, equally famous, Ghirardelli chocolate. They also made good use of a coast rich in seafood—not unlike the one at home—to create dishes such as cioppino, a rich seafood stew, or one of my childhood favorites, local barracuda baked in parchment with sliced lemon, tomatoes, basil, and onions.

Italian cooking has always been a true fusion cuisine, combining foods and cooking styles from many lands—Egyptian wheat, Chinese pasta, Arabian flatbread, Indian eggplant and rice, and tomatoes, peppers, and corn from the New World—into a distinct collection of regional flavors. (There are twenty regions of Italy, each with its own cooking style.) In California the fusion continued. California Italian cooking is altogether different from that of the East, not only because California Italians came from different regions in Italy, but also because California contributed its own ingredients to the cuisine.

Yet, as most California Italians will testify, Italian is still Italian. And despite their differences, most will say that family is still family, linked by blood, tradition, culture, and faith. Gathered together in love, we can touch past, present, and future while joined around the common table to celebrate life. Surely this is the essence of Sunday dinner.

CANNELLINI BEAN AND CLAM SOUP
8 SERVINGS

The cold sands along the central California coast produce some of the most succulent, sweet, briny clams to be had. Whether they are tossed with pasta, steamed and served with crusty bread or paired with these savory beans, clams give off the perfectly balanced flavors of the sea.

NOTE: *You can substitute 2 cans of baby clams, along with their liquid, for the fresh clams and clam juice in this recipe.*

BEANS

1 cup dried cannellini or navy beans
1 celery rib with leaves
1 small onion
1 bay leaf
2 whole cloves garlic

PREPARE THE BEANS:

~ **FIRST,** place the beans in a large pot, cover them with water and soak for 8 hours or overnight.

~ **SECOND,** drain the beans and return them to the pot; fill the pot with enough fresh water to cover the beans by 2 inches. Cut the celery and onion into large pieces; then add the celery, onion, bay leaf and garlic to the pot. Bring to a boil, then reduce the heat and simmer until the beans are tender, approximately 1 hour.

~ **THIRD,** drain the beans through a colander, reserving the liquid, and set both aside. When the beans are cool, remove and discard the celery, onion, bay leaf and garlic. Pour enough reserved cooking liquid over the beans to just submerge them.

CLAMS

4 to 5 dozen small clams
4 tablespoons olive oil
2 cups clam juice

PREPARE THE CLAMS:

~ **FIRST,** rinse the clams in several changes of cold water, scrubbing them vigorously with a stiff brush each time to remove any grains of sand. Discard any clams that do not remain closed when held under running water or tapped on the edge of the sink.

~ SECOND, working in 2 batches, pour 2 tablespoons of the olive oil into a large skillet and heat until the oil just begins to smoke; then quickly add in half of the clams with a slotted spoon and toss with the olive oil for 1 minute. Pour in 1 cup of the clam juice, cover the skillet with a tight-fitting lid and steam until all the clamshells have opened, 3 to 4 minutes. Use the slotted spoon to transfer the clams to a stainless bowl; strain and reserve the cooking liquid through a fine sieve, being especially careful to avoid any sandy sediment that may have settled to the bottom. Set both the clams and the strained cooking liquid aside to cool. Repeat this process with the remaining clams.

~ THIRD, remove the clam meat from the clamshells, holding them over the bowl to retain the juices; discard the shells. Most of the clams will come out of their shells easily, but any clams that do not open all of the way can be pried open using the back edge of a sturdy paring knife. When you have finished, add the clam meat to the reserved cooking liquid. (*Note:* You may want to set aside a few clams, still in their shells, for garnishing the bowls of soup.)

SOUP

¼ cup olive oil
4 cloves garlic, thinly sliced
½ cup diced onion
⅛ teaspoon crushed red pepper
½ cup packed fresh basil leaves
2 cups packed fresh spinach leaves
Salt to taste

PREPARE THE SOUP:

~ FIRST, heat the olive oil in a skillet. Add in the garlic and onion and cook over medium-high heat, stirring from time to time, until the garlic and onion are beginning to brown, 3 to 4 minutes.

~ SECOND, add the beans and the reserved liquid from the beans and clams to the garlic and onions, then add in the crushed red pepper and simmer until the beans are soft and the liquid is reduced to a full-bodied soup consistency, about 20 minutes. Add in the clam meat, basil and spinach. Continue to cook over medium-high heat for 2 to 3 more minutes. Season to taste with salt and serve immediately.

If the divine Creator

has taken pains

to give us delicious

and exquisite things to eat,

the least we can do

is prepare them well and

serve them with ceremony.

~

FERNAND POINT

MARINATED ARTICHOKE
AND FENNEL SALAD

8 SERVINGS

In most Mediterranean cultures, vegetables are an integral part of every meal—a tradition that works especially well in California, with its warm climate and incredible produce. Castroville, on the Monterey Bay, hails as the artichoke capital of the world, which may explain the many wonderful artichoke recipes found in California's Italian-inspired cooking.

ARTICHOKES

4 fresh artichokes
1 lemon, quartered
2 whole cloves garlic
2 tablespoons olive oil, as needed

FENNEL SALAD

4 bulbs fresh fennel
¼ cup extra-virgin olive oil
Juice of 1 lemon
Salt and pepper to taste
2 tablespoons balsamic vinegar

PREPARE THE ARTICHOKES:

~ **FIRST,** snap off all the tough outer leaves of the artichokes, then cut off the top third of each trimmed artichoke with a serrated knife. Use a sharp paring knife to peel away the tough dark green area around the base of each artichoke, and trim the stems to 1 inch. Quarter each artichoke and cut away the fuzzy interior. Rub the quartered artichokes with 2 of the lemon quarters to prevent discoloration; reserve the squeezed lemons for cooking the artichokes.

~ **SECOND,** place the artichokes, along with the 2 squeezed lemon quarters, the garlic and a splash of olive oil, into a skillet. Add enough cold salted water to cover them completely. Bring to a boil over medium heat, then cover with a tight-fitting lid and cook the artichokes until tender, approximately 20 minutes. Drain the artichokes, transfer to a stainless bowl, squeeze the juice from the remaining 2 lemon quarters over them and drizzle with a little olive oil. Set aside.

PREPARE THE FENNEL:

~ Cut the long, fernlike stalks off the fennel bulbs, reserving a few of the sprigs. Trim away any outer bottom leaves that are discolored. Cut the bulbs in half lengthwise, then lay each half flat on a clean cutting board and finely shred into thin slices with a sharp kitchen knife. Finely chop 1 tablespoon of the reserved fennel fronds and toss together with the shredded bulbs in a stainless bowl, along with the extra-virgin olive oil and lemon juice. Season to taste with salt and pepper.

ASSEMBLE THE SALAD:

~ Mound the marinated fennel in the center of a platter and arrange the artichokes around the outside. Drizzle the salad with a little more extra-virgin olive oil and the balsamic vinegar.

ONION FOCACCIA
MAKES 1 RECTANGULAR LOAF

These flat rustic loaves are a favorite throughout Italy and in California, where the recipe most likely arrived with families from Liguria. Focaccia in Liguria is topped with onions and enjoyed primarily as a snack. It is the perfect bread for sopping up the olive oil–balsamic dressing in the fennel and artichoke salad.

FOCACCIA

1 package (2¼ teaspoons) active dry yeast
¼ cup warm water, about 110°F
2 tablespoons olive oil
1½ cups water, room temperature
3½ cups bread flour
1 teaspoon coarse salt

MAKE THE FOCACCIA:

~ **FIRST,** sprinkle the yeast over the warm water and let the mixture stand for 1 minute, then stir until the yeast is dissolved.

~ **SECOND,** combine the olive oil with 1½ cups water in a mixing bowl and blend in the dissolved yeast. Use a wooden spoon to add in 2 cups of the bread flour; stir until the mixture reaches the consistency of thick batter. Continue stirring until the dough is smooth and elastic, about 200 strokes; then scrape down the sides of the bowl with a rubber spatula. Cover with a clean tea towel and set in a draft-free place until the dough is bubbly and has doubled in volume, about 1 hour.

~ **THIRD,** whisk the remaining 1½ cups bread flour with the salt in a separate bowl. Place the bubbly dough under an electric mixer fitted with a dough hook and add in the flour mixture on low speed, ½ cup at a time; the dough should be sticking just a little to the sides of the bowl. Add in additional flour if necessary, and knead on low speed for about 10 minutes. Transfer the dough to a clean, lightly oiled bowl; cover with a clean tea towel and set in a draft-free place until it has again doubled in volume, about 1 hour.

TOPPING

2 teaspoons olive oil
2 cups thinly sliced onion
Olive oil for brushing
Pinch of coarse salt

PREPARE THE TOPPING:

~ Heat 2 teaspoons of olive oil in a skillet over medium heat. Add in the sliced onion and sauté just long enough to soften, about 1 minute. Set aside to cool.

ASSEMBLE THE FOCACCIA:

~ **FIRST,** shape the dough by gently pulling it, starting from the middle, until it forms a 12-by-18-inch rectangle. Transfer it to a lightly oiled baking sheet and use two fingers to make little indentations over the entire surface. Lightly brush the dough with lukewarm water and let it rise uncovered for 30 minutes.

~ **SECOND,** carefully brush the focaccia with a little olive oil, sprinkle the surface evenly with the sautéed onions and season with a pinch of coarse salt. Bake the focaccia in a 400°F oven until crusty and brown, 20 to 25 minutes.

FAMILY-STYLE ROLLED VEAL SHOULDER ROAST
8 SERVINGS

Few of us think of roasts when we envision Italian food, but succulent roasts are actually quite common on the Italian-American table. In my neighborhood while I was growing up, the aromas coming from the homes of our Italian neighbors was always inviting. While my mom would make a stew from our leftover roast, our Italian friends would enjoy a hearty Bolognese sauce for the weekday pasta from theirs.

NOTE: *Have your butcher prepare a boneless shoulder roast that weighs between 4 and 4½ pounds and has a ¼-inch covering of fat; also have him roll the roast and securely tie it with kitchen twine.*

SHOULDER ROAST

1 4- to 4½-pound rolled veal or pork shoulder roast
2 cloves garlic, mashed
2 teaspoons fresh chopped rosemary
2 tablespoons olive oil
Coarse salt and freshly-ground black pepper
6 whole cloves garlic
⅓ cup chopped carrot
⅓ cup chopped celery
⅓ cup chopped onion
1 cup dry white wine
2 bay leaves
2 sprigs fresh rosemary

~ Preheat the oven to 325°F.

PREPARE THE ROAST:

~ **FIRST,** remove the roast from the refrigerator. Combine the mashed garlic cloves and the rosemary with 1 tablespoon of the olive oil. Rub the mixture over the surface of the roast, season with salt and pepper and leave at room temperature for at least 30 minutes before roasting.

~ **SECOND,** heat the remaining 1 tablespoon olive oil over medium heat in a heavy roasting pan. Brown the roast, beginning with the fat side down, for 10 to 12 minutes; turn every 2 to 3 minutes until the entire roast is evenly browned. Transfer the roast to a platter. Add the whole garlic cloves to the roasting pan, along with the chopped carrot, celery and onion. Scrape the meaty drippings from the bottom of the pan, then pour in the wine and simmer over medium heat for about 2 minutes.

~ **MEANWHILE,** slip the bay leaves alternately with the rosemary sprigs under the kitchen twine on each side of the roast.

~ **THIRD,** return the roast to the pan, fat side up, and place it in the oven. For veal, cook until the internal temperature reaches between 130°F and 135°F, about 1½ hours; for pork, roast to an internal temperature of 150°F, about 2 hours.

~ **FOURTH,** carefully remove the roast from the oven and allow the meat to rest in the roasting pan for 20 minutes before slicing. The temperature will rise by 5 to 10 degrees during this time, giving you a perfect serving temperature.

SERVE THE ROAST:

~ **FIRST,** transfer the roast to a clean cutting board. Cut away and discard the kitchen twine, bay leaves and rosemary.

~ **SECOND,** place the roasting pan over a burner set at medium heat. When the juices begin to simmer, remove from heat and strain through a sieve into a small bowl, pressing on the vegetables to extract the aromatic flavors.

~ **THIRD,** slice the roast and arrange on a decorative platter. Add any juices that accumulate on the cutting board to the juices in the bowl and pour over the sliced roast just before serving.

BAKED SEMOLINA GNOCCHI
8 SERVINGS

Gnocchi, which are little dumplings, can be made at least a hundred different ways. Some gnocchi recipes call for mashed potatoes, others use cornmeal, and still others are made with ricotta cheese and spinach. The methods of cooking also vary: Gnocchi might be dropped into boiling water, sautéed in hot oil or—like these—cut into shapes and baked. These gnocchi are also wonderful poached in boiling water and smothered in a tomato or Bolognese sauce.

GNOCCHI

4 cups whole milk
½ teaspoon salt
1½ cups fine semolina
8 tablespoons (1 stick) butter
1½ cups coarsely grated Parmesan cheese
2 large egg yolks, room temperature

MAKE THE GNOCCHI:

~ **FIRST,** bring the milk to a rolling boil over medium-high heat in a heavy-bottomed saucepan. Add in the salt and then, stirring constantly with a wooden spoon, slowly add in the semolina. Reduce the heat to low and stir until the mixture is thick and smooth, about 10 minutes. Remove the pan from heat and beat in 6 tablespoons of the butter and all of the Parmesan cheese. Allow the mixture to cool slightly, then beat in the egg yolks.

~ **SECOND,** spread the mixture into a lightly oiled glass dish or casserole; brush the top lightly with oil and cool to room temperature, then cover with plastic wrap and refrigerate for at least 2 hours.

~ **THIRD,** melt the remaining 2 tablespoons of butter. Use a regular household spoon to scoop out rounded oval portions of the chilled gnocchi dough, each about 2 tablespoons in volume, and with your fingers gently form the dough into egg-shaped dumplings about 1¾ inches in length. Layer the gnocchi in alternating circles in the bottom of a lightly oiled casserole, brushing melted butter over each layer. Mound them layer by layer like a small pyramid. Bake uncovered in a 400°F oven until golden, about 20 minutes.

FRESH PEPPERONATA

8 SERVINGS

Pepperonata is a slow-simmered stew made with peppers and tomatoes and seasoned with either basil or Italian parsley; it can also include carrots, zucchini and olives. This particular variation, prepared with roasted peppers, tastes similar to fresh pasta sauce. It is really quite wonderful served as a side dish with the baked gnocchi and the aromatic roast.

PEPPERONATA

2 red bell peppers
2 yellow bell peppers
½ cup olive oil
2 cloves garlic, thinly sliced
1 small onion, quartered and separated
6 large plum tomatoes, peeled and seeded *or*
1 24-ounce can Italian plum tomatoes
¼ cup dry white wine
2 teaspoons fresh chopped Italian parsley
Salt and pepper to taste

MAKE THE PEPPERONATA:

~ **FIRST,** brush the outside of each pepper lightly with a little olive oil. Using tongs to turn them, grill the peppers directly over a gas flame for about 10 minutes; or place them on a baking sheet and broil 3 inches under the heat, using tongs to turn them, for approximately 10 minutes. When they are done, the skins of the peppers should be completely charred and blistered. Transfer them to a sealed plastic bag and let them steam for 10 minutes. Then clean away the charred skin, stems and seeds, and quarter each pepper lengthwise.

~ **SECOND,** heat the olive oil over medium heat in an 8-inch oval casserole and sauté the garlic and onion until translucent, 2 to 3 minutes.

~ **THIRD,** if you are using fresh tomatoes, cut each peeled and seeded tomato into large chunks. Toss the peppers and tomatoes with the sautéed garlic and onion in the oval casserole; add the dry white wine and let simmer for 2 to 3 minutes. Stir in the Italian parsley, then season to taste with salt and pepper. Drizzle a little extra olive oil over the top and simmer, covered, over low heat for 20 minutes.

Easy time-saving
AND DO-AHEAD TIPS:

FRIDAY EVENING
Prepare the gnocchi dough and refrigerate. Bake the cheesecake and refrigerate.

SATURDAY
Prepare the artichokes and refrigerate in a stainless bowl. Prepare the vegetables for the pepperonata and refrigerate in well-sealed containers. Soak the beans for the soup. Prepare the clams for the soup and refrigerate.

SUNDAY MORNING
Bake the focaccia. Drain and cook the beans for the soup. Prepare the gnocchi for the oven.

CHOCOLATE APRICOT
AMARETTI CHEESECAKE

10 SERVINGS

During the early 1970s, my mother was the business manager for one of the finest restaurants in Beverly Hills, which specialized in French and Italian cuisine. As I was beginning my career, I'd moonlight there on busy weekends just to gain experience. Some of the truly splendid desserts served at that restaurant included crepes, tiramisu and zabaglione. I was intrigued by what the pastry chef often chose to box up for his family's Sunday dinner: a rustic ricotta cheesecake just like this one, chock-full of bittersweet chocolate and candied fruit.

BISCOTTI CRUST

1 8-ounce package almond biscotti
¼ cup (½ stick) butter, melted

~ Adjust the rack to the center of the oven and preheat to 300°F.

PREPARE THE CRUST:

~ Break the biscotti into pieces and place in the bowl of a food processor fitted with a steel blade; pulse to make fine crumbs. Pour in the melted butter and pulse until well blended. Press the crust into the bottom and about 1 inch up the sides of a 9-inch springform pan.

CHEESECAKE FILLING

2 teaspoons orange zest
4 ounces bittersweet chocolate
3 ounces dried apricots
3 ounces amaretti cookies (Italian almond macaroons)
1 8-ounce package cream cheese
1 cup granulated sugar
½ teaspoon salt
½ tablespoon pure almond extract
2 pounds whole-milk ricotta cheese
6 large eggs, room temperature
½ cup all-purpose flour

PREPARE THE FILLING:

~ **FIRST,** pour in just enough water to cover the orange zest and heat in a small pan for 2 to 3 minutes or in a small dish of water in the microwave for 1 to 2 minutes; this process will extract the bitter oil. Drain the zest thoroughly and set aside.

~ **SECOND,** chop the chocolate into pieces about half the size of chocolate chips; set aside. Dice the apricots into small pieces (you should end up with about ⅔ cup) and set aside. Place the amaretti in a resealable plastic bag and gently crush with a rolling pin (you should end up with about 1 cup of tiny pieces); set aside.

~ **THIRD,** combine the cream cheese and sugar in the bowl of a mixer fitted with a paddle and beat on medium speed until there are no lumps.

~ **FOURTH,** turn the mixer speed to low, add in the salt and almond extract and beat for 1 minute. Turn the machine off and scrape down the sides of the bowl with a rubber spatula.

~ **FIFTH,** return the mixer speed to low and add in the ricotta, a cup at a time, until fully blended and smooth. Add in the eggs one at a time, allowing each egg to blend into the cheese mixture before adding the next. Then add in the flour, a tablespoon at a time, and mix just long enough to fully incorporate all the ingredients. (*Note:* It is important that you don't overmix the filling when making a cheesecake; air beaten into the batter will cause the cake to crack when it is baked.)

~ **SIXTH,** use a rubber spatula to fold the orange zest, chopped chocolate and apricots into the ricotta mixture; then fold in the crushed amaretti. Pour the filling into the prepared crust. Smooth the top and lightly tap the sides of the pan to knock out any air bubbles.

BAKE THE CHEESECAKE:

~ **FIRST,** bake the cheesecake on a baking sheet in the center of the oven for 50 minutes; this will allow the thick center of the cake to rise evenly to temperature. Increase the oven temperature to 350°F and continue baking for another 25 to 30 minutes. The cheesecake is completely baked when the edges begin to brown and rise slightly above the center. The center will still jiggle slightly, like a baked custard.

~ **SECOND,** turn off the oven, set the oven door ajar and allow the cheesecake to cool for 30 minutes undisturbed; this will keep the center from falling.

~ **THIRD,** transfer the cheesecake to a cooling rack and carefully run a thin knife about 1 inch deep around the inside rim of the pan. (As the cheesecake cools, it will pull into the center; loosening the cake from the edges of the pan will reduce the chance of cracks forming on the surface.) Cool to room temperature in the pan, then cover tightly with plastic wrap and refrigerate for at least 4 hours and up to 2 days.

PRESENT THE CHEESECAKE:

~ Run a thin knife around the inside edge of the cake pan, then carefully loosen the spring and remove the ring. Transfer the cheesecake to a decorative cake platter and cut into 10 slices. (*Note:* It is helpful to cut each slice of cheesecake with a thin sharp knife that has been dipped in warm water.)

Good food

is a matchless

expression of love

because it gives life,

brings pleasure,

and excites the senses.

RC

A Sunday for Thanksgiving

>> >> >>   SAVORY TURKEY AND VEGETABLE POT PIE

MOLDED CRANBERRY, APPLE AND ORANGE RING

SWEET POTATO BISCUITS WITH MAPLE-WALNUT BUTTER

SPICED PUMPKIN MOUSSE CAKE

Throughout history and around the world, harvest festivals have been held to celebrate the gathering of the year's crops. They acknowledge God's "manifold blessings" and the earth's plentiful abundance. In 1621, however, when the Pilgrims invited their Indian neighbors to a dinner in honor of their first harvest, a distinctly American tradition was born. Today, in fact, we are one of the few nations to observe an official day of thanksgiving. On the fourth Thursday of November, Americans of all backgrounds gather to give thanks with a feast of traditional foods harvested from our land: turkey, corn, squash, pumpkin, sweet potatoes, and cranberries.

Thanksgiving has always been more than just a harvest festival, however. It has also traditionally been a time to refocus our attention on what is important and give God thanks for His grace and protection. George Washington was the first to proclaim a national day of thanksgiving. Later, during the Civil War, President Lincoln set aside the last Thursday of November "as a day of Thanksgiving and Praise to our beneficent Father." After that it became a tradition for each president to proclaim annually a day of thanksgiving. This continued until 1941, when Congress finally established it as a national holiday.

Thanksgiving has always been one of my favorite holidays. Each year our family gathers together to share a traditional meal complete with hearty seafood chowder, juicy herb-scented roasted turkey, savory cornbread dressing, sparkling cider, and rich homey desserts. This is a joyous time to remember our heritage, our family, our faith, and all the blessings we have enjoyed throughout the year. Every year, however, we seem to face the same universal challenges: How do we fit all those leftovers into the crowded refrigerator? What do we do with that picked-over turkey carcass?

My wife and I met these challenges years ago when we began the tradition of making turkey pot pie from our leftover bird and serving it the Sunday following Thanksgiving. We've come to anticipate this savory and satisfying entrée as much as the Thanksgiving dinner itself. It is a perfect Sunday dinner: very easy, mostly prepared ahead, and memorably delicious. I think you'll agree that leftovers never tasted better! Of course, you don't have to wait until November. After all, Sunday dinner should be a bit like having Thanksgiving each and every week; it's a time for both thankful reflection and joyful feasting.

SAVORY TURKEY AND VEGETABLE POT PIE
8 SERVINGS

Creating this excellent pot pie couldn't be easier. One way to save on time is by making a little extra crust when you prepare your Thanksgiving pies (pastry crust will stay fresh for days when refrigerated). Then, when those Thanksgiving dinner dishes are being scraped and stacked, take a few moments to prepare a rich stock from the turkey carcass and a few of the vegetables and herbs you'll no doubt have on hand. Trust me: As you organize things to prepare the stock, a lot of that leftover Thanksgiving mess on the stovetop will disappear in the process!

NOTE: *When making a stock, I generally fortify the flavor by using a quality bouillon in lieu of using salt. (Most bouillon cubes are for the most part sodium anyway, so I really think of this as salt with a little extra flavor.)*

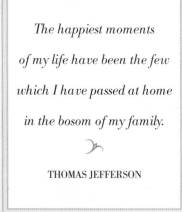

> The happiest moments
>
> of my life have been the few
>
> which I have passed at home
>
> in the bosom of my family.
>
> ❧
>
> THOMAS JEFFERSON

TURKEY STOCK

1 whole turkey carcass
8 cups cold water
1 carrot, peeled and chopped
2 ribs celery, chopped
1 leek, white part only, thinly sliced
1 medium onion, diced
1 whole clove garlic
1 bay leaf
1 small bouquet of fresh herbs: parsley, rosemary, sage and thyme
6 to 8 white peppercorns
2 chicken bouillon cubes

PREPARE THE STOCK:

~ **FIRST,** cut away the extra meat from the turkey breast and remove the legs and thighs. Trim the remaining meat from the legs and thighs, keeping the larger pieces for sandwiches or other favorites, and set aside about 4 cups of the smaller pieces, as well as any little bits of extra white and dark meat, for the pie filling. Scrape any lingering dressing from the carcass, but don't worry if a little remains—the flavor will only enhance the pie. Use a pair of poultry shears to carefully cut through the breastbone and back.

~ **SECOND,** place the turkey carcass, as well as the leg, thigh and wing bones, into a large pot and pour in the 8 cups cold water. Add the chopped carrot, celery, leek, onion, garlic, bay leaf, bouquet of fresh herbs, white peppercorns and bouillon cubes.

~ **THIRD,** heat the stock until the water just begins to boil. Reduce the heat and simmer uncovered until the liquid is reduced by half, about 3 hours; this should yield about 4 cups of stock. Cool slightly, discard the turkey bones and strain through a fine sieve; then cool to room temperature. The stock may be refrigerated in a well-sealed container for up to a week.

PASTRY DOUGH

3 cups all-purpose flour
1 teaspoon salt
½ cup (1 stick) unsalted butter
½ cup shortening
4 to 5 tablespoons cold milk, as needed

PREPARE THE PASTRY DOUGH:

~ FIRST, whisk the flour and salt together using a stiff wire whisk. Cut in the butter and shortening with a pastry cutter, or pulse for several seconds in a food processor, until the mixture reaches the consistency of coarse crumbly meal.

~ SECOND, add in the milk, a tablespoon at a time, and toss together with a fork or by pulsing a second or two until the liquid is incorporated and the moistened dough is just beginning to come together. Remove the mixture from the bowl or food processor, turn out onto a clean dry surface and knead the dough just enough to form a pliable, tender ball. Divide into two portions and roll into balls. Flatten each ball into a disk by gently pressing it between your hands.

~ THIRD, wrap the disks in plastic wrap and chill for at least 30 minutes. The dough may be kept in the refrigerator, wrapped tightly, for up to a week.

POT PIE FILLING

½ cup (1 stick) butter
½ cup diced celery
2 cloves garlic, minced
½ cup diced onion
1 cup peeled sliced carrots
1 cup peeled pearl onions
6 tablespoons all-purpose flour
4 cups turkey stock
Salt and white pepper to taste
4 cups roasted turkey, cubed
1 cup fresh blanched peas or frozen peas, thawed
1 tablespoon combined fresh chopped herbs:
parsley, rosemary, sage and thyme

PREPARE THE FILLING:

~ FIRST, melt the butter in a skillet over medium heat. Add in the celery, garlic and onion and sauté until the onion becomes translucent, 2 to 3 minutes; regulate the heat carefully to ensure that the butter doesn't brown. Add in the carrots and pearl onions and sauté for 2 more minutes. Sprinkle the flour over the sautéed vegetables and stir until the flour combines with the butter to form a *roux*.

~ SECOND, pour in the stock, stirring constantly to keep lumps from forming, and simmer until the sauce has thickened to the desired consistency, 3 to 4 minutes. Season to taste with the salt and white pepper and remove the pan from the stove. Fold in the cubed turkey meat, peas and fresh herbs and cool the mixture to room temperature. This filling may be used right away or refrigerated in a well-sealed container for up to 4 days.

ASSEMBLE THE TURKEY POT PIE:

~ FIRST, lightly dust a rolling pin and a clean work surface with a little flour, then roll out one of the chilled pastry disks into a circle that is about ¼-inch thick and about 12 inches in diameter. Carefully drape the pastry over the rolling pin and transfer it to a 10-inch deep-dish pie pan.

~ SECOND, spoon the filling into the dish. Roll out the second piece of dough so that it is slightly smaller in diameter and just a bit thicker than the bottom crust, and carefully place it over the filling. Use a sharp knife or poultry shears to trim away any excess dough, then crimp the edges. Cut several slits into the top of the crust and brush with a little milk. (*Note:* Extra pieces of dough can be cut into attractive shapes and arranged decoratively over the surface of the pie.)

~ THIRD, bake in a 350°F oven until the crust is golden and the filling is bubbling hot, 60 to 70 minutes. Remove the pot pie from the oven and let it rest at room temperature for 20 minutes before serving.

MOLDED CRANBERRY,
APPLE AND ORANGE RING
10 SERVINGS

The tang of cranberries and orange with crunchy apples makes a festive salad— leftover cranberry sauce never had it so good!

CRANBERRY, APPLE AND ORANGE RING

2 whole oranges
1 12-ounce package fresh cranberries
1½ cups granulated sugar
2 tablespoons unflavored gelatin
2 cups cranberry-apple juice cocktail
2 cups whole-cranberry sauce
2 cups diced red or green apples

PREPARE THE CRANBERRY, APPLE AND ORANGE RING:

~ **FIRST,** wash the oranges thoroughly and cut them into quarters (leave the peels on); remove any seeds and slice the quarters into chunks. Combine the orange chunks with the fresh cranberries and ½ cup of the sugar in the bowl of a food processor fitted with a steel blade. Roughly chop by pulsing for 5 to 10 seconds. Set this mixture aside.

~ **SECOND,** sprinkle the gelatin and the remaining 1 cup of sugar into the cranberry-apple juice in a small saucepan. Bring the mixture to a boil over medium heat and stir until the sugar and gelatin are completely dissolved, about 5 minutes.

~ **THIRD,** combine the hot cranberry-apple juice mixture and the whole-berry cranberry sauce in a stainless bowl. Stir together well, let stand for 5 minutes and then partially submerge in a bowl of ice water; stir until cool. When the mixture has cooled completely, fold in the diced apples and the chopped orange-cranberry mixture.

~ **FOURTH,** pour into a 2-quart plastic mold or ceramic dish and cover with plastic wrap. Chill until the salad is set, at least 8 hours or overnight.

SERVE THE SALAD:

~ Take the salad out of the refrigerator and dip the bottom into hot water to loosen the gelatin. Remove the plastic wrap and carefully invert the salad onto a decorative platter. If desired, garnish with fresh orange slices and sugar-frosted cranberries.

Crisp linens,

gleaming silver and glass,

cherished linens

and lovingly prepared foods

graciously set for the scene

for giving thanks.

PEGGY KENNEDY

SWEET POTATO BISCUITS
WITH MAPLE-WALNUT BUTTER
18 BISCUITS

For this recipe you can bake a couple of extra sweet potatoes when preparing your Thanksgiving dinner. Or simply use leftover mashed sweet potatoes—the little extra brown sugar that you seasoned them with will only enhance the flavor of the biscuits. The biscuits are especially good served hot and oozing with creamy maple-walnut butter.

BISCUITS

2½ cups all-purpose flour
2 tablespoons baking powder
Pinch of allspice
Pinch of ground cloves
½ teaspoon salt
¼ cup packed light brown sugar
¼ cup (½ stick) unsalted butter, chilled
½ cup shortening, chilled
1½ cups mashed sweet potatoes or yams

~ Adjust the rack to the center of the oven and preheat to 425°F.

MAKE THE BISCUITS:

~ **FIRST,** sift the flour, baking powder, allspice, ground cloves and salt into a large bowl. Use the tips of your fingers to blend in the brown sugar.

~ **SECOND,** cut in the chilled butter and shortening with a pastry cutter or pulse in a food processor until the mixture resembles coarse crumbly meal. Then stir in the mashed sweet potatoes and knead until the dough just holds together.

~ **THIRD,** turn the dough out onto a lightly floured surface. Knead gently for 1 minute, adding a little extra flour as necessary to incorporate all the ingredients and ensure that the biscuits will rise evenly. Pat the dough into a ½-inch-thick circle and let it rest, covered with a clean tea towel, for 10 to 15 minutes.

~ **FOURTH,** cut out the biscuits with a 2-inch round cutter dipped in flour. Gather the scraps, pat out again and cut into biscuits. Arrange them about ¾-inch apart on an ungreased baking sheet and brush the tops with a little milk.

~ **FIFTH,** bake the biscuits until golden brown, 10 to 12 minutes. Cool the biscuits on racks and brush with a little melted butter.

MAPLE-WALNUT BUTTER

½ cup (1 stick) unsalted butter, softened
2 tablespoons pure maple syrup
2 tablespoons ground walnuts

MAKE THE BUTTER:

~ **FIRST,** whip together the softened butter with the maple syrup and ground walnuts using an electric mixer set at high speed, or pulse in a food processor fitted with a steel blade, until the butter is light and fluffy.

~ **SECOND,** spoon the maple butter into a small serving dish or use a pastry bag fitted with a decorative tip to pipe the butter into small ramekins. The butter can be kept at room temperature until ready to serve; or you can cover with plastic wrap and refrigerate, then return to room temperature before serving.

*S*omething happens in my human heart when I approach that place—a perpetual place, Yeats calls it—where time and space and family have grounded me: my parents' Sunday dinner table. It was never grand, but it was ever constant. During lean, hard times when hailed-out crops or plunging cattle prices brought us to the brink of ruin, my parents still bowed their heads in thanks and showed us how to live.

Ranch life lingered on, but with the "work all done" in fall, Thanksgiving marked a season of rest as well as feast, and we enjoyed pheasants fattened on our corn and the bounty of garden vegetables—God's provision redeemed from the soil and put up for winter's store.

Our five original family members now number twenty-three, and when we gather together, the grandchildren sleep in tents or under the open sky. At dinnertime the youngest ones take their plates to the lawn to eat, and Sunday dinners still last most of the afternoon. Now the stories are of our own diaspora, for modernity has scattered us from coast to coast. But here, in the vast spaces of Wyoming, the children learn that they are part of a larger story.

A tall chocolate cake layered with fresh fruit welcomes us home each year, and once again we celebrate the continuity of holy things—communion around God's table, followed by communion around our own.

MARY ANN BELL

SPICED PUMPKIN MOUSSE CAKE
12 SERVINGS

There always seems to be at least one unused can of pumpkin left in the cupboard after Thanksgiving (you'll need a 29-ounce can for this recipe). If your home is anything like ours, you'll no doubt have plenty of leftover whipped cream on hand, as well. This amazing cake is rich and creamy, light and airy—and the combination of spices creates a fabulous dessert!

PUMPKIN CAKE

1 cup all-purpose flour
¾ teaspoon baking soda
¼ teaspoon ground allspice
½ teaspoon ground cinnamon
¼ teaspoon ground nutmeg
¼ teaspoon salt
½ cup (1 stick) unsalted butter
½ cup granulated sugar
½ cup packed dark brown sugar
1 large egg, room temperature
1⅓ cups canned pumpkin
½ cup dark raisins

~ Adjust the rack to the center of the oven and preheat to 350°F.

MAKE THE CAKE:

~ **FIRST,** lightly grease a 9-inch springform pan.

~ **SECOND,** sift the flour, baking soda, allspice, cinnamon, nutmeg and salt into a mixing bowl; set aside.

~ **THIRD,** thoroughly cream the butter with the granulated sugar and brown sugar in the bowl of an electric mixer fitted with a paddle until light and fluffy, about 6 minutes. Scrape down the sides of the bowl with a rubber spatula. Then, with the mixer running at medium speed, add in the egg; beat until the egg is fully incorporated into the butter mixture.

~ **FOURTH,** turn the mixer speed to low and add the sifted dry ingredients in 3 stages alternately with the pumpkin, mixing well after each addition. Increase the mixer speed to medium and beat for about 30 seconds. Then scrape down the sides of the bowl and fold in the raisins.

~ **FIFTH,** spread the batter evenly in the springform pan and bake until a wooden pick comes out clean when inserted into the middle, 35 to 40 minutes. (The cake will only rise to a height of approximately 1 inch.) Cool the cake in the pan.

Easy time-saving
AND DO-AHEAD TIPS:

THANKSGIVING NIGHT
Make the turkey stock.

FRIDAY EVENING
Bake the cake. Prepare the turkey pot pie filling and the pastry dough; refrigerate separately.

SATURDAY
Prepare the mousse and assemble the cake. Prepare the molded salad; seal with plastic wrap and refrigerate.

SUNDAY MORNING
Assemble the turkey pot pie. Prepare the biscuit dough.

When the cake is cool, wipe along the inside edge of the springform pan with a damp paper towel, then lightly butter the clean edge.

MOUSSE FILLING

2 cups half-and-half
⅓ cup brandy *or* ¼ cup water plus 1 tablespoon brandy flavoring
2 tablespoons unflavored gelatin
4 large egg yolks, room temperature
1⅔ cups canned pumpkin
¾ cup granulated sugar
½ cup packed light brown sugar
1 teaspoon ground allspice
1 teaspoon ground cinnamon
½ teaspoon ground cloves
2 cups heavy whipping cream

MAKE THE MOUSSE:

~ **FIRST,** scald the half-and-half in a saucepan by heating it just to the point of boiling; then quickly remove the pan from heat and cool until it is lukewarm.

~ **SECOND,** pour the brandy into a small bowl and sprinkle the gelatin over it, then stir until the gelatin has dissolved.

~ **THIRD,** combine the egg yolks with the pumpkin, granulated sugar, brown sugar, allspice, cinnamon and cloves in the top of a double boiler or in a stainless bowl. Stir well to incorporate.

~ **FOURTH,** whip the heavy cream in a separate bowl until stiff peaks form; cover and refrigerate.

~ **FIFTH,** add the softened gelatin to the scalded half-and-half and stir to dissolve so that there are no lumps, then slowly pour it into the pumpkin mixture, stirring constantly. Place the bowl over a double boiler or pan of rapidly boiling water—do not allow the pan to touch the water—and stir with a heat-resistant rubber spatula until the pumpkin mousse has thickened slightly and is barely bubbling around the edges, about 5 minutes. Remove the mousse from the pan of boiling water, submerge it partially in a pan of ice water and cool, stirring constantly, to room temperature. As the custard cools, it will begin to set up and have the consistency of cake batter.

~ **SIXTH,** just when the custard begins to set up, add half of the stiffly whipped cream to it and stir until fully incorporated; then quickly but gently fold in the remaining whipped cream. Pour the mousse over the cake in the cake pan, tapping the edges of the pan to get rid of any air bubbles. Chill uncovered in the refrigerator until the mousse is completely cool, about 1 hour; then cover tightly with plastic wrap. Refrigerate for at least 8 hours or overnight.

SERVE THE CAKE:

~ Wrap a warm damp tea towel around the outer rim of the pan for a minute or so, then carefully run a thin sharp knife around the inside of the pan. Loosen the springform ring and transfer the cake to your favorite cake stand. If desired, garnish the cake just before serving with rosettes of whipped cream and lightly dust the top with pumpkin pie spice.

A Sunday to Remember

> ❧ ❧ ❧

OLD WORLD BRAISED BEEF ROULADES

POTATO DUMPLINGS

SWEET-AND-SOUR RED CABBAGE

SCALLOPED CAULIFLOWER AND LEEK GRATIN

FARMHOUSE CARAWAY RYE ROLLS

DARK CHERRY–ALMOND KUCHEN

Americans observe many holidays throughout the year, days that hold special meaning, that spark memories, that recall struggle or celebrate triumph and that bring to mind a unique heritage. For many Americans of German descent, Reformation Day is one of these. Though this holiday may not be widely recognized, it holds significance not only for those of German-Protestant heritage, but for all those who treasure freedom of thought, freedom of conscience, and freedom of worship.

In 1517, on the eve of All Saint's Day, a gifted young German monk and professor named Martin Luther posted a paper outlining his objections to current church policies on a church door in Wittenberg. Among Luther's concerns was the sale of "indulgences"—or exemption from punishment for sins—to finance the building of St. Peter's Basilica in Rome. Luther was deeply troubled by this practice, which implied that one could buy or earn grace and favor from God. His ongoing study of such issues brought him to a kind of personal reformation, a rethinking of his Catholic beliefs and practice. He stressed that each person can have personal access to God, that salvation is an act of God's grace, and that people are justified (made righteous) by faith alone.

Luther refused to recant his controversial views and was excommunicated. But he set in motion a revolution that would not only transform the church, but ultimately change the world—the Protestant Reformation.

On the last Sunday of October, therefore, Lutherans and Reformed Christians celebrate Martin Luther's courage in confronting church corruption, his refusal to back down in the face of imprisonment and threatened death, and his fostering of the ideals of individual responsibility, which helped plant seeds of freedom of thought. For American Germans, a special Sunday dinner is often part of the celebration.

Sunday dinner has always been a valued tradition in German households. The midday meal, or *mittagessen,* was always the main meal of the day. On Sundays, mittagessen became a more formal affair. A typical Sunday mittagessen might begin with soup or poultry. A roast, or *braten,* with cauliflower and potatoes was often the centerpiece. Dessert might be a fresh fruit tart served with whipped cream and robust coffee and, of course, thoughtful conversation.

To Americans of German heritage, an invitation to someone's home for such a dinner is among the most prized expressions of hospitality. A table set with flowers, embroidered tablecloths, and special dishes is an essential part of the welcome. Enjoying a meal while remembering, exploring, and celebrating a shared spiritual heritage adds even greater value to those treasured times.

OLD WORLD BRAISED BEEF ROULADES
8 SERVINGS

My wife, who was born in Germany, crossed into the West with her family during the Berlin crisis in the early 1960s, just before the building of the Berlin Wall. She was in Berlin to hear John F. Kennedy's famous "Ich bin ein Berliner" speech. We have always incorporated her rich heritage into our family celebrations. Beef roulades are one of our favorites, just as they are a favorite for many Americans of German ancestry.

NOTE: *For this recipe, have your butcher trim all the fat from the round steak and slice it into 8 pieces, each about 6 ounces in weight and ¼-inch thick.*

ROULADES

3 pounds round steak, sliced into 8 pieces
8 strips bacon, diced
¼ cup deli-style mustard
1 cup finely diced onion
¼ cup fresh chopped parsley
8 dill pickle spears
¼ cup (½ stick) butter
Salt and pepper to taste
Flour for dredging
2 cups beef broth

MAKE THE ROULADES:

- **FIRST,** sandwich the meat slices between layers of plastic wrap and place on a clean work surface. Use a meat mallet to pound the slices into 4-by-8-inch rectangles that are ⅛-inch thick.

- **SECOND,** combine the bacon, mustard, onion and parsley in a small mixing bowl; then spread the mixture evenly onto each slice of pounded beef. Place a pickle at the end nearest you and roll the meat lengthwise around the pickle, then secure with wooden picks or tie with kitchen twine. Repeat with remaining roulades.

- **THIRD,** heat the butter in a large skillet over medium heat until it is melted and just beginning to bubble. Season the roulades with salt and pepper and dredge them in flour, then transfer them to the hot skillet. Sear the roulades until they are dark brown, 2 to 3 minutes on each side; then transfer to a clean platter.

- **FOURTH,** pour the beef broth into the skillet and bring to a boil over medium-high heat. Scrape the bottom and sides of the skillet with a whisk to loosen any brown bits. Return the beef roulades to the pan, cover with a tight-fitting lid and reduce the heat to low. Simmer the roulades until the meat is tender and a fork inserts easily into them, about 1 hour; turn them two or three times as they cook and add water as needed to maintain the same broth level. When the roulades are done, transfer them to a clean platter. Leave the skillet on the stovetop.

GRAVY

3 tablespoons flour
¼ cup water
Salt and pepper to taste

MAKE THE GRAVY:

~ **FIRST,** blend the flour with the water in a small bowl, using a stiff wire whisk to form a smooth paste. Turn the burner to medium-high heat; when the liquid in the skillet begins to simmer, add in about half of the paste, whisking constantly; add in the remaining paste, a little at a time, until the gravy has thickened. Let the gravy simmer for 5 minutes, then season to taste with salt and pepper.

~ **SECOND,** place the roulades in the gravy to keep them warm until you are ready to serve.

NOTE: *If you wish to prepare the roulades a day ahead, simply follow the directions through the first step of making the gravy. Cool the gravy to room temperature, then whisk in an extra ¼ cup of cool water. Place the cooked roulades in an ovenproof casserole and pour the gravy over them; then cover the casserole with a tight-fitting lid and refrigerate overnight. Warm the roulades, still covered, in a 325°F oven until they are completely heated through, about 45 minutes.*

POTATO DUMPLINGS
8 SERVINGS

One can say

everything best

over a meal.

GEORGE ELIOT

Potatoes have been at the center of the German table almost since the time they were imported from the New World. This is due in part to Frederick the Great, who had his vast army distribute seed potatoes to peasant farmers countrywide and then issued a decree that "encouraged" planting them. Potato-based soups, dumplings, salads, pancakes and breads were soon to follow.

DUMPLINGS

3¾ cups mashed potatoes
½ cup all-purpose flour
½ cup farina or cream of wheat
1 tablespoon salt
¼ teaspoon white pepper
Pinch of nutmeg
2 large eggs, lightly beaten
24 ¾-inch-square croutons

MAKE THE DUMPLINGS:

FIRST, peel and boil about 5 medium potatoes. When they are cooked completely, drain thoroughly; then spread them out on a baking sheet to fully evaporate the moisture. Cool the potatoes to room temperature, then mash by hand or pass through a ricer. Do not add any additional liquid. Measure out 3¾ cups. (*Note:* These can be made a day in advance.)

SECOND, whisk the flour and farina together with the salt, white pepper and nutmeg in a small bowl. Use a wooden spoon to beat this flour mixture, a few tablespoons at a time, into the mashed potatoes. When all the dry ingredients are incorporated into the potatoes, add in the eggs. Beat just until the eggs are fully incorporated and the dough is smooth and holds its shape. If the dough is too thin, add in a little more flour.

THIRD, lightly dust your hands with flour. Scoop off about 2 tablespoons of the dough and form into a rough ball. Place 1 crouton in the center of the ball and reshape until it is smooth and round. Repeat the process with the rest of the dough and croutons. As you work, transfer the dumplings to a lightly buttered dish, spacing them apart so they do not touch one another.

FOURTH, bring 4 quarts of salted water to a boil in a large pot. Drop in the dumplings one at a time, stirring the water gently as you do to keep them from sticking to one another. When the dumplings begin to float to the surface, reduce the heat to medium and simmer for 12 to 15 minutes. Remove the dumplings from the water using a slotted spoon and transfer to a serving bowl. If desired, dot with a little butter and sprinkle with chopped parsley.

SWEET-AND-SOUR RED CABBAGE
8 SERVINGS

You'll love this sweet-and-sour red cabbage. It is especially great with roulades or sauerbraten, but we also serve it for Christmas dinner alongside roast duck or venison.

SWEET-AND-SOUR CABBAGE

1 medium head of red cabbage
⅔ cup red wine vinegar
2 tablespoons granulated sugar
2 teaspoons salt
2 tablespoons lard or bacon fat
1 medium apple, peeled, cored and sliced
1 small onion, thinly sliced
1 bay leaf
1 whole clove
¼ cup red currant jelly
½ cup boiling water
Salt and pepper to taste

MAKE THE CABBAGE:

~ **FIRST,** rinse the head of cabbage under cold running water and remove the tough outer leaves. Slice into quarters and cut out the core. Thinly shred the cabbage using a serrated knife or food processor fitted with a steel blade.

~ **SECOND,** place the shredded cabbage in a stainless mixing bowl. Sprinkle with the vinegar, sugar and salt and toss together until the cabbage is thoroughly coated.

~ **THIRD,** melt the lard or bacon fat over medium heat in a heavy 4-quart casserole or stainless pot. Add in the apple and onion slices and sauté for 4 to 5 minutes, stirring frequently, until the onions are lightly browned. Add in the seasoned cabbage, bay leaf and clove; toss thoroughly and sauté for another 5 minutes. Lightly whisk together the red currant jelly and the boiling water in a small bowl, then pour into the sweet-and-sour cabbage.

~ **FOURTH,** cover the pot with a tight-fitting lid and reduce the heat to low. Check every so often to make sure the cabbage has enough moisture to keep it from sticking to the bottom of the pot; add in a little more hot water, if needed. Simmer until the cabbage is tender but still has some bite left to it, 40 to 50 minutes. The cabbage is done when it has turned a deep vibrant red, like the color of pickled beets, and all the liquid has been fully absorbed.

~ **FIFTH,** remove the bay leaf and clove. Adjust the seasoning to taste with salt and pepper and transfer to your favorite serving bowl.

SCALLOPED CAULIFLOWER AND LEEK GRATIN

8 SERVINGS

Cauliflower arrived in Europe in the sixteenth century and is cultivated today in countries known for their cool climates. A common practice known as frost-sweetening, in which the cauliflowers are not harvested until after the first frost, is still used to increase their natural sweetness. They get their snowy hue from the large leaves that shelter the head from sunlight. Select a large head of cauliflower that is creamy-white and without spots or blemishes; make sure that the florets are firm and the leaves are green and still covering much of the flower.

GRATIN

1 head cauliflower
4 medium leeks
2 cups whole milk
1 chicken bouillon cube
1 teaspoon dry mustard
2 tablespoons butter
2 tablespoons all-purpose flour
Salt and white pepper to taste
¾ cup grated Swiss cheese
¼ cup fresh white bread crumbs

~ Preheat the oven to 350°F.

MAKE THE GRATIN:

~ **FIRST,** wash the head of cauliflower well. Remove the outer leaves and any small bruised sections. Use a paring knife to remove the core and break the cauliflower into florets.

~ **SECOND,** pour 1 inch of water into a saucepan and add the cauliflower florets. Cover the pan, bring the water to a boil, and steam until tender yet still firm, 6 to 8 minutes. Remove the pan from heat and set aside, keeping the lid on.

~ **MEANWHILE,** cut the root end and tough dark green leaves from the leeks, leaving only the white and tender green parts; thinly slice the leeks and rinse well under cool running water.

~ **THIRD,** scald the milk in a small pan over medium-high heat; thoroughly whisk in the chicken bouillon and the dry mustard. Remove from heat and cover to keep warm.

~ **FOURTH,** melt the butter in a medium skillet over medium-high heat and sauté the leeks until they are tender and translucent in color, 3 to 4 minutes. Sprinkle the flour over the leeks and stir until the flour blends with the butter to form a *roux*. Whisk in the scalded milk; then season to taste with the salt and white pepper. Simmer until thickened, about 5 minutes.

~ **FIFTH,** thoroughly drain the cauliflower and transfer to a large buttered casserole. Arrange the grated Swiss cheese over the cauliflower and pour in the creamed leek mixture. Sprinkle the fresh bread crumbs evenly over the top of the casserole and bake for about 40 minutes.

FARMHOUSE CARAWAY
RYE ROLLS
MAKES 18 ROLLS

Because white flour was once very expensive, white bread was a symbol of wealth and prosperity in American German communities. White bread came from the city, dark bread from the country. Hearty grains such as rye, barley and corn make satisfying, nourishing loaves of bread—the perfect accompaniment to this meal or served alongside a steaming bowl of soup.

ROLLS

1 package (2¼ teaspoons) active dry yeast
¼ cup warm water, about 110°F
¼ cup molasses
2 tablespoons shortening, melted
1 cup water, room temperature

1¼ cups whole-grain rye flour
1½ cups bread flour
½ tablespoon salt
1 teaspoon caraway seeds

MAKE THE ROLLS:

FIRST, sprinkle the yeast over the ¼ cup water and let stand for 1 minute. Then stir until the yeast is dissolved.

SECOND, whisk the molasses and the melted shortening together in the bowl of a mixer; whisk in 1 cup of water and the dissolved yeast. Stir in the rye flour with ½ cup of the bread flour using a wooden spoon; continue stirring until the mixture is smooth, elastic and the consistency of thick batter, about 200 strokes. Scrape down the sides of the bowl with a rubber spatula. Cover the bowl with a clean tea towel and set in a draft-free place until the dough is bubbly and has doubled in volume, about 1½ hours.

THIRD, whisk the remaining cup of bread flour together with the salt. Use an electric mixer fitted with a dough hook to slowly incorporate the flour into the bubbly dough, adding in a little extra flour if needed, a tablespoon at a time, until the dough pulls away from the bowl and forms into a ball. Turn the mixer speed to low and knead for about 8 minutes. The dough should be smooth, densely textured and stiff enough to hold its shape.

FOURTH, transfer the dough to a lightly oiled bowl. Cover the bowl with a clean tea towel and set in a draft-free place until the dough has again doubled in volume, about 1 hour. Punch the dough down, cover with plastic wrap and refrigerate for at least 30 minutes and up to 4 hours.

FIFTH, turn the dough out onto a clean work surface that has been lightly dusted with flour. Sprinkle the caraway seeds evenly over the dough and knead them in using the heels of your hands. Divide the dough into 18 equal pieces and shape into rolls. Place the rolls on a baking sheet that has been lightly dusted with cornmeal and let them rest at room temperature, covered with a clean tea towel, for 40 minutes. Brush with a little water and, if desired, sprinkle with more caraway seeds and a pinch of coarse salt. Bake in a 375°F oven for 15 to 18 minutes.

DARK CHERRY–ALMOND KUCHEN
12 SERVINGS

German homemakers brought to America simple cakes known as kuchen. *These delicacies are somewhere between a crumb cake and a tart, and are excellent with fresh fruit, such as peaches, apricots, plums or apples. Sweet dark cherries, fresh or canned, are my favorite. Kuchen are best made a day ahead and served at room temperature, topped with mounds of freshly whipped cream.*

CRUST

¼ cup granulated sugar
½ cup whole milk
1 package (2¼ teaspoons) active dry yeast
3 cups all-purpose flour
½ teaspoon salt
12 tablespoons (1½ sticks) unsalted butter, softened
Zest of 1 lemon
2 large eggs, room temperature

MAKE THE CRUST:

~ **FIRST,** whisk the sugar into the milk and scald in the microwave or in a small pan over medium heat just to the point of boiling; cool until lukewarm (about 110°F) and then sprinkle the yeast over the top. Let the yeast stand for 1 minute, then stir until thoroughly dissolved.

~ **SECOND,** whisk the 2 cups of the flour and the salt together in a separate bowl; set aside.

~ **THIRD,** beat 4 tablespoons of the butter together with the lemon zest and the eggs in the bowl of a mixer fitted with a paddle; then beat in the lukewarm milk mixture. Set the mixer to low speed and add in the flour mixture, ½ cup at a time, until the dry ingredients are fully incorporated. Continue mixing at low speed until the dough is silky and elastic, about 3 minutes. Then slowly add in the remaining 8 tablespoons of butter, a tablespoon at a time, until the butter is completely blended into the dough.

~ **FOURTH,** cover the bowl with a clean tea towel and let rise until doubled in volume, about 1 hour. Punch down the dough, then transfer to a clean, lightly floured work surface and knead in the remaining 1 cup of flour. Roll into a 10-by-14-inch rectangle. Transfer to a 13x9-inch baking pan, fitting the dough into the pan so that it extends ½-inch up the sides. Prick the crust all over with a fork, then cover the pan with a clean tea towel and let the dough rise for an additional 20 minutes.

My kitchen is...

a place where

the surfaces seem

to have significance,

and odors may

carry meaning that

transfers from the past

and bridges to the future.

PEARL BAILEY

ALMOND FILLING

4 ounces almond paste
½ cup granulated sugar
½ cup (1 stick) unsalted butter
2 large eggs, room temperature
6 tablespoons all-purpose flour

PREPARE THE ALMOND FILLING:

~ Combine the almond paste and sugar in the bowl of a mixer fitted with a paddle; beat until the two are thoroughly creamed, about 3 minutes. Add in the butter and beat until smooth, about 2 more minutes. Turn the mixer speed to low and add in the eggs one at a time, beating just enough after each addition to fully incorporate. Add in the flour and mix just enough to blend.

STREUSEL TOPPING

¾ cup all-purpose flour
½ cup packed light brown sugar
Pinch of salt
¼ cup (½ stick) unsalted butter

PREPARE THE STREUSEL TOPPING:

~ Combine the flour with the brown sugar and a pinch of salt; whisk together thoroughly. Slice the butter into ½-inch pieces and use a pastry cutter to blend the butter into the flour mixture until large, tender clumps form.

CHERRY FILLING

½ cup cherry jam
2 cups pitted dark cherries, fresh or canned
1 tablespoon cornstarch

ASSEMBLE THE TART:

~ Spread the cherry jam evenly over the crust; then spread the almond filling inside the crust so that it reaches just below the top edge of the dough and seals in the jam. Mix the cherries with the cornstarch and spread them evenly over the almond filling, making sure they remain inside the top edge of the dough. Sprinkle the streusel topping over the surface of the filling and the crust, covering the top of the tart from edge to edge. Bake in a 375°F oven for 35 to 40 minutes.

No one who cooks,

cooks alone.

Even at her most

solitary, a cook

in the kitchen

is surrounded

by generations

of cooks past,

the advice and menus

of cooks present,

and the wisdom

of cookbook writers.

LAURIE COLWIN

Harvest of the Lakes

ROAST DUCK WITH CHERRY CIDER AND DRIED CRANBERRIES
HERB-SCENTED MUSHROOM WILD RICE
MAPLE-GLAZED RUTABAGAS AND WINTER SQUASH
SOUR CREAM–APPLE BUNDT CAKE

Along our northern border, among the great north woods, Americans have long enjoyed the harvest of the lakes. Although Vikings visited Minnesota in 1362, the French were among the first to explore and settle in these northern territories. They were followed by a wave of other groups, who further enriched the area with their traditions, customs, and cooking styles.

These newcomers settled near the of headwaters of the mighty Mississippi, along the St. Croix and St. Louis rivers, with easy outlets to the Great Lakes and the Mississippi. St. Paul and her twin city, Minneapolis, soon became centers for manufacturing, mining, timber, and trade. The vast lands from Montana across the rugged Dakotas and to the Mississippi River were incorporated into our nation as part of the Louisiana Purchase.

This is the northernmost section of the great Mississippi flyway in the United States. Millions of birds and waterfowl migrate to and from these vast wetlands yearly. Mere shadows gliding over waves of wheat and corn, they journey across the rolling plains, soaring above silos and red barns and to rest in the interior lowlands. This is the Land of Ten Thousand Lakes and the Superior uplands. It's a country of wild woods, dense forests, rolling plains, and family farms.

Mushrooms are found in abundance. Wild cherries and sugar maples provide a sweet harvest. Mossy bogs blink bright red with cranberries.

Among the native harvests is wild rice, the seed of the long marsh grass native to the western Great Lakes region. Indian tribes harvested this grain and relied on it first for sustenance and later as a trading commodity. Life in this area revolved around the wild rice harvest. Local tribes set up summer camps in the north to hunt game and gather the grains, wild berries, and mushrooms growing in the marshes and on the forest floors. The berries and mushrooms were dried and stored for winter meals. Several tribes even created wild rice "farms" by wrapping the plants with ropes and sectioning off boundaries. Many tribal wars were fought over control of the marshes, but eventually the Chippewa became the dominant force. And though much of the wild rice is now produced in cultivated paddies, state laws still protect the Chippewa's access to the grain.

Slow-roasted, succulent, and full of flavor, duck is a traditional autumn and winter feast long associated with the harvest, the joyous seasons of Advent, Christmas, and the Epiphany. Here is a menu to mark such a feast. It's a menu that celebrates the abundant harvest of the lakes.

ROAST DUCK WITH CHERRY CIDER AND DRIED CRANBERRIES

8 SERVINGS

In our home, my family and I enjoy duck each Christmas—roasted crisp and seasoned with fresh herbs. Our celebration begins on the fourth Sunday before Christmas Eve, which is the first Sunday of Advent—a four-week-long time of anticipation when we prepare our hearts and home for the coming of the Christ-child. On the first Sunday of Advent, we purchase and trim our tree; on each consecutive Sunday, we invite friends for dinner. After all, Christmas is not just one day; it's a season (a season with four Sunday dinners)!

NOTE: *A tender, well-fed duckling will have a good amount of fat, which renders and drains from the bird while cooking. This natural fat can be refrigerated in a crock and used for flavoring recipes, such as the "Herb-Scented Mushroom Wild Rice" recipe found later in this menu.*

ROAST DUCKS

2 whole 5-pound ducklings
1 tablespoon fresh chopped rosemary
2 tablespoons fresh chopped thyme

PROCESS THE DUCKS:

~ **FIRST,** remove the necks and giblets. Thoroughly rinse each duck inside and out under cold running water and pat dry with paper towels. Cut away the excess skin from around the neck opening and discard. Cut the wing tips and first wing joint from each duck and reserve, along with the giblets, to be used for the sauce.

~ **SECOND,** carefully separate the legs from the ducks by pulling them away from the body and cutting the skin between the thigh and the breast as you would a chicken. Then separate the whole leg from where the joint is attached to the back. Break off the large piece of the back from where it is attached to the whole breast.

~ **THIRD,** use a sharp knife or poultry shears to cut the remaining backs from each whole duck breast and split each breast by cutting down each side of the remaining backbone and down the middle of the breastbone, leaving the small wing bone attached. Carefully cut away the small rib bones and trim any pieces of excess fat and skin. You will have four whole breasts with the small wing bones attached, four whole legs, and the pieces of backbone and wing tips for the sauce.

~ **FOURTH,** season the breasts and legs with the rosemary and thyme, cover with plastic wrap and refrigerate overnight. Then trim the fat and skin from the large pieces of back and discard, reserving the bones with the necks and giblets for making the sauce.

BASIC DUCK SAUCE

Reserved duck necks, wing tips, backs and giblets
1 carrot, peeled and chopped
1 rib celery, chopped
2 whole cloves garlic
1 leek, white part only, thinly sliced
1 medium onion, diced
2 tablespoons all-purpose flour
2 tablespoons tomato paste
¼ cup brandy or cognac
¾ cup fruity white wine
2 cups chicken stock
2 cups water
1 bay leaf
1 sprig fresh rosemary
1 sprig fresh thyme
6 to 8 black peppercorns

MAKE THE DUCK SAUCE:

~ **FIRST,** heat a skillet over high heat, then add in the reserved necks, wing tips, backs and giblets. Reduce the heat to medium and brown the pieces, undisturbed, for 4 to 5 minutes. Turn each piece over and continue to brown for 2 to 3 minutes longer; then scatter the chopped carrot, celery, garlic, leek and onion over the top. Toss with the bones until the onion and carrot begin to caramelize, 4 to 5 minutes.

SECOND, sprinkle the flour into the pan and then add in the tomato paste. Use a wooden spoon to toss all of this together—the flour and tomato paste will blend with the fat to form a *roux* (or what looks like a sticky mess clinging to the vegetables and bones). Cook for 1 to 2 minutes more, being careful that the flour does not scorch.

THIRD, remove the pan from heat and slowly pour in the brandy or cognac, taking care that you don't splatter yourself with the hot fat. Let the skillet rest away from heat for 1 minute to allow the alcohol to evaporate; then add in the wine and return the pan to medium heat. Stir everything together with a wooden spoon.

FOURTH, add in the chicken stock and then the water; stir to combine. Do not salt the sauce—the drippings from the bottom of the roasting pan, when added into the finished sauce, will provide exceptional flavor. Add in the bay leaf, rosemary, thyme and peppercorns. Bring to a boil, reduce the heat to low and simmer, stirring occasionally, until the liquid is reduced to 2 cups, about 90 minutes. When the sauce is reduced, strain it through a fine sieve and reserve. Discard the bones and vegetables.

PAN-ROASTING INGREDIENTS

1 tablespoon coarse salt
½ tablespoon coarse-ground black pepper
2 carrots, peeled and chopped
2 ribs celery, chopped
2 whole cloves garlic
2 medium onions, peeled and chopped

PAN-ROAST THE DUCKS:

FIRST, transfer the ducks from the refrigerator to a clean work surface; remove the plastic wrap and discard. Without piercing the meat, prick the skin all over with the tip of a sharp paring knife. This will allow some of the fat, which is layered between the skin and the meat, to release while the ducks self-baste. Season with the salt and pepper.

SECOND, heat a large skillet or Dutch oven over high heat. First add the whole duck legs to the skillet, skin side down; turn down to medium heat and cook until golden, about 6 to 8 minutes on each side. Remove the duck legs to a separate dish; drain and reserve the excess fat in the skillet. Then add the duck breasts to the skillet and brown for 4 to 5 minutes on each side. Again, drain and reserve the fat in the skillet.

THIRD, scatter the carrots, celery, garlic and onions in the bottom of the skillet and then place the browned pieces of duck, skin side up, on top of the vegetables. This will add extra flavor for finishing the sauce and prevent the pieces of duck from sitting in the fat as they roast. Transfer the skillet to a 350°F oven and bake until the duck is tender and the juices run clear when the legs are pieced between the thigh and leg, 60 to 70 minutes.

FOURTH, transfer the duck pieces to a baking sheet. Remove the vegetables from the drippings with a slotted spoon and discard. Carefully pour off all of the duck fat and reserve—you should have about 1 cup. Leave any drippings in the bottom of the skillet.

CHERRY CIDER–CRANBERRY SAUCE:

1 cup cherry cider or cherry juice
2 cups basic duck sauce
½ cup cherry preserves
1 cup dried cranberries
1 tablespoon orange zest
Salt and pepper to taste

MAKE THE CHERRY CIDER–CRANBERRY SAUCE:

Set the skillet back over medium-high heat, pour in the cherry cider and blend the cider with the drippings. Simmer for 3 to 4 minutes to reduce the juice, then add in the duck sauce, cherry preserves, cranberries and orange zest. Simmer for 4 to 5 minutes; season to taste, if necessary, with salt and pepper.

SERVE THE DUCKS:

Crisp the skin by placing the baking pan full of duck pieces under the broiler for 2 to 3 minutes. Arrange the crisp pieces of duck on a serving platter; if desired, garnish with orange slices and sprigs of fresh herbs. Lace the roasted duck with the sauce and pass the remaining sauce in a gravy boat.

Easy time-saving

AND DO-AHEAD TIPS:

FRIDAY EVENING

Trim the ducks, quarter and season. Prepare the basic duck sauce and refrigerate.

SATURDAY

Par-cook the wild rice and refrigerate covered in a stainless bowl. Bake the apple cake.

SUNDAY MORNING

Pan-roast the duck quarters. Cut the squash and rutabagas into pieces and refrigerate in well-sealed containers.

HERB-SCENTED MUSHROOM WILD RICE
8 SERVINGS

Wild rice, which is known for its distinctly nutty flavor, is a perfect accompaniment to duck. The birds love to feed on this wild grain, so what could be more natural than serving them together? This is a really ethereal dish, with the heady mushrooms, leeks and fresh herbs. It is also great with pheasant or quail, and especially good alongside game hen.

WILD RICE

2 cups wild rice, thoroughly rinsed	1 cup chopped leeks (white part only)
6 cups water	½ cup diced onion
½ ounce dried wild mushrooms	Pinch of salt
½ pound assorted fresh mushrooms	1 tablespoon fresh chopped rosemary
¼ cup duck fat or butter	1 tablespoon fresh chopped thyme
½ cup diced celery	1 cup chicken broth
2 cloves garlic, chopped	Salt and pepper to taste

PAR-COOK THE WILD RICE:

Combine the rice and water in a heavy-bottomed saucepan over medium-high heat. Bring to a boil and reduce the heat to low; then cover with a tight-fitting lid and simmer, stirring occasionally, until the rice is just tender but still firm and the grain has not yet split open, about 40 minutes. Drain, cool and reserve.

MAKE THE MUSHROOM WILD RICE:

FIRST, soak the dried mushrooms in warm water for 45 minutes; rinse and drain. Clean the fresh mushrooms with a damp paper towel and discard any tough or woody stems. Roughly chop all of the mushrooms.

SECOND, heat the duck fat in a skillet over medium-high heat and sauté the celery, garlic, leeks and onion until the onion begins to brown, 4 to 5 minutes. Add in the chopped mushrooms, season with a pinch of salt and toss with the rosemary and thyme; turn the heat to medium-low, cover the pan and simmer until the mushrooms are tender, 2 to 3 minutes.

THIRD, toss in the par-cooked wild rice and stir in the chicken broth. Raise the heat to medium, cover and simmer until the rice is fully cooked, 10 to 15 minutes. Season to taste with salt and pepper.

MAPLE-GLAZED RUTABAGAS
AND WINTER SQUASH
8 SERVINGS

Rutabagas, or "Swedish turnips," are thought to be a cross between turnips and cabbage. They have a spicy, slightly sweet flavor that is very much like a turnip. They are wonderful and pair perfectly with any variety of winter squash, like Hubbard or Butternut.

RUTABAGAS AND SQUASH

2 large rutabagas
1½ pounds winter squash
¼ cup (½ stick) butter
Pinch of nutmeg
Salt and pepper to taste
¼ cup pure maple syrup

PREPARE THE RUTABAGAS AND SQUASH:

~ **FIRST,** peel the rutabagas and cut into 1-inch pieces. Remove the seeds from the squash, slice away the hard outer shell and cut into 1-inch pieces.

~ **SECOND,** place the rutabagas and the squash into a large skillet and cover with cold salted water. Bring to a boil over high heat, cover the skillet with a tight-fitting lid and cook the vegetables until they are tender when pierced with the tip of a sharp knife, 8 to 10 minutes. Drain the water from the skillet, return the pan to the stove and reduce the heat to medium.

~ **THIRD,** cut the butter into small pieces and add to the skillet, tossing with the vegetables as it melts. Season with the pinch of nutmeg, salt and pepper. Pour in the maple syrup and cook for 2 to 3 minutes for a nice even glaze.

Planning special

Sunday celebrations

shows how much

we truly care

as we build traditions

that add luster and color

to this mosaic

we call "family."

RC

SOUR CREAM–APPLE BUNDT CAKE

12 SERVINGS

The bundt cake was invented in Minnesota, which might explain why one finds so many bundt recipes in the Upper Midwest. With just the right hint of spice and crumbly goodness, this one is sure to become a family favorite. The cooked apples keep this rich, buttery cake really moist. I prefer to use mellow Golden Delicious apples, which stay firm and retain their shape when baked.

APPLES

6 medium Golden Delicious apples
¼ cup (½ stick) unsalted butter
¼ cup granulated sugar
1 teaspoon cardamom

~ Adjust the rack to the center of the oven and preheat to 350°F.

PREPARE THE APPLES:

~ Peel, core and quarter the apples; slice each quarter into 3 slices lengthwise. Melt the butter in a skillet over medium-low heat; when it begins to bubble, add in the apples, along with the sugar and cardamom, and sauté over low heat until the apples are tender but still firm, 3 to 4 minutes. Remove the apples from heat and cool to room temperature. Drain the apple slices and reserve the syrup—you should have 2 or 3 tablespoons.

CAKE BATTER

½ cup (1 stick) unsalted butter
2 cups all-purpose flour
1¼ cup granulated sugar
2 teaspoons baking powder
1 teaspoon baking soda
¼ teaspoon allspice
½ teaspoon cinnamon
½ teaspoon salt
1 cup sour cream
2 large eggs, room temperature

1 teaspoon pure vanilla extract
Reserved syrup from the apples
½ cup fresh bread crumbs

FOR THE PAN

2 tablespoons unsalted butter
½ cup fresh bread crumbs

MAKE THE CAKE:

~ FIRST, melt the butter and cool to room temperature.

~ SECOND, in a large bowl combine the flour, sugar, baking powder, baking soda, allspice, cinnamon and salt; whisk together thoroughly.

~ THIRD, combine the cooled butter and sour cream in a separate bowl and beat until smooth; add in the eggs and beat until they are fully blended.

~ FOURTH, add the dry ingredients, ½ a cup at a time, into the sour cream mixture, mixing on low speed just long enough after each addition to fully incorporate. Scrape down the sides of the bowl with a spatula. Add in the vanilla and the reserved apple syrup, then increase the mixer speed to medium and beat for about 1 minute. Toss the cooked apple slices with the ½ cup of bread crumbs and fold them into the batter.

~ FIFTH, liberally butter a 9-inch bundt pan with the 2 tablespoons butter and sprinkle the inside with the fresh bread crumbs. Make sure the pan is completely coated before tapping out the excess.

~ SIXTH, spoon the prepared batter into the bundt pan and bake for 50 to 60 minutes. When it is done, the cake should be pulling away from the edges of the pan and a wooden pick should come out clean when inserted. Cool on a wire rack for 20 minutes, then run a thin metal spatula around the edges of the pan to loosen. Gently invert the cake onto the cooling rack and cool to room temperature.

SERVE THE CAKE:

~ If desired, lightly dust each slice with powdered sugar and serve with mounds of freshly whipped cream.

A Timeless Sensibility

>> >> >>   SCALLOP AND CORN CHOWDER
OLD-FASHIONED YANKEE POT ROAST
BAKED TOMATOES
PARKER HOUSE ROLLS
VICTORIAN GINGERBREAD

Call it merchant savvy or Yankee ingenuity—this energetic blend of enterprise, industry, and plain old common sense helped shape the American character and define the American experience. From the time the Dutch East India Company financed an expedition to America (ten years before the Pilgrims landed at Plymouth Rock) and purchased the lands that are now Manhattan Island, commerce has been the lifeblood of this land we call home.

Merchant savvy and Yankee know-how continued to flourish in the nineteenth century, but it was always balanced by a powerful love of home and family. The home was the center of Victorian-era city life, an oasis from the busy workaday world. While city life bustled outside, the interior of the house glowed with warmth. Homemaking was elevated to a fine craft and celebrated in publications like *Godey's Lady's Book* and *The American Woman's Home*. Crafts, music, family games, and story time were the hallmarks of a serene, well-ordered life.

And Sunday was always special—a day of lingering charm, white linen and lace, content and secure children, providence and protection. Families enjoyed a wholesome afternoon filled with fun and frolic, relished long into the evening and hushed only by the fall of night.

Our world today is not so different. We busily engage in commerce and pursue excellence in our chosen vocations. We work hard, and our children study hard—but to what end, if we don't take pleasure in just a few uninterrupted hours together one day a week?

Today we celebrate an appropriate balance: family ideals and comforting foods, enjoyed in the refuge of our home: a hearty, slow-simmered chowder; a tender, juicy pot roast; a simple, warm-from-the-oven slice of gingerbread crowned with a mound of sweetened whipped cream. And the family all gathered together, reveling in the values that give meaning and purpose to everything we do.

What could possibly be more important?

SCALLOP AND CORN CHOWDER

8 SERVINGS

Chowder was an early offering to American cooking. The rich, thick seafood stew was once a staple along the coastal European lowlands—in Holland, Belgium and France—and is mother to the now-famous soups enjoyed all over our own Atlantic seaboard. Early recipes were not, however, milk based; nor did they include potatoes until late in the eighteenth century. The chowders we know today are classically American—especially those made with corn.

CHOWDER

4 ears of sweet corn, shucked

2 cups half-and-half

4 tablespoons (½ stick) butter

½ cup diced celery

2 cloves garlic, minced

1 cup sliced leeks

½ cup diced onion

1 pound bay scallops

1 teaspoon fresh thyme leaves

¼ cup all-purpose flour

4 cups fish stock or clam broth

Salt and white pepper to taste

MAKE THE CHOWDER:

~ **FIRST,** steam the ears of corn until they are tender, about 5 minutes. Refresh the ears in an ice bath and cut the kernels from the cobs with a sharp knife. Reserve the kernels and the cobs.

~ **SECOND,** heat the half-and-half in a medium saucepan until it just begins to boil, then reduce the heat to low and steep the cobs in the half-and-half for about 20 minutes to extract all the sweet flavor of the corn. Remove and discard the cobs; keep the half-and-half warm.

~ **THIRD,** melt 2 tablespoons of the butter in a 2½-quart heavy-bottomed saucepan over medium-low heat. Add in the celery, garlic, leeks and onion and sauté in the melted butter for 1 minute, stirring frequently. Cover the pan with a tight-fitting lid and allow the vegetables to steam until they are tender and translucent, 2 to 3 minutes.

~ **FOURTH,** make a well in the center of the saucepan by pushing the vegetables to the sides of the pan. Add the remaining 2 tablespoons of butter into the center of the well. When the butter begins to bubble, add in the scallops and thyme leaves. Continue cooking for 1 to 2 minutes, until the scallops are opaque and the fragrant aroma of the thyme is steaming from the pan; then gently stir together with the vegetables.

~ **FIFTH,** increase the heat to medium, sprinkle the flour into the pan and carefully but thoroughly mix it in with a wooden spoon or a heat-resistant spatula. As you stir, the flour, butter and juices will combine to form a light *roux*. Quickly pour in the fish stock or clam juice and stir until the mixture is smooth, thick and bubbly, about 1 minute. Slowly stir in the reserved scalded half-and-half and then add in the corn. Continue stirring gently and cook for 3 to 4 minutes more. Season the chowder to taste with salt and white pepper.

To me as a child, Sunday dinners were about the beauty of the ordinary and the sanctity of Sunday and family. "Dinner" in our Dutch community was one of five meals served each day: breakfast; midmorning coffee time; dinner at noon; midafternoon coffee time; and supper, which followed the evening chores. Coffee time consisted of what many nonfarmers would call lunch—ham on buns, a cookie or pastry, and coffee. Dinner was always a hot meal.

But Sunday dinner was set apart. It was a special time for family. After the morning church service each Sunday, my parents, brother, and I journeyed the twenty miles through the cornfields to my grandparents' house. We gathered with uncles and aunts and cousins around the large rectangular table in the kitchen. Every Sunday I looked forward to the same foods: canned beef, mashed potatoes and gravy, and applesauce. I'm sure other things were served, but I can't remember them. I always focused on the salty, browned shredded beef my grandmother had canned from their own livestock. The gravy, of course, was homemade. The potatoes came from their garden, which encompassed more square footage than their house. The applesauce came from the apple trees in the orchard, where the sheep kept the grass short.

We would eat and talk during dinner, discussing Sunday sermons and news from town. Church bulletins from our respective churches were exchanged; their content was often more informative than our small-town newspapers.

Our custom at every meal was to pray before we ate and then afterward read the Bible or a devotional book and pray again. This is what I remember the most about Sunday dinner: my grandfather reading the Bible. Grandfather, whose parents' primary language was Dutch, had less than an eighth-grade education and wasn't a man given to long oratories. I'm not sure if these factors influenced his reading style, but I do know that he read slowly and carefully, almost haltingly, and with a sense of reverence and awe. And through his reading I heard the Scriptures afresh—especially when he read the Psalms. To me, it was as if God spoke.

GINA VOS

OLD-FASHIONED YANKEE POT ROAST
8 SERVINGS

The origin of this humble American favorite is generally attributed to the Dutch, who first settled in New York. The pot roast and its many variations—including daube, pot-au-feu, estouffade and potjevfleisch—were slowly simmered with vegetables in Dutch ovens. They were often prepared the day before and reheated on Sunday, but sometimes they were placed in a moderate oven that morning to slow-cook for hours and be ready after church—which may explain why this exceptional choice has remained a favorite for generations.

POT ROAST

1 4- to 5-pound beef chuck roast, 2 inches thick
2 teaspoons salt
1 teaspoon coarse-ground black pepper
2 tablespoons all-purpose flour
1 tablespoon vegetable oil
2 cups beef broth
1 cup water, as needed
1 bay leaf
2 cloves garlic, sliced
Pinch of marjoram or summer savory

PREPARE THE ROAST:

~ **FIRST,** season the meat with the salt and pepper and coat well with the flour. Use a wooden mallet or tenderizer to pound the flour into the meat.

~ **SECOND,** heat the oil over medium-high heat in a Dutch oven or heavy casserole fitted with a lid. When the oil is just beginning to smoke, reduce the temperature to medium, add the meat and brown it slowly, turning it every minute or so. When the roast is evenly browned on all sides, pour in all the beef broth and just enough water to cover the roast a little more than halfway; add in the bay leaf, sliced garlic and marjoram or summer savory. Cover the pan and simmer on the stovetop over low heat or in a 300°F oven for 2 to 2½ hours.

FRIDAY EVENING

Bake the gingerbread, cool to room temperature and seal with plastic wrap.

SATURDAY

Prepare the chowder, cool and refrigerate in a well-sealed container. Prepare the vegetables for the pot roast and refrigerate in well-sealed containers.

SUNDAY MORNING

Prepare the dough for the rolls and refrigerate. Prepare and refrigerate the tomatoes. Remove the pot roast from the refrigerator and bring to room temperature.

VEGETABLES

4 large carrots
4 ribs celery
2 large onions
2 large turnips
8 medium potatoes
Salt and pepper to taste

PREPARE THE VEGETABLES:

~ **FIRST,** peel the carrots and cut into 1½-inch-thick rounds. Trim the celery and cut into 1-inch pieces. Peel the onions and cut into quarters. Peel the turnips and cut into quarters. Peel the potatoes and cut in half.

~ **SECOND,** after the roast has been cooking for 2 hours, test the meat to be sure it is tender by gently inserting a fork into the thickest part. If the roast does not yield easily to the fork, add in a little water as needed and continue cooking until the fork can be inserted effortlessly. Then add all the vegetables except for the potatoes into the liquid around the roast; replace the lid and cook for another 15 minutes.

~ **THIRD,** increase the oven temperature to 350°F, place the potatoes on top of the vegetables, season with a little salt and pepper, replace the lid and cook for 30 minutes more or until the potatoes are done. At this point the meat should be tender, just falling away from the fat and easy to pull apart from each section, but still firm enough to slice easily.

~ **FOURTH,** let the roast rest in the pan at room temperature for 15 minutes, then transfer the roast and vegetables to a platter. Cover with foil to keep warm and leave the cooking liquid in the roasting pan.

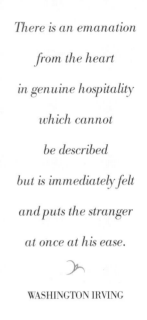

There is an emanation

from the heart

in genuine hospitality

which cannot

be described

but is immediately felt

and puts the stranger

at once at his ease.

WASHINGTON IRVING

GRAVY

3 tablespoons all-purpose flour
½ cup water
Salt and pepper to taste

PREPARE THE GRAVY:

~ **FIRST,** combine the 3 tablespoons flour with ½ cup of water in a small bowl and use a stiff wire whisk to form a smooth paste.

~ **SECOND,** place the roasting pan with the cooking liquid over medium-high heat; when the liquid begins to simmer, add in about half of the paste, whisking constantly. Add more paste, a little at a time, until the gravy thickens to the desired consistency. Turn the heat to low and let the gravy simmer for 5 minutes. Season to taste with salt and pepper.

SERVE THE ROAST:

~ Transfer the roast to a clean cutting board and use a sharp knife to slice the roast across the grain. Serve the pot roast on the platter, garnished with the vegetables. Pass the gravy separately in a gravy boat.

BAKED TOMATOES
8 SERVINGS

Tomatoes—"love apples," as they were once known—were introduced into New England cooking in the late eighteenth century. They became quite popular and were prepared in a variety of ways: sliced and seasoned with sugar, stewed, scalloped or home-canned. This is a wonderfully simple recipe and a perfect accompaniment to the pot roast.

TOMATOES

2 strips smoked bacon, diced
½ cup grated onion
1 tablespoon fresh chopped parsley
½ cup dry bread crumbs
8 medium ripe tomatoes
1 teaspoon salt
1 teaspoon granulated sugar

~ Preheat the oven to 350°F.

MAKE THE BAKED TOMATOES:

~ **FIRST,** sauté the bacon over medium-high heat in a small skillet until the bacon just begins to crisp. Add in the grated onion and the parsley; sauté for 1 minute more. Then combine the bacon mixture with the bread crumbs in a small bowl.

~ **SECOND,** slice the bottom from each tomato so they stand evenly; cut the top off and remove all of the stem. Grease the bottom of a ceramic baking dish with a little butter or bacon fat and arrange the tomatoes so that they are not touching one another. Sprinkle the tomatoes with the salt and sugar, then top with equal amounts of the bread crumb mixture. Bake in the preheated oven for 20 minutes, until the bread crumb topping is browned and the tomatoes are heated through.

The smell of good bread baking, like the sound of lightly flowing water, is indescribable in its evocation of innocence and delight.

M. K. FISHER

PARKER HOUSE ROLLS

18 ROLLS

*T*he Parker House in Boston was founded by coachman Harvey Parker and has been in operation since 1855. On one memorable occasion, Charles Dickens, Henry Longfellow, Oliver Wendell Holmes and Ralph Waldo Emerson dined together there. Perhaps they enjoyed these rolls, which are now an American classic.

ROLLS

1 package (2¼ teaspoons) active dry yeast
¼ cup warm water, about 110°F
1 cup whole milk
2 tablespoons granulated sugar
7 tablespoons unsalted butter
3 cups all-purpose flour
1 teaspoon salt

MAKE THE ROLLS:

FIRST, sprinkle the yeast over the warm water and let the mixture stand for 1 minute, then stir until the yeast is dissolved.

SECOND, heat the milk with the sugar just to the point of boiling in a small saucepan, then remove the pan from heat. Add 3 tablespoons of the butter and swirl until the butter has melted. Cool the mixture in the saucepan until lukewarm.

THIRD, combine the yeast mixture with the lukewarm milk in a mixing bowl and stir in 2 cups of the flour. The mixture will now be the consistency of a thick batter. Continue stirring for about 120 strokes. Cover the bowl with a clean tea towel and set in a draft-free place until it is bubbly and has doubled in volume, about 1 hour.

FOURTH, whisk the remaining cup of flour into the salt using a stiff wire whisk. Use an electric mixer fitted with a dough hook to slowly incorporate the flour mixture into the bubbly dough on low speed. Scrape down the sides of the bowl with a rubber spatula. Increase the mixer speed to medium and add in a little extra flour as necessary, until the dough begins to pull away from the sides of the bowl and form a ball. Reduce the mixer speed to low and knead the dough for about 5 minutes. The dough will have a smooth, soft texture. Dust the dough with a little flour to keep it from sticking to your hands; form it into a ball and place in a lightly oiled bowl, then cover with plastic wrap. Refrigerate for at least 30 minutes and up to 4 hours.

FIFTH, preheat the oven to 400°F. Melt the remaining 4 tablespoons of butter in a shallow bowl. Divide the dough into 18 equal pieces and roll them into balls. Place the balls on a clean dry surface that has been dusted with a little flour. Sprinkle the balls with a little more flour and flatten each with the palm of your hand. Brush each generously with the melted butter and fold in half. Place the rolls about 2 inches apart on a lightly greased baking sheet. Let the rolls rise in a draft-free place until they have doubled in size, about 1 hour, then bake for 12 to 15 minutes. Brush with any remaining melted butter.

VICTORIAN GINGERBREAD
9 SERVINGS

ingerbread has been made in this country since the Mayflower first arrived, and it reached the height of popularity during the Victorian years. Gingerbread was originally served alongside baked beans and roast pork, rather than as a dessert. My grandmother always substituted hot coffee for the water found in most recipes; she did the same with her delicious, old-fashioned applesauce cake.

GINGERBREAD

2¼ cups all-purpose flour
2 teaspoons baking soda
1 teaspoon ground cinnamon
½ teaspoon ground cloves
2 teaspoons ground ginger

½ teaspoon salt
⅔ cup shortening
⅔ cup packed light brown sugar
¾ cup molasses
2 large eggs, room temperature, well beaten
1 cup hot coffee

~ Adjust the rack to the center of the oven and pre-heat to 375°F.

MAKE THE GINGERBREAD:

~ **FIRST,** grease and lightly flour a 9x9x2-inch baking pan.

~ **SECOND,** whisk the flour, baking soda, cinnamon, cloves, ginger and salt together in a mixing bowl; set aside.

~ **THIRD,** combine the shortening and brown sugar in the bowl of an electric mixer fitted with a paddle; beat together at medium speed for 3 to 4 minutes. Pour in the molasses, then scrape down the sides of the bowl with a rubber spatula. Add in the beaten eggs and mix until the eggs are fully incorporated into the batter, about 1 minute.

~ **FOURTH,** turn the mixer speed down to low. Add in the dry ingredients, ½ cup at a time, mixing after each addition for about 10 seconds. When ⅔ of the dry ingredients are mixed in, quickly pour in half of the hot coffee, followed by the remaining dry ingredients, and finally the remaining coffee; mix until just combined.

~ **FIFTH,** scrape down the sides of the bowl with a rubber spatula and beat by hand for 20 to 30 strokes. Pour the batter into the prepared baking pan. Bake until a cake tester or wooden pick comes out clean, though still a little moist, when inserted into the middle, 40 to 45 minutes. Cool the cake in the pan.

SERVE THE GINGERBREAD:

~ Cut the gingerbread into 9 equal pieces and serve with mounds of sweetened freshly whipped cream.

Return to the Heartland

> HERB-ROASTED CHICKEN WITH SAGE STUFFING AND GIBLET GRAVY
> BUTTERY MASHED POTATOES
> ROASTED CARROT AND PARSNIP PURÉE
> CREAMED PEAS AND PEARL ONIONS
> KNOTTED HONEY–WHOLE WHEAT ROLLS
> HEARTLAND RAISIN-BUTTERMILK PIE

There's a reason we call the Midwest the heartland, and it's not just because it's in the center of the continent. In a sense, the sweeping region known as the Great Plains, with its heritage of hard work, self-reliance, and persevering faith, lives at the heart of American faith and values.

This vast area stretches from Illinois and Iowa across Kansas and Nebraska to eastern Colorado and from the Dakotas. The landscape is pancake flat or gently rolling, a subtle patchwork of farmland, pasture, and prairie under an enormous sky. This is the country of Frank Lloyd Wright, Laura Ingalls Wilder, and William Jennings Bryan; of quilting bees and county fairs; and of Holsteins and harvest moons. The land is written into our memories and celebrated in song for its tall grass, sweeping vistas, and amber waves of grain.

Much of America's heartland was settled during the great migration of the 1860s, when homesteading families arrived in droves to seek a better life. They were ambitious, self-reliant, do-it-yourself pioneers determined to carve a new homeland from the prairie. Soon they would be molded by the very land they sought to mold.

These were farmers who were used to working hard and performing the most difficult chores by themselves. Many came from Europe, especially Germany and the Scandinavian countries, fleeing poverty and war. Others ventured from homes back east in search of land and opportunity. They were Baptists, Amish, Mennonites, Lutherans, Methodists, and Quakers who saw their life of hard work as an expression of their quiet faith: A job worth doing was worth doing well.

Few things remind us of God's faithful provision and constancy as much as this understated, but bountiful, countryside, with its acres of grain and grazing livestock. (It's why this area is called America's "breadbasket.") Yet few things remind us of our dependence on God's grace as much as the massive storms, droughts, fires, and insect invasions that sometimes sweep across the unobstructed prairies. Living here has always called for an extra portion of enduring faith. We plow, we plant, we hope, but it is God who preserves us and brings the increase.

These realities took firm hold in the hearts of those who lived in this area during the Great Depression, when drought baked the prairie, and the overtilled soil blew away in great clouds. Those who stuck it out during the dust bowl developed particular habits of perseverance and thrift that shaped their very character.

Today we once again celebrate the heartland with satisfying and time-honored recipes that make good use of its bounty and resources. Wholesome, filling foods, garden vegetables thriftily prepared, simple but delicious pies, and whole-grain breads—these are the pride of the Great Plains Sunday dinner table.

HERB-ROASTED CHICKEN
WITH SAGE STUFFING AND GIBLET GRAVY
8 SERVINGS

We all have

hometown appetites.

Every other person

is a bundle of longing

for the simplicities

of good taste

once enjoyed on the farm

or in the hometown

left behind.

CLEMENTINE PADDLEFORD

This is roasted chicken at its very best! Use any combination of your favorite fresh herbs, such as parsley, sage, rosemary and thyme, for the chicken. In the southern U.S., stuffing is called dressing *and is often made with corn bread. This midwestern favorite, however, can made with either bread stuffing mix or corn bread mix.*

NOTE: *The 7- to 8-pound roaster called for in this recipe can be substituted by two 3- to 4-pound roasting chickens.*

SAGE STUFFING	ROASTED CHICKEN
¼ cup (½ stick) butter	1 7- to 8-pound roasting chicken
½ cup diced celery	1 tablespoon coarse salt
½ cup diced onion	2 tablespoons combined fresh chopped herbs
2 cups day-old bread cubes	Vegetable oil
1 tablespoon rubbed sage	¼ cup (½ stick) butter, melted
4 cups packaged dry stuffing	
¼ teaspoon salt	
¼ teaspoon white pepper	
¾ cup giblet stock (recipe follows) or chicken broth	

MAKE THE SAGE STUFFING:

➛ FIRST, melt half of the butter in a skillet over medium heat. Add in the diced celery and onion and sauté until the onions are soft and just beginning to brown, about 5 minutes. Make a well in the center of the pan by pushing the vegetables to the edges. Add in the remaining butter; when it begins to bubble, toss in the day-old bread cubes, sprinkle the sage over them and toss lightly for 1 minute, then stir together with the vegetables.

➛ SECOND, combine the dry stuffing mix in a mixing bowl with the salt and white pepper. Add in the sautéed bread cube mixture; toss together with as much of the giblet stock as needed to moisten. Allow the stuffing to cool to room temperature before preparing the chicken.

PREPARE THE CHICKEN:

➛ FIRST, preheat the oven to 375°F. Rub the inside of the chicken with the salt and half of the fresh chopped herbs. Stuff the chicken with the cooled dressing. Tuck the wings securely under the chicken and then tie the legs together with kitchen twine.

➛ SECOND, rub the outside of the chicken with a little vegetable oil, place in a shallow roasting pan and season the outside with salt. Bake for 30 minutes, then reduce the heat to 350°F and bake for approximately 2 more hours. Thirty minutes before the chicken is fully cooked, brush the skin with the melted butter and sprinkle with the remaining fresh chopped herbs.

~THIRD, the chicken is done when an instant-read thermometer reads 160°F when inserted into the thickest part of the thigh. The drumstick should move up and down easily in its socket and the juices should flow clear when a knife is inserted into the area between the leg and the thigh. Transfer the chicken to a clean cutting board and allow it to rest at room temperature for 15 minutes before carving.

GIBLET STOCK

NOTE: *The following easy-to-make giblet stock adds a great slow-cooked taste to the dressing and the gravy. And you can always chop the giblets to add to either. But if you're pressed for time, simply use a quality chicken broth or bouillon in its place.*

Neck and heart reserved from the chicken
1 small carrot, peeled and chopped
1 rib celery with leaves, chopped
1 whole clove garlic
1 small onion, chopped
4 cups chicken broth
1 bay leaf
1 thyme sprig
4 white peppercorns

PREPARE THE GIBLET STOCK:
~ FIRST, place the neck and heart into a medium saucepan along with the carrot, celery, garlic and onion. Pour in the chicken broth and bring to a boil. Reduce the heat to a simmer and use a ladle to skim off any residue that rises to the surface.

~ SECOND, add in the bay leaf, thyme sprig and white peppercorns; simmer until the giblets are tender, about 45 minutes. Cool and strain through a fine sieve. Reserve the giblets to chop and add to the gravy, if desired.

GRAVY

3 tablespoons all-purpose flour
2 cups giblet stock or chicken broth
Chopped reserved giblets (optional)
Salt and white pepper to taste

PREPARE THE GRAVY:
~ FIRST, pour the juices from the roasting pan into a cup and skim off the excess fat. Scrape the drippings free from the bottom of the pan. Place the roasting pan over medium heat and sprinkle the flour into the pan; pour in the pan juices and whisk into a paste using a stiff wire whisk.

~ SECOND, blend in the 2 cups giblet stock or chicken broth, reduce the heat to low and simmer for 5 minutes. Add in the chopped giblets, if desired, and season with salt and white pepper to taste.

CARVE THE CHICKEN:
~ Cut away the twine from the legs. Use a spoon to remove the stuffing from the cavity and transfer it to a serving bowl, then place the chicken on a platter. Pull each leg up and away from the body and slice the skin between the leg and the breast—the legs will come away easily—then cut between the drumstick and the thigh. Slice the breast meat just as you would carve a turkey: by holding the chicken firmly with a serving fork and cutting in a single motion from the top of the breastbone and down toward the side.

BUTTERY
MASHED POTATOES
8 SERVINGS

Americans love mashed potatoes seasoned in a variety of ways. Next time you make this recipe, try replacing the salt with a couple of chicken bouillon cubes added to the water while cooking the potatoes, along with a few slices of fresh garlic and a sprig of rosemary or thyme. Replacing the milk in the recipe with ⅔ cup of the seasoned potato water makes for a more savory mashed potato.

MASHED POTATOES

8 medium potatoes
½ cup (1 stick) butter
⅔ cup whole milk
Salt and pepper to taste

MAKE THE MASHED POTATOES:

— **FIRST,** peel the potatoes, pare away any eyes, and cut into quarters. Place the potatoes in a large pot filled with enough cool salted water to cover them completely. Heat the water to a low boil and simmer until the potatoes are completely cooked, 20 to 25 minutes.

— **SECOND,** drain the water from the potatoes, leaving them in the pot. Return the pot to the stove and let them cook for a minute, shaking the pan while the excess moisture evaporates. Add in the butter and continue to shake the pan until the butter melts completely and coats all of the potatoes (this will keep them from becoming sticky when they are mashed). Pour in the milk and bring to a boil, then remove the pan from heat and mash until fluffy. Season to taste with salt and pepper.

ROASTED CARROT
AND PARSNIP PURÉE
8 SERVINGS

Roasting the carrots and parsnips brings out their natural sugars and adds a hint of caramel flavor, which is a perfect complement to their juicy sweetness.

PURÉE

2 pounds carrots, scrubbed
1 pound parsnips, scrubbed
12 tablespoons (1½ sticks) butter
Salt to taste
2 tablespoons packed brown sugar
1 cup apple juice or white grape juice

— Preheat the oven to 325°F.

MAKE THE PURÉE:

— **FIRST,** bake the carrots and parsnips on a lightly oiled baking sheet until they are just beginning to soften, about 1 hour. Cool them enough to handle and peel away the skins with a sharp paring knife or vegetable peeler. Cut into ½-inch-thick rounds.

— **SECOND,** melt 4 tablespoons of the butter in a skillet over medium heat and sauté the roasted vegetables for 5 minutes. Season to taste with a little salt, add in the brown sugar and cook for another minute or so, stirring so that the sugar and butter combine thoroughly. Then pour in the apple or white grape juice and continue to cook over medium heat until the vegetables are completely cooked and the liquid has been reduced by half, 15 to 20 minutes. Turn off the heat and cover the pan until you are ready to purée.

— **THIRD,** purée the vegetables in a food processor or grind through a food mill. Whip in the remaining 8 tablespoons of butter and adjust the salt to taste.

CREAMED PEAS
AND PEARL ONIONS
8 SERVINGS

Tender peas and pearl onions, sweetened with just a touch of fresh cream and butter, are hard to beat for sheer simplicity. The addition of fresh mint and snipped chives is near culinary perfection.

CREAMED PEAS AND PEARL ONIONS

16 ounces (1 dry pint) pearl onions
2 tablespoons butter
4 cups freshly blanched peas or frozen peas, thawed
½ cup heavy cream
Salt to taste
1 tablespoon fresh snipped chives
1 teaspoon fresh chopped mint

PREPARE THE CREAMED PEAS AND ONIONS:

~ **FIRST,** place the onions in a medium bowl and cover them with boiling water. Steep for 5 minutes, then drain well; trim off the root ends with a paring knife and peel away the skin, leaving the onions whole.

~ **SECOND,** melt the butter in a small skillet over medium heat. When the butter just begins to bubble, add in the pearl onions and sauté for 2 minutes. Add in the peas and sauté for 1 minute more. Pour in the cream, season with salt and simmer until the cream is reduced and beginning to thicken, 4 to 5 minutes.

~ **THIRD,** add in the chives and mint and toss to combine. Serve immediately.

KNOTTED HONEY–WHOLE WHEAT ROLLS
18 ROLLS

Robust, whole-grain breads cooked on the open hearth are the hallmark of heartland baking. These breads have a simple, satisfying European influence that celebrates the bounty of the field.

HONEY–WHOLE WHEAT ROLLS

1 package (2¼ teaspoons) active dry yeast
¼ cup warm water, about 110°F
1 cup whole milk
¼ cup (½ stick) unsalted butter
¼ cup honey
1 large egg, room temperature, lightly beaten
2 cups whole wheat flour
1½ cups all-purpose flour
½ cup wheat germ
2 teaspoons salt

MAKE THE ROLLS:

FIRST, sprinkle the yeast over the warm water and let the mixture stand for 1 minute, then stir until the yeast is dissolved.

SECOND, heat the milk in a small saucepan to the point of boiling; remove it from heat and swirl in the butter until it is melted. Cool in the pan until lukewarm.

THIRD, combine the yeast with the lukewarm milk. Blend in the honey and the lightly beaten egg. Using a wooden spoon, stir in 1 cup of the whole wheat flour and then 1 cup of the all-purpose flour. The mixture should be the consistency of thick batter. Continue stirring for about 200 strokes; scrape down the sides of the bowl with a rubber spatula. Cover with a clean tea towel and set in a draft-free place until it is bubbly and has doubled in volume, about 2 hours.

FOURTH, in a separate mixing bowl combine the remaining 1 cup whole wheat flour and ½ cup all-purpose flour with the wheat germ and the salt. Blend thoroughly with a stiff wire whisk.

FIFTH, transfer the bubbly mixture to the bowl of an electric mixer fitted with a dough hook. Turn the speed to low and slowly add in the blended flour mixture, ½ cup at a time; scrape down the sides of the bowl between additions. Increase the mixer speed to medium and add in a little extra flour as necessary, until the dough pulls away from the sides of the bowl and forms a ball. At this point the dough will be firm and densely textured. Reduce the mixer speed to low and knead for 10 minutes.

SIXTH, divide the dough into 18 equal pieces. Roll each piece between the palms of your hands into a 5- to 6-inch rope. Tie each rope loosely into a simple knot and place on a lightly greased baking sheet. (*Note:* The rolls can prepared up to this point, wrapped in plastic and refrigerated for up to 4 hours.)

SEVENTH, cover the rolls with a clean tea towel that has been dusted with a little flour. Set the rolls in a draft-free place and let them rise until they have doubled in size, about 1 to 1½ hours (or 2 hours, if they were refrigerated). Lightly brush the tops with a little milk and then bake at 400°F for 12 to 15 minutes. Brush the tops with a little butter before serving.

HEARTLAND RAISIN-BUTTERMILK PIE
8 SERVINGS

The tangy buttermilk and lemon bring a bit of zest to this simple, unadorned Old World custard pie. The sweet, buttery pie crust is more in keeping with the tradition of central European pastries, and the addition of zesty lemon is an excellent surprise!

PIE CRUST

1 cup all-purpose flour
¼ cup granulated sugar
½ teaspoon salt
¼ cup (½ stick) unsalted butter
1 large egg yolk, room temperature
1 teaspoon pure vanilla extract
1 to 2 tablespoons cold water, as needed

MAKE THE CRUST:

FIRST, combine the flour, sugar and salt in the bowl of a food processor fitted with a steel blade. Cut the butter into pieces and add to the flour mixture; pulse until the mixture resembles coarse crumbly meal, about 20 seconds. Then add in the egg yolk, vanilla and a sparse tablespoon of cold water, and pulse just long enough for the dough to hold together. Add a few extra drops of water as needed for the dough to reach the consistency of cookie dough. Roll into a ball, flatten into a disk and wrap in plastic. Chill the dough in the refrigerator for at least 20 minutes and up to 5 days.

SECOND, sprinkle a clean dry surface with a little flour and roll the chilled dough into a 12-inch circle. Brush off any excess flour, then line a 9-inch pie or tart pan with the dough and chill in the refrigerator for 30 minutes.

THIRD, line the bottom of the chilled crust with foil, fill it with pie weights and bake in a 400°F oven for 10 minutes. Cool on a baking rack and remove the foil and pie weights. The crust will be partially baked and have a pale golden hue.

Easy time-saving
AND DO-AHEAD TIPS:

FRIDAY EVENING

Mix together the pie crust and refrigerate. Prepare the giblet stock and refrigerate.

SATURDAY

Blanch the peas (if using fresh) and peel the pearl onions; refrigerate in well-sealed containers. Roast the carrots and parsnips. Prepare the sage stuffing; cover and refrigerate. Make the buttermilk filling for the pie and bake.

SUNDAY MORNING

Prepare the dough for the rolls; cover and refrigerate. Stuff the chicken.

BUTTERMILK FILLING

⅔ cup dark raisins
3 large eggs, room temperature
2 tablespoons unsalted butter, softened
1 cup granulated sugar
¼ cup all-purpose flour
2 cups buttermilk
1 teaspoon pure vanilla extract
2 tablespoons fresh lemon juice
Zest of 1 lemon
¼ teaspoon nutmeg

MAKE THE FILLING:

~ **FIRST,** plump the raisins by soaking them for 30 minutes in a bowl of warm water; then drain thoroughly. Whisk together the eggs, butter and sugar in a stainless mixing bowl.

~ **SECOND,** whisk the flour into the buttermilk until smooth. Heat the buttermilk in a small saucepan, stirring constantly, until it just begins to thicken and bubble. Stir a scant ½ cup of the thickened buttermilk into the egg mixture to temper it, then blend both together completely.

~ **THIRD,** whisk in the vanilla, lemon juice and zest and add in the plumped raisins. Pour the filling into the prebaked pie shell and sprinkle the nutmeg on top.

~ **FOURTH,** bake the pie at 350°F for 30 to 35 minutes. The pie is done when the custard has begun to rise evenly and a knife inserted into the custard comes out clean. The pie can be cooled to room temperature and served immediately, or it can be made the day before and then chilled overnight, covered.

From morning till night,

sounds drift

from the kitchen,

most of them familiar

and comforting....

On days when warmth

is the most important need

of the human heart,

the kitchen is the place

you can find it.

E. B. WHITE

In the Neighborhood

> ❧ ❧ ❧

BRAISED PAPRIKA VEAL SHANKS

HOMEMADE EGG NOODLES
with PARSLEY AND TOMATO BUTTER

BUTTERED KOHLRABI

BRAISED SWISS CHARD

WARM PEAR STRUDEL WITH VANILLA SAUCE

America was once a country of neighborhoods. Even in the biggest cities, life typically revolved around neighborhood schools and churches, local bakeries, butcher shops, grocers, bookstores, restaurants, and so on. Each neighborhood had its own distinctive flavor. There were Catholic or Jewish or Muslim neighborhoods, and each was energized by rich traditions. The people were Irish or Czech or Chinese, white or black, united by a shared culture and shared problems. Yes, these neighborhoods could be insular or exclusive—they could inspire stereotypes—but they also offered their people an oasis of familiarity in an overwhelming sea of change. Each, too, added its own rich flavoring to the melting pot that is America.

More and more these days, we see ourselves first as Americans. And we should. We are from so many places, of so many faiths, yet we are still united by the ideal of freedom. We are "one nation under God." Our neighborhood differences have also been sources of division at times, rather than something we can explore, learn from, and celebrate. We are Americans of Scottish, African, Hungarian, Armenian, Polish, Mexican, Swedish, Cherokee, Vietnamese, or Italian descent. Many of us claim such diversity in our heritage that *American* really is the only possible label. But that very diversity is still something to appreciate and preserve.

In many ways the homogenization of America is a sad reality. Colorless suburbs, featureless fast-food restaurants, indistinguishable chain-store shopping malls, and familiar logos diminish the unique character for which neighborhoods were once known. But surely the key to healing our divisions lies in allowing our differences to enrich us all, not washing out those differences in a sea of sameness.

The flavors that make up the traditional American table, the foods from our neighborhoods, celebrate our diversity and provide a window to our varied but united past. Indeed, our melting pot is a simmering, savory dish made from a wide variety of tasty ingredients.

So take a Sunday walk with me through an old neighborhood in all its particular glory. Picture little markets with meats hanging in the window. Squeeze some fruit at the greengrocers and admire the glossy array of vegetables: garlic, leeks, turnips, tomatillos. Stand on the corner and listen to the gossip as the intoxicating aromas from little restaurants and bakeries drift down the block, beckoning us with every passing breeze. Lift a lid in a kitchen to enjoy the old-world ambience of slow-braised veal with garlic and paprika, aromatic herbs and vegetables, or even mushrooms. And smile, because this is America in all her diverse glory; it's a Sunday celebration straight from the heart of the neighborhood.

BRAISED PAPRIKA VEAL SHANKS
6 SERVINGS

One of the best cuts for braising is the shank—particularly lamb or veal. The shank is the lean calf muscle of the leg. Shanks have long been underappreciated cuts of meat, but they are still enjoyed in old-world neighborhoods, where skilled butchers carefully trim and prepare select pieces from whole sides that are hung cold and aged to perfection.

NOTE: *Have your butcher cut the veal shanks into 1½-inch-thick slices and tie each piece securely with kitchen twine to help it retain its shape. Each slice should be about 4 inches in diameter and weigh about 12 ounces—a hearty portion.*

VEAL SHANKS

6 12-ounce veal shanks	2 tablespoons tomato paste
Salt and white pepper	2 tablespoons all-purpose flour
1 tablespoon olive oil	1 cup dry white wine
2 tablespoons butter	2 cups veal or chicken broth
1 carrot, peeled and chopped	1 bay leaf
1 rib celery, chopped	1 tablespoon paprika
4 whole cloves garlic	2 sprigs fresh thyme
1 leek, white part only, chopped	4 to 5 white peppercorns
1 small onion, quartered	Salt and pepper to taste

~ Adjust the rack to the bottom of the oven and preheat to 300°F.

PREPARE THE VEAL SHANKS:

~ **FIRST,** season the veal with the salt and white pepper. Heat the oil in a covered casserole or Dutch oven over medium-high heat; when the oil just begins to smoke, add the meat to the skillet and sear the shanks until they are evenly browned, 4 to 5 minutes per side. Transfer the shanks to a warm platter.

~ **SECOND,** add the butter to the casserole; when it is melted, scatter in the carrot, celery, garlic, leek and onion. Sauté the vegetables until they begin to brown, 4 to 5 minutes.

THIRD, whisk the tomato paste into the vegetables; then sprinkle in the flour and whisk to form a *roux*. Pour in the wine and allow the wine to cook for 1 to 2 minutes. When the mixture becomes thick and bubbly, add in the broth, bay leaf, paprika, thyme and peppercorns. Return the shanks to the casserole, cover with a tight-fitting lid and transfer to the oven; braise for 1½ hours.

FOURTH, transfer the shanks from the casserole to a warm platter and tent with foil to keep warm. Skim off any excess fat that may have risen to the top of the sauce. Strain the remaining sauce through a fine sieve into a small bowl, pressing on the vegetables with a rubber spatula so that all of the flavorful juices are extracted. Discard the vegetables and season the sauce to taste with salt and pepper.

MUSHROOM SAUCE

2 tablespoons (¼ stick) butter
8 ounces sliced button mushrooms
1 medium onion, thinly sliced
Pinch of salt
¼ cup dry white wine
Reserved veal sauce
¼ cup sour cream
Salt and pepper to taste

PREPARE THE MUSHROOM SAUCE:

Melt the 2 tablespoons of butter over medium heat in the same casserole that was used for the shanks; when the butter begins to bubble, add in the mushrooms and sliced onion and season with a pinch of salt. Sauté until the onion slices are translucent and the mushrooms are tender, 2 to 3 minutes; pour in the wine and simmer for 1 to 2 more minutes. Blend in the sauce reserved from the veal, then carefully remove the kitchen twine from the shanks and add the veal to the sauce. Reduce the oven to 200°F, cover the casserole and transfer the shanks to the oven for 20 to 30 minutes before serving.

SERVE THE SHANKS:

Transfer the shanks to a warm serving platter. Whisk the sour cream into the sauce and season to taste. Lace the shanks with sauce and serve the remainder of the sauce in a gravy boat.

Although some fabulous meals have been served on it, the people and the diversity undertaken as our family evolved are what make this table's story so rich and unique. A variety of fine shoes and bare feet, both of assorted sizes and colors, have rested under its oak leaves.

ANNETTE SMITH

HOMEMADE EGG NOODLES
WITH PARSLEY AND TOMATO BUTTER
6 SERVINGS

Making noodles is a bit of work, but oh, what a difference! Like so much of home cooking, making noodles is all about love. It can also be fun to do with the kids; they will come to appreciate the time and care good cooking takes, especially since the rewards are in the eating. You can, of course, substitute fresh store-bought noodles when time is a factor.

EGG NOODLES

2 cups all-purpose flour
½ teaspoon salt
2 large eggs, lightly beaten
¼ cup whole milk

MAKE THE NOODLES:

~ **FIRST,** sift the flour together with the salt into a large shallow mixing bowl. Beat the eggs with the milk in a separate bowl. Make a well in the center of the flour and slowly pour the liquid ingredients into the well. Use a dinner fork to gently blend the flour into the beaten eggs by whisking the eggs in a circular motion and drawing the flour into the eggs, a tablespoon at a time (the process should take 10 to 12 minutes). The mixture will at first become a thick liquid, then a soft dough, and finally reach the firmness of pastry dough. Once the soft dough begins to form, you will need to use the tips of your fingers to roll the dough in a circular motion until there is just a thin rim of flour left around the edges of the bowl. Form the dough into a ball and knead in the remaining flour, as well as any bits of dough stuck to the bottom of the bowl. Knead until the dough is the consistency of pastry dough and just a little sticky to the fingers when pressed; if needed, add a little more flour.

~ **SECOND,** turn the ball of dough onto a clean work surface that has been lightly dusted with flour. Continue kneading, pressing the dough firmly with the heel of your hand to flatten the ball, folding it in half back over itself so it is doubled up again and pressing flat again in a continuous motion for 8 to 10 minutes, until completely smooth.

~ **THIRD,** allow the dough to rest for 20 minutes covered with a clean tea towel. Flatten and shape the dough in as close to a square as possible; divide the dough into 4 equal pieces. Press the pieces one at a time onto a clean work surface that has been lightly dusted with flour and flatten with a rolling pin. Lightly dust

Easy time-saving
AND DO-AHEAD TIPS:

FRIDAY EVENING
Prepare the vanilla sauce, cool to room temperature and refrigerate.

SATURDAY
Prepare and cut the noodles; seal in plastic bags. Clean the chard, peel and cut the kohlrabi and refrigerate in sealed plastic bags. Prepare the vegetables for the shanks.

SUNDAY MORNING
Braise the veal shanks. Prepare the strudel to the point of baking and refrigerate.

the dough with flour and roll out into 12-by-5-inch rectangles that are a little less than ¹/₁₆-inch thick (about half the thickness of pie dough). Use a knife or pizza wheel to cut the dough, guiding with a ruler or straightedge, into ½-inch-wide, 5-inch-long noodles. If the noodles aren't thin enough, don't worry—simply lay each noodle flat on the work surface and give it one firm roll to attain the desired thinness. The noodles won't have the same uniform cut, but this method will be well worth the extra effort.

～ **FOURTH,** transfer the noodles to a pasta rack or lay them flat on sheets of waxed paper. Let the noodles dry for about 1 hour. (*Note:* They can be made the night before, lightly dusted with a little additional flour and loosely packed and sealed in plastic bags, then refrigerated.)

COOK THE NOODLES:

～ Drop them into a large pot of boiling salted water. After 1 minute, separate the noodles gently with a cooking fork so that they don't stick to the bottom of the pot or each other; then continue cooking until tender yet firm (al dente), about 5 minutes. Drain thoroughly and set aside.

TOMATO BUTTER

½ cup (1 stick) butter
2 cloves garlic, minced
¼ cup minced onion
1 cup peeled, seeded and diced fresh tomatoes
1 tablespoon fresh chopped parsley
½ cup dry white wine
Salt and pepper to taste

MAKE THE TOMATO BUTTER:

～ Melt the butter in a skillet over medium heat until it just begins to bubble. Add in the garlic and onion and sauté until translucent, 2 to 3 minutes. Add in the tomatoes and parsley and sauté for about 1 minute. Pour in the wine and simmer for 2 to 3 minutes. Season to taste with salt and pepper.

ASSEMBLE THE DISH:

～ Shake any excess water from the noodles and add them to the sauce. (If the noodles stick together in the colander, run a little hot water over them and shake off the excess water.) Toss together well and adjust the seasoning to taste. Transfer to a wide bowl and serve immediately.

Just as it is good to get

one's fingers into the soil

and plant seeds,

so it is good to get

one's fingers and fists

into bread dough

to knead and punch it.

There is something

very positive in being

involved in the creativity,

which is so basic to life itself.

EDITH SCHAEFFER

BUTTERED KOHLRABI

6 SERVINGS

This really is an unusual vegetable. It originated in the cabbage family, though it has the snappy flavor of a turnip and, when steamed to perfection, the taste and texture of an artichoke heart. Kohlrabi is especially wonderful steamed and served with a touch of mayonnaise or hollandaise sauce.

KOHLRABI

8 large kohlrabi
¼ cup (½ stick) butter
Juice of 1 lemon
Salt and pepper to taste

PREPARE THE KOHLRABI:

~ **FIRST,** cut the tops and bottoms from the kohlrabi and break off any remaining leaf stems. Peel away the tough outer skin layer, then cut each into 6 to 8 wedges. Place the wedges in a pan with a tight-fitting lid. Season with a pinch of salt and pour in enough water to barely cover.

~ **SECOND,** bring the water to a boil and steam the kohlrabi over medium-high heat until they are tender, about 12 minutes, then drain. Return the pan to the burner, add in the butter and lemon juice, replace the lid and simmer over low heat for 2 to 3 more minutes. Season to taste with salt and pepper and, if desired, dot with a little more butter just before serving.

BRAISED SWISS CHARD

6 SERVINGS

Swiss chard is actually the leaves of beet tops. It is a wonderful green, with a sweet flavor and crunchy texture. It is especially good wilted and seasoned with a splash of vinegar. Sliced apples or a little orange juice can also be a great addition.

SWISS CHARD

¼ cup (½ stick) butter
¼ cup thinly sliced red onion
2 bunches Swiss chard
1 tablespoon tarragon or sherry vinegar
Salt and pepper to taste

MAKE THE SWISS CHARD:

~ Heat the butter in a large skillet over medium heat until it is melted and bubbling. Add in the sliced onion and sauté for 1 minute, then add in the chard. Pour in the vinegar and cover the skillet; steam for 2 to 3 minutes, tossing the chard occasionally so that it wilts evenly. Season to taste with salt and pepper.

My grandmother, Mary Pakarick, was sixteen years old when she left Prague for Chicago. Her possessions consisted of one boat ticket, the clothes on her back, a letter for her sister (already in America), and a sturdy little cutting board her father had carved.

Many years later, after she had established a home and raised a family, Grandma's Sunday dinner preparations were an unbearable temptation for me. The rich aroma of her cooking permeated the house, and it always seemed like time slowed down right before dinner.

As family conversations rose and fell throughout the house, voices wafting rhythmically from room to room, I often stood mesmerized beside the set dinner table: the clean, formal linens; the polished silverware; the dishes each standing at soldierlike attention, ready to present Grandma's Sunday feast.

My chair was always next to Grandma's at one end of the long table. As the plates and platters whirled past me, Grandma would dab a little helping of everything onto my plate. Golden chicken paprikash clung to steaming homemade dumplings. Pickled beets and green beans flashed red and green from silver serving spoons. Bright yellow kernels of corn, cut in strips from the cob, glided onto my plate. Crisp green onions stood tall in cut crystal vases. Black and green olives rolled into place. A spoonful of my personal favorite, red Jell-O salad with fruit suspended inside, slid next to the dumplings—the heat of the paprikash always caused the Jell-O to melt slightly.

When every delectable morsel was in place, we would then fold our hands for prayer. At six years of age, I perceived this as torture. The rich, steaming foods were only inches from my bowed head!

And then came dessert. Strudels were Grandma's particular pride and joy. My favorite kind of strudel, cherry, always looked smaller than its voluptuous apple counterpart. As the coffeepot happily perked its rich, dark brew on the stove, we lined up around the kitchen table, dessert plates in hand. This ritual was always observed in the same way: The family watched as the strudels were cut, revealing layers of paper-thin pastry and soft, magical fruit centers. Even at age six, I somehow understood that we were sharing a heritage as well as a dessert.

LENORE SAME

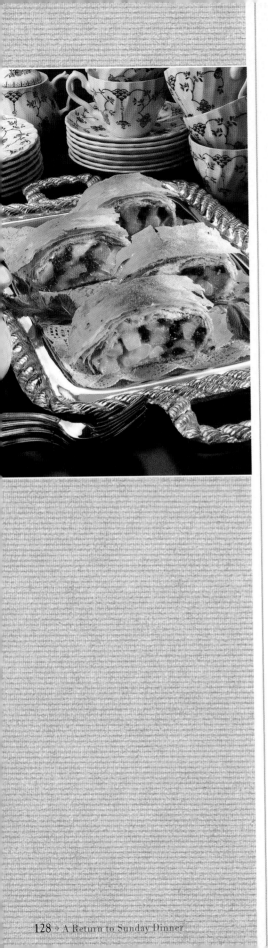

WARM PEAR STRUDEL
WITH VANILLA SAUCE
6 SERVINGS

ew desserts in the world are as satisfying as warm, freshly prepared strudel. Making the delicate dough by hand is something else altogether: You must slowly stretch it over a linen sheet and carefully pull it until it is thin and silky enough to read a newspaper through. It is something everyone should try at least once. After gaining an appreciation for all the work involved, you'll gratefully go back to using store-bought sheets of phyllo, as we do in this recipe.

FILLING

4 medium firm ripe pears
Lemon juice
¼ cup dried currants
2 tablespoons all-purpose flour
2 tablespoons granulated sugar
¼ teaspoon ground allspice

MAKE THE STRUDEL FILLING:

~ Working with one pear at a time, peel and quarter it, then carefully remove the thin stem and core and slice into ½-inch chunks (this should yield about 4 cups). Transfer the chunks to a stainless bowl and toss with a little lemon juice to prevent discoloration. When you have tossed the last pear chunks with lemon juice, fold in the currants and then sprinkle the flour, sugar and allspice over the mixture; gently toss together until the pears are evenly coated.

STRUDEL

½ cup (1 stick) unsalted butter
1 tablespoon vegetable oil
8 frozen phyllo dough sheets,
each about 12 by 15 inches
3 tablespoons ground hazelnuts
6 tablespoons fresh white bread crumbs
1 tablespoon granulated sugar

CLARIFY THE BUTTER:

~ Melt the butter, then bring it to a boil in a small saucepan over medium-low heat or in a glass dish for 30 seconds in the microwave—the butter will foam up when it begins to boil. Swirl it around in the pan for about 30 seconds until the foam subsides, then allow it to cool undisturbed for 4 to 5 minutes. Use a small ladle or spoon to skim the foam from the top, then tip the pan ever so gently. Carefully transfer the clear oil, ladleful by ladleful, to a small dish, leaving the milky sediment in the pan. Discard the sediment and blend the vegetable oil into the clarified butter.

PREPARE THE STRUDEL:

- **FIRST,** thaw the phyllo dough according to package directions.

- **SECOND,** remove 8 phyllo sheets from the package and carefully lay them flat on a cool clean work surface. Immediately cover them with a damp paper towel or damp clean tea towel to keep them from drying out. (*Note:* As you work with the phyllo, be sure to remove only one sheet at a time from under the damp towel.)

- **THIRD,** lay one sheet of phyllo on a cool clean surface and carefully brush it with a thin amount of the clarified butter. Lay a second sheet on top, brush it with butter and sprinkle it lightly with 1 tablespoon of the ground hazelnuts and 2 tablespoons of the fresh bread crumbs. Repeat this process three times. (Do not sprinkle hazelnuts or crumbs over the top layer.)

ASSEMBLE THE STRUDEL:

- **FIRST,** spoon the pear filling lengthwise in an even mound over the top sheet of phyllo, 3 inches from the bottom edge of the dough; leave a 1-inch border at each end without any filling. Roll the 3-inch area of dough over the mounded filling and then continue to roll up the layers of dough into a cylinder. Flatten each end of the phyllo to seal in the filling. Liberally brush the outside with the remaining clarified butter and sprinkle with 1 tablespoon of sugar.

- **SECOND,** use a long metal spatula to carefully transfer the strudel seam-side down to a lightly greased baking sheet. Use a sharp serrated knife to cut through the top layers of the dough to make 6 equal portions; this will keep the strudel from breaking apart when you slice each portion. Bake in a 375°F oven until the dough is golden and the filling is just beginning to bubble, 35 to 40 minutes.

VANILLA SAUCE

3 large egg yolks, room temperature
1 teaspoon pure vanilla extract
½ cup granulated sugar
1 cup half-and-half
½ cup heavy cream

MAKE THE VANILLA SAUCE:

- **FIRST,** combine the egg yolks and vanilla in a stainless bowl or in the top of a double boiler. Slowly beat in the sugar with a wire whisk—it's important that the sugar dissolves slowly and completely into the yolks (beating the mixture too rapidly will make the yolks frothy and full of air).

- **SECOND,** scald the half-and-half and the cream in a small saucepan over medium heat just to the point of boiling; then remove from heat immediately. Temper the yolks by whisking ½ cup of the hot cream into the yolk mixture until fully blended; then whisk in the remaining hot cream.

- **THIRD,** place the bowl over a pan of simmering water, making sure that the bowl does not touch the water. Cook the sauce, stirring constantly with a heat-resistant rubber spatula, until thickened, 6 to 8 minutes. To test for thickness: Dip a spoon into the sauce and hold it horizontally over the pan, making sure that the sauce coats the spoon evenly; then run your finger through the sauce on the spoon—if the line doesn't fill back up, it has thickened enough. Strain through a fine sieve and cool.

SERVE THE STRUDEL:

- Carefully slice the strudel into portions using a serrated knife. Ladle a generous amount of sauce on each of 6 dessert plates, and place the strudel slices in the sauce. If desired, garnish each serving with additional pear slices, currants and fresh mint leaves.

At Home in New England

≫ ≫ ≫ | STUFFED CENTER–CUT PORK CHOPS
FRIED APPLE RINGS
PICKLED RED BEET SALAD
MOLASSES BAKED BEANS
BOSTON BROWN BREAD
VERMONT MAPLE–WALNUT TART

The political, religious, and cultural life of New England— and the nation—was dramatically shaped by the region's first English settlers, the Puritans. These reformed Protestants came to America to escape religious persecution. They wanted to form churches and a social order that conformed to the teachings they discerned from the Bible. These hardy, determined people ended up doing much more, however; they influenced our national work ethic, our educational ideals, and our constitutional principles of democratic and local-based rule, free exercise of religion, and separation of church and state.

The first group of Puritans founded Plymouth Colony in 1620. Subsequent decades saw dozens of independent villages sprout up all along New England's rugged shoreline and inland rivers as the industrious Puritans established a vibrant economy based on farming, fishing, and mills. Hard work, love of education, the pursuit of excellence, and an earnest piety informed all aspects of Puritan life, from their unassuming dress and well-ordered homes to the plain white Congregationalist church buildings, whose tall spires still grace the picturesque New England landscape.

The Puritans' food, like their lives, was practical and hearty, gratefully prepared from the bounty of land and sea that surrounded them. Though many new-world foods were unfamiliar to the Puritans, they quickly learned to use what was available. The Wampanoag Indians generously helped the Puritans by teaching them to harvest and prepare corn, tap maple trees for clear golden syrup, and cultivate a variety of sweet, nutritious squash.

Beans, especially, became a staple for the Puritans, who adapted the native practice of baking them slowly in earthen pots buried beneath the ground. The Wampanoags seasoned their beans with game, but the Puritans preferred to use the pigs they had imported from home. The culinary result of this cultural blend was a new American classic: pork and beans.

The technique of slow-baking the beans proved especially useful to the Puritans, who took seriously the biblical command to honor the Sabbath by refraining from work. A large pot of beans could be prepared for Saturday supper, then reheated and eaten both for Sunday breakfast and Sunday dinner.

This simple and savory Sabbath meal, though varied in its preparation from region to region, is still widely enjoyed throughout New England. The sweet, juicy pork is a perfect match for the nutty flavor of the beans, and the sweet and savory flavors of herbs, onions, and molasses add an exceptional balance of taste and texture. The make-ahead ease of preparation offers the kind of restful Sabbath the Puritans appreciated and the rest of us desperately need: one that is peaceful, prayerful, and purely delicious.

STUFFED CENTER-CUT PORK CHOPS

6 SERVINGS

Stuffed pork chops is an authentic New England dish that seems to have no previous origin. I love the addition of dried fruit—especially apricots, cherries and plums—to this savory bread stuffing. It keeps the pork chops moist while the seasonings and the natural pan juices infuse their flavors into the meat.

NOTE: *For this recipe, have your butcher cut 6 bone-in pork loin chops that weigh about 8 ounces each and are at least 1 inch thick.*

STUFFING

1 cup mixed dried fruit, diced
½ cup apple or cherry juice
2 tablespoons butter
½ cup diced celery
½ cup diced onion
1 tablespoon fresh chopped parsley
1 teaspoon dry rubbed sage
3 cups day-old bread cubes
¼ teaspoon coarse salt
¼ teaspoon white pepper

MAKE THE STUFFING:

FIRST, soak the dried fruit in the fruit juice until plump, about 1 hour. Heat the butter over medium heat in a small skillet until it is just melted and beginning to bubble. Add in the diced celery and onion and sauté until the onion is soft and translucent, 2 to 3 minutes; remove from heat, add in the parsley and sage and cool to room temperature.

SECOND, drain the plumped fruit, reserving the liquid. Combine the bread cubes with the sautéed celery and onion in a stainless mixing bowl; season with the salt and white pepper and toss together with the fruit. Mix well, adding in the reserved fruit juice, a tablespoon at a time, until the stuffing is moist and just a little sticky. (*Note:* The stuffing can be made a day ahead and refrigerated overnight.)

PORK CHOPS

6 8-ounce bone-in pork loin chops
Salt and pepper
¼ cup (½ stick) butter
½ cup pork or chicken broth

MAKE THE PORK CHOPS:

FIRST, use a thin sharp knife to cut a 2-inch slit in each pork chop. Slicing through the fat, use the tip of the knife to form a pocket by cutting into the meat and toward the bone. Fill each pocket with stuffing and secure with wooden picks. Allow the chops to rest for at least 4 hours, covered and refrigerated, so that they can absorb some of the flavor from the stuffing.

SECOND, preheat the oven to 325°F, then season the pork chops with the salt and pepper. Melt the butter in a skillet or heavy baking dish large enough that the chops will lie flat on the bottom. Sear the chops over medium-high heat, turning once, about 3 minutes per side. Transfer the skillet to the preheated oven, cover loosely with foil and cook until the chops are done and the stuffing is heated above 140°F, 25 to 30 minutes.

THIRD, remove the skillet from the oven. Transfer the chops to a serving platter and remove the wooden picks. Place the skillet on a burner set to medium heat. Scrape any glazed meat drippings from the bottom. Quickly pour in the broth and blend with the pan juices. Simmer for 2 to 3 minutes, to reduce the liquid and fully incorporate the rich flavors. Serve laced over the platter of chops.

FRIED APPLE RINGS
6 SERVINGS

Serving apples with pork is a natural choice, whether it is in the form of applesauce, baked apples, spiced apples or these wonderful fried apple rings. I love the distinctive flavor of fried apples, especially when they are lightly sautéed in bacon fat—the perfect complement to the juicy pork.

FRIED APPLE RINGS

4 sweet-tart apples
¼ cup bacon fat or butter
1 tablespoon granulated sugar
Pinch of ground cinnamon

MAKE THE APPLE RINGS:

~ **FIRST**, carefully core each apple, then use a thin sharp knife to slice the apples into ⅓-inch-thick rings.

~ **SECOND**, melt the bacon fat or butter in a skillet over medium-high heat and fry the rings for 2 to 3 minutes. Sprinkle the rings with sugar, dust with a pinch of cinnamon and carefully turn over using a spatula. Fry for another 2 to 3 minutes. (This can be done in 2 batches.) When the apple rings are nicely browned, transfer them to a clean dry paper towel and blot the excess oil. Serve warm arranged on the platter around the stuffed chops.

Easy time-saving
AND DO-AHEAD TIPS:

FRIDAY EVENING
Prepare the tart dough and refrigerate sealed in plastic wrap. Sift together the dry ingredients for the brown bread and store in a plastic container.

SATURDAY
Prepare the stuffing for the pork chops, cool to room temperature, and refrigerate in a well-sealed container. Bake the tart, cool, and store at room temperature. Prepare and steam the Boston brown bread. Prepare and marinate the beet salad. Soak the beans overnight.

SUNDAY MORNING
Par-cook and bake the beans. Stuff the pork chops, cover and refrigerate.

PICKLED RED BEET SALAD
6 SERVINGS

eets, as well as other root vegetables brought to our shores by English and Dutch settlers, are still common fare throughout New England. You may use any fruity vinegar for this recipe, but I think you will agree that raspberry vinegar lends exceptional flavor to this dish.

BEET SALAD

4 large fresh firm beets
1 teaspoon salt
1 medium onion, thinly sliced
⅓ cup raspberry vinegar
¼ cup granulated sugar
2 whole cloves
6 black peppercorns

MAKE THE SALAD:

~ **FIRST,** cut the top and bottom from each beet; peel and cut horizontally into ¼-inch-thick slices. Place the beets into a large skillet and cover with cold water. Add the salt, bring to a boil, cover the skillet and steam for 4 to 5 minutes—the beets should still be firm when pierced with the tip of a sharp knife. Drain off all the liquid and cool the beets uncovered in the pan.

~ **SECOND,** transfer the cooked beets to a work surface that has been covered with waxed paper to keep the surface from staining. Cut the beets into matchstick-size strips. Transfer to a glass dish and toss with the sliced onion.

~ **THIRD,** whisk the vinegar with the sugar, cloves and peppercorns in a small saucepan over high heat until the sugar is dissolved, 1 to 2 minutes. Pour the mixture over the beets and onions so they are covered completely. Cool to room temperature, cover with plastic wrap and refrigerate for at least 24 hours.

SERVE THE SALAD:

~ Discard the cloves and peppercorns and toss lightly just before serving.

MOLASSES BAKED BEANS
6 SERVINGS

I still savor fond memories of childhood Sunday dinners, which from time to time entailed a simple meal of traditional baked beans, slices of homemade Boston brown bread, and for dessert, either baked apples or apple pie. Those who were fortunate enough to grow up eating delicious, home-baked beans warm from the oven know that there is no comparison. Slow, even cooking is the key to tender, full-flavored baked beans.

BAKED BEANS

1 cup dried northern beans
1 quart cold water
¼ pound salt pork fat or slab bacon
3 tablespoons packed dark brown sugar
1 bay leaf
1 whole clove garlic
1 medium onion, diced
⅓ cup molasses
3 tablespoons deli-style mustard
Coarse salt to taste

MAKE THE BAKED BEANS:

~ **FIRST,** wash and pick over the beans, then soak them for 8 hours or overnight.

~ **SECOND,** place the beans into a heavy-bottomed pot with 1 quart of cold water and bring to a boil. Reduce the heat to medium-low and simmer until the beans are tender and the skins begin to break, about 50 minutes.

~ **THIRD,** drain off any excess liquid, leaving only enough to cover the beans by half an inch. Cut the rind from the salt pork fat or slab bacon and slice into 2 or 3 chunks. Add the salt pork fat, brown sugar, bay leaf, garlic, onion, molasses and mustard to the beans. Transfer to a ceramic casserole or Dutch oven, then cover and bake in a 250°F oven without stirring until the beans are tender, about 2½ hours. Check the water level from time to time to make sure the beans are covered.

~ **FOURTH,** when the beans are tender, remove the lid and continue cooking for an additional 30 minutes. Season to taste with salt. Remove and discard the bay leaf before serving.

Whenever I'm in my kitchen,

smelling the aroma of beans

slowly cooking

for our evening meal,

my mind goes back to

my childhood....

I still enjoy cooking up a

"potful of the past."

ONETA M. WHITLOCK

BOSTON BROWN BREAD
MAKES 1 LOAF

Steamed breads were born of necessity long before the advent of modern ovens, and they kept well when sealed and stored in a cool root cellar. Many modern Boston brown bread recipes call for replacing the rye flour with all-purpose flour; this works, but the dense texture and nutty flavor are not the same.

NOTE: *For this recipe you'll need an empty 1-pound coffee can (or equal-sized can) or a 1-quart steamed-pudding mold in which to bake the bread.*

BROWN BREAD

½ cup whole-grain rye flour
½ cup whole wheat flour
½ cup cornmeal
½ teaspoon salt
1 cup buttermilk
½ teaspoon baking soda
1 tablespoon hot water
¼ cup dark molasses
½ cup raisins

MAKE THE BROWN BREAD:

FIRST, whisk the rye flour, whole wheat flour and cornmeal together with the salt in a mixing bowl. Use a wooden spoon or a mixer fitted with a paddle to slowly incorporate the buttermilk into the dry ingredients. Dissolve the baking soda in the hot water in a separate small bowl and add, along with the molasses, into the dough. Mix on low speed until smooth, about 2 minutes; then fold in the raisins.

SECOND, butter and flour the 1-pound coffee can or 1-quart mold. Spoon the batter into the can; it should be about ⅔ full. Cover the can tightly with plastic wrap, then secure the wrap by tying a piece of kitchen twine or a second piece of plastic wrap rolled into a long strand around the top.

Cover with aluminum foil to keep the bread from browning. Place the can in a large pot fitted with a round cooling rack or a slotted bottom like you'd have in a pressure cooker, and pour boiling water into the pot until it reaches between 2 and 3 inches up the sides of the can. Cover the pot with a tight-fitting lid and simmer over medium heat for 3 hours, adding more water as necessary to maintain the water level.

THIRD, when the bread is fully steamed, remove the can from the water and cool to room temperature, about 2 hours. Once the bread has cooled, you can serve it or keep the loaf sealed in the can. To remove the bread from the can, turn it over, cut the bottom free with a can opener and gently but firmly push the loaf out.

VERMONT MAPLE–WALNUT TART

8 SERVINGS

When the Wampanoag Indians introduced maple syrup to the Puritans, I doubt they had something as incredible as this rich, buttery, nutty tart in mind! Maple syrup is harvested throughout eastern North America, but nowhere can better, sweeter maple syrup be found than in Vermont. Maple syrup is enjoyed in so many ways, and the addition of walnuts creates a truly heavenly dessert.

NOTE: *For this recipe you'll need one 10-inch fluted false-bottom tart pan.*

BROWN SUGAR CRUST

1¼ cups all-purpose flour
¼ cup packed light brown sugar
½ teaspoon salt
¼ cup (½ stick) unsalted butter
1 large egg yolk, room temperature
1 teaspoon pure vanilla extract
2 tablespoons whole milk, cold

MAKE THE CRUST:

FIRST, combine the flour, brown sugar and salt in the bowl of a food processor fitted with a steel blade. Cut the butter into ½-inch pieces and add to the flour mixture; pulse until the mixture resembles coarse crumbly meal, about 20 seconds. Then add in the egg yolk, vanilla and a sparse tablespoon of cold milk, and pulse long enough for the dough to just hold together. Add a few extra drops of milk as needed for the dough to reach the consistency of cookie dough. Roll into a ball, flatten into a disk and wrap in plastic. Chill the dough in the refrigerator for at least 20 minutes and up to 5 days.

SECOND, on a clean dry surface that has been lightly dusted with a little granulated sugar, roll out the chilled tart dough into a 12-inch round. Carefully transfer the dough to the tart pan and gently press into the edges, leaving about a ¼-inch overhang. Fold the edges of the dough inward and press firmly into the fluted pan so that the double edge extends about ⅛-inch above the rim. Place the tart shell in the freezer for 20 minutes.

THIRD, adjust the rack to the center of the oven and preheat to 400°F. Remove the crust from the freezer.

MAPLE-WALNUT FILLING

¼ cup (½ stick) unsalted butter, softened
1 cup packed dark brown sugar
3 large eggs, room temperature
1 cup pure Vermont maple syrup
1 teaspoon pure vanilla extract
½ teaspoon salt
2 cups chopped walnuts

PREPARE THE FILLING:

FIRST, cream the butter and brown sugar together in a mixing bowl; whisk in the eggs until they are well blended. Beat in the maple syrup, vanilla and salt.

SECOND, scatter the walnut pieces evenly over the bottom of the unbaked tart shell; pour in the filling. Place the tart on a baking sheet and bake for 10 minutes; then reduce the oven temperature to 350°F and continue baking until the filling is set, 30 to 40 more minutes. Remove from the oven and cool the tart to room temperature. If desired, serve topped with vanilla ice cream and warm maple syrup.

Travelin' Through

CHICKEN AND SAUSAGE GUMBO
BAKED FLOUNDER WITH CRAB STUFFING
HOPPIN' JOHN
DILLY SUMMER SQUASH SAUTÉ
SKILLET CORN BREAD
LEMON 'N' LIME MERINGUE PIE

I love traveling through the Southern coastal plains—from the Mississippi Delta along the Gulf of Mexico to the southern Atlantic coast and up through the low country of South Carolina—through the backwoods, waterways, marshes, and lowlands some call Hurricane Alley. The pace of life here is slow, like the tides and rivers that ebb and flow through the lowlands. And the foods are truly special; they are spicy yet subtle and always alive with flavor.

The culinary influences are many: African, Creole, Spanish, French, Caribbean, Gullah (a kind of African Creole that developed in the coastal South), and native. Each micro-region is distinct, yet all share familiar ingredients and cooking styles. From Charleston to Savannah to Mobile and New Orleans—and countless points in between—you'll be served chunky, spicy gumbos, golden corn bread, and an array of fresh fish. You'll also come across dishes with curious names such as she-crab soup, limpin' Susan, frogmore stew, shrimp bog, and Hoppin' John. You'll find an abundance of succulent ingredients harvested from the wetlands: shrimp, crab, duck, oysters, and crawfish. And there's rice—always rice—the quintessential lowland grain. (You'll eat gumbo with rice, red beans and rice, dirty rice, rice with gravy, and rice pudding.) For dessert there are sweet, gooey delicacies such as pecan pie, blackberry cobbler, Key lime tarts, or rich bread pudding.

Despite the natural abundance of these regions, poverty has also been a familiar companion in the lowland South. The people here learned long ago, however, that poverty of worldly wealth does not necessarily mean poverty of soul. That's why Sunday is more than just tradition. The day of rest always takes on greater meaning in a world born of struggle. So folks still dress up for church—women with their Sunday hats, children at their best, men in coats and ties—and enjoy the privilege of taking time off and honoring God in all things.

I love the great preaching in so many lowland churches. It's poetic and spoken in slow cadence, like the tides. And I especially love gospel music, with its deep roots in rhythmic folk songs and field hollers. These are work songs, sorrow songs, songs of faith in the face of hardship. They tell the story of poverty, slavery, misunderstanding, and injustice. They offer strength for trials and hope for the future. And though they remind us, again and again, that this world is not really our home, that all of us are really just traveling through, they also remind us of the wonderful truth that shines behind every Sunday: that even in this "vale of tears," we don't have to travel alone.

CHICKEN AND SAUSAGE GUMBO
8 SERVINGS

In Louisiana, gumbo—big chunks of spicy goodness—is often served as a main dish over rice. It is also served as a first course throughout the lowland South. Many different types of meat and seafood are excellent in gumbo, including duck, chicken and shrimp. Gumbo is made using a dark roux, *and it is often thickened and flavored with the powdered young leaves of sassafras called* Gumbo filé.

CHICKEN AND SAUSAGE GUMBO

4 chicken thighs	1 cup diced onion
½ teaspoon cayenne pepper	3 tablespoons all-purpose flour
1 teaspoon granulated garlic	2 tablespoon Gumbo filé
1 teaspoon onion powder	4 cups chicken broth
1 teaspoon ground thyme	1 cup sliced okra
2 teaspoons salt	6 ounces sliced Andouille sausage
2 teaspoons pepper	Salt to taste
6 tablespoons olive oil	¼ to ½ teaspoon Tabasco sauce
1 cup diced green bell pepper	½ cup sliced green onions
1 cup diced celery	

MAKE THE GUMBO:

~ **FIRST,** pull the skin from each thigh and discard. Carefully cut out the bone, discard, and cut the chicken into chunks. Whisk together the cayenne, garlic, onion powder, thyme, salt and pepper in a small mixing bowl. Mix the seasoning thoroughly with the chunks of chicken. Cover and refrigerate for at least 4 hours and up to 24 hours.

~ **SECOND,** heat 4 tablespoons of the olive oil in a heavy-bottomed skillet over medium-high heat. Add the seasoned chicken to the skillet and sauté in the hot oil until the chicken is browned, 6 to 8 minutes. Use a slotted spoon to transfer the chicken from the skillet into a dish to cool.

~ **THIRD,** pour in the remaining 2 tablespoons of olive oil, reduce the heat to medium and add in the bell pepper, celery and onion; sauté for 2 to 3 minutes.

~ **FOURTH,** make a well in the center of the pan by pushing the vegetables to the edges; then tip the pan from side to side so most of the oil flows into the center. Sprinkle the flour into the well—it will immediately begin to absorb some of the oil. Reduce the heat to medium-low and let the flour cook undisturbed for 4 to 5 minutes, then scrape the bottom of the skillet. (This will allow the flour to brown evenly.) Leave it to cook undisturbed for another 4 to 5 minutes.

~ **MEANWHILE,** blend the Gumbo filé into the chicken broth in a separate bowl.

~ **FIFTH,** when the flour turns a deep even brown, stir it together with the vegetables and oil around the edges of the pan. Add in the okra, sausage and cooked chicken with all of its juices; stir together and cook for 2 more minutes.

~ **SIXTH,** pour in the chicken broth. Bring to a boil, reduce the heat to low and simmer for about 40 minutes, stirring from time to time until the okra is fully cooked and beginning to fall apart. Season the gumbo to taste with salt and Tabasco sauce; garnish with chopped green onions.

*O*nce a month for every year I can remember of my childhood, my parents transported us kids ninety miles from our home in New Orleans to my grandparents' sugarcane farm near Thibodaux, Louisiana. Situated on the banks of Bayou Lafourche, the farmhouse was Acadian in style and nestled under the broad, moss-draped branches of two ancient oak trees. In that house where my father was raised, we enjoyed Sunday dinner with my grandparents and other members of the extended Faucheux family.

My favorite Sunday dinners came in the springtime, when Grandmother augmented her standard Sunday fare with the bounty of the Louisiana wetlands. It was then that the whole family enjoyed a special and ancient dish she called crawfish bisque—in Cajun, *bisque d'ecrevisse*—served over rice. It was of course delicious, and it was made even tastier by the accompaniment of fresh produce from my grandfather's mule-plowed garden.

After dinner, everyone would gather for dessert under the oak trees. It was not unusual for all of my cousins to show up around this time. As children we played together on the twin oaks' manila rope swings while my parents, aunts, and uncles prepared the desserts we would share together as a family. After-dinner sweets were forms of handmade folk art—as one would expect, many of them were prepared with cane sugar. Each aunt had her specialty: pralines from the farm's giant pecan tree; brittle from peanuts grown in grandfather's garden; wild-blackberry cobbler; hand-cranked ice cream with fresh peaches; and shaved ice flavored with a variety of syrups.

Today it isn't so much the sweets as the family togetherness that I and my thirty-plus cousins really remember. These warm memories of la famille Faucheux, as we refer to the family experience, were provided by parents, aunts, and uncles who knew the real value of a family Sunday dinner on the bayou.

GUY FAUCHEUX

BAKED FLOUNDER WITH CRAB STUFFING AND REMOULADE SAUCE

8 SERVINGS

Stuffed fish is a wonderful Sunday treat. In the low coastal plains, delicate flat-fish such as flounder are often stuffed with shrimp, crawfish or crab. Blue crabs are what you find in the Southeast—when steamed, the sweet, succulent lump meat makes wonderful crab cakes, while the flaky backfin is used for stuffing and soups. Out West, Dungeness crabs are a good alternative.

REMOULADE SAUCE

1 cup mayonnaise	1 teaspoon paprika
2 tablespoons fresh lemon juice	Pinch of cayenne pepper
3 tablespoons minced onion	2 to 3 drops Worcestershire sauce
3 tablespoons minced sweet pickles	Pinch of salt
3 tablespoons fresh chopped parsley	

MAKE THE REMOULADE SAUCE:

~ Whisk the mayonnaise together with the lemon juice in a small stainless mixing bowl. Fold in the minced onion, sweet pickles and parsley. Season with the paprika, cayenne, Worcestershire sauce and a pinch of salt. Cover and refrigerate for 4 hours or overnight to allow the flavors to meld.

STUFFING

¼ cup (½ stick) butter	1 teaspoon dry mustard
⅓ cup diced green bell pepper	1 teaspoon paprika
⅓ cup diced celery	½ teaspoon celery salt
⅓ cup diced onion	1 teaspoon Worcestershire sauce
1 pound steamed crabmeat	4 or 5 drops Tabasco sauce
2 tablespoons all-purpose flour	¼ cup chopped green onions
1 cup fish stock or clam juice	2 tablespoons fresh chopped parsley
¼ teaspoon cayenne pepper	2 cups fresh bread crumbs

MAKE THE STUFFING:

~ FIRST, melt the butter in a large skillet over medium heat. Add in the bell pepper, celery and onion; sauté until the vegetables are soft, 2 to 3 minutes. Add in the crabmeat and toss lightly with the vegetables, then sprinkle the flour into the pan and blend with the crab mixture to form a paste. Cook together for 2 to 3 minutes, stirring gently.

~ **SECOND,** pour in the fish stock or clam juice and stir until thick and bubbly. Season with the cayenne, dry mustard, paprika and celery salt; then add the Worcestershire sauce and Tabasco sauce. Remove the pan from heat and fold in the green onions, parsley and bread crumbs. Cool to room temperature. The stuffing can be made up to this point a day ahead and refrigerated in a well-sealed container.

FLOUNDER

8 5- to 6-ounce skinless fillets	1 teaspoon paprika
Salt for seasoning	2 tablespoons chopped green onions
½ cup (1 stick) butter	1 tablespoon fresh chopped parsley
2 lemons, halved	

PREPARE THE FLOUNDER:

~ **FIRST,** butter a large glass or ceramic dish. Divide the cooled stuffing into 8 equal mounds and place the mounds a couple of inches apart in the casserole so the fish fillets will not touch one another. Place 1 flounder fillet (or 2 smaller ones, if larger fish are unavailable) on top of each mound, skinned side up; press gently on the fillets.

~ **SECOND,** sprinkle the fillets with a little salt and dot the top of each with a tablespoon of butter. Juice the 2 lemons over the top and then lightly dust with paprika. Bake in a 350°F oven for 20 to 25 minutes.

SERVE THE FLOUNDER:

~ Transfer the fillets to a warm platter. Sprinkle with the chopped green onions and parsley and pour the pan juices over the top. If desired, garnish with fresh lemon slices. Serve the remoulade sauce on the side.

HOPPIN' JOHN
8 SERVINGS

Black-eyed peas are traditionally eaten in Southern homes on New Year's Day to symbolize prosperity for the year to come. The Southern classic Hoppin' John combines black-eyes peas with that lowland staple—rice. Clever stories abound to explain how this wonderfully simple dish got its name. They involve young children hopping around the table in anticipation of or a hearty welcome call for dinner guests to "hop on in" and enjoy the food before them. But the name is more likely derived from the Creole dish Pois á Pigeon, *or pigeon peas, which was similar to black-eyed peas and was enjoyed throughout the Caribbean. Whatever its origin, Hoppin' John is a dish that contains both memories and hope.*

HOPPIN' JOHN

1 cup dried black-eyed peas
1 tablespoon peanut oil
1 4-ounce piece of country ham
½ cup diced onion
½ teaspoon pepper
2 tablespoons butter
½ teaspoon salt
1 cup long-grain white rice

PREPARE THE BLACK-EYED PEAS:

~ **FIRST,** pick through the black-eyed peas and rinse them thoroughly. Soak the peas for 8 hours or overnight in 1 quart of cold water; then drain.

~ **SECOND,** heat the peanut oil in a skillet over medium heat and brown the ham, turning once, until crusty on each side, about 5 minutes. Add in the onion and the black-eyed peas. Pour in enough water to barely cover the peas and season with the pepper. Reduce the heat to medium-low and simmer until the peas are tender, about 45 minutes. Drain the peas and reserve the liquid and peas separately.

MAKE THE RICE:

~ Add enough water to the reserved liquid from the peas to equal 2¼ cups and pour into a 2-quart saucepan. Bring to a vigorous boil over high heat and add in the butter and salt; stir in the rice, reduce the heat to low, cover the pan with a tight-fitting lid and continue cooking for 15 minutes. Turn off the heat and let the rice stand for an additional 10 minutes. (Do not lift the lid.)

ASSEMBLE THE HOPPIN' JOHN:

~ Use a fork to lightly toss the steamed rice together with the black-eyed peas; serve immediately.

> *The pleasure*
> *of the table*
> *may be enjoyed*
> *every day,*
> *in every climate,*
> *at all ages,*
> *and by all*
> *conditions of men.*
>
> BRILLAT-SAVARIN

DILLY SUMMER SQUASH SAUTÉ
8 SERVINGS

I prefer to use tender little pattypan squash for this dish. If you can't find pattypan, use small crookneck or any variety of summer squash. If the squash are large, cut them in half lengthwise and use a spoon to scrape out the seeds and spongy centers, which tend to become bitter during cooking.

SQUASH

2 pounds tiny yellow squash
1 tablespoon vegetable oil
2 tablespoons butter
1 small sweet onion
Salt to taste
2 tablespoon granulated sugar
1 tablespoon cider vinegar
2 tablespoons fresh snipped chives
1 tablespoon fresh chopped dill

PREPARE THE SQUASH:

Trim the ends from each of the squash and cut them into ½-inch slices. Heat the oil and butter in a skillet over medium heat. Cut the onion in half crosswise and then slice the halves into slivers. Add the onion slivers to the skillet and sauté until soft and translucent in color, about 2 minutes; then add in the squash, season with salt and sauté until the squash are tender, 3 to 4 minutes. Sprinkle the sugar over the squash and add in the vinegar. Toss in the chives and the dill and cover for 1 minute more, allowing the squash to absorb the flavors.

SKILLET CORN BREAD
8 SERVINGS

Skillet corn bread was baked on hearths long before most people had ovens. Those who didn't have a skillet often baked the dough directly on the hearth or even on the blade of a hoe out in the fields. Corn bread was traveling bread—what New Englanders called "journey" or "johnnycake" and Southern folks called "pone" or "hoecake." My grandmother called it "crumblin,'" because she often crumbled it over a bowl of black-eyed peas or into a glass of buttermilk and ate it with a spoon. Double corn bread is made with the addition of fresh or creamed corn.

CORN BREAD

2 cups yellow cornmeal

1½ cups all-purpose flour

¼ cup granulated sugar

1 tablespoon baking powder

2 teaspoons salt

3 large eggs, room temperature

⅔ cup whole milk

1 8-ounce can cream-style corn

¼ cup (½ stick) unsalted butter

¼ cup bacon fat or lard

⌐ Adjust the rack to the center of the oven and preheat to 400°F.

MAKE THE CORN BREAD:

⌐ **FIRST,** combine the cornmeal, flour, sugar, baking powder and salt in the bowl of a mixer fitted with a paddle; whisk together thoroughly. Lightly beat the eggs into the milk in a separate bowl. Add the egg mixture into the dry ingredients and mix together on low speed to form a smooth paste; then mix in the cream-style corn until just blended.

⌐ **SECOND,** heat a 10-inch heavy-bottomed or cast-iron skillet over medium heat. Add in the butter and the bacon fat or lard and allow it to bubble. Pour all but about 2 tablespoons of the melted butter mixture into the corn bread batter and stir to combine thoroughly. Return the skillet to the stove; when the butter just begins to brown, pour in the batter. Let the corn bread cook on top of the stove just long enough for the fat to absorb into the batter, about 2 minutes; gently shake the skillet back and forth to keep the batter from sticking to the bottom. Transfer the skillet to the oven and bake until a wooden pick comes out clean when inserted into the center, about 25 minutes.

LEMON 'N' LIME MERINGUE PIE
8 SERVINGS

I love lemon meringue pie, and I really love this lemon-lime pie! Lemon pies can often be too sweet or too slight on that real-fresh-lemonade flavor, but here's a recipe that has true-lemony lemon-lime flavor with a light meringue and an easy crust made with zesty lemon snaps. It is a prized recipe, worthy of a Junior League bake sale or church supper dessert!

PIE CRUST

2 cups crushed lemon- or gingersnaps
¼ cup granulated sugar
5 tablespoons unsalted butter, melted

~ Adjust the rack to the center of the oven and preheat to 400°F.

PREPARE THE CRUST:

~ Combine the lemon snaps and the sugar in the bowl of a food processor fitted with a steel blade. Pulse until you have fine crumbs; then pour in the melted butter and pulse until thoroughly combined. Press the mixture into the bottom and up the sides of a 1-inch-deep pie dish. Bake until brown, 8 to 10 minutes. Cool.

FILLING

1½ cups granulated sugar	Zest of 1 lemon
5 tablespoons cornstarch	Zest of 1 lime
Pinch of salt	½ tablespoon unflavored gelatin
1½ cups lemon-lime soda	2 tablespoons cold water
⅓ cup fresh lemon juice	4 large egg yolks, room temperature
⅓ cup fresh lime juice	3 tablespoons unsalted butter

MAKE THE FILLING:

~ **FIRST,** combine the sugar, cornstarch and salt with the lemon-lime soda in a 2-quart heavy-bottomed saucepan; whisk together until smooth. Cook over medium heat, stirring constantly, until the mixture begins to boil; then immediately turn the heat to low and add in the lemon juice, lime juice, lemon zest and lime zest. Continue cooking until bubbles begin to break over the entire surface, 2 to 3 minutes more.

~ **MEANWHILE,** sprinkle the gelatin over the water and let stand for 4 to 5 minutes, then stir to dissolve.

~ **SECOND,** lightly whisk the egg yolks in a medium mixing bowl; add about ½ cup of the hot lemon filling to the egg yolks to temper them, whisk in the dissolved

FRIDAY EVENING

Prepare the crab stuffing and the remoulade sauce; cover and refrigerate.

SATURDAY

Bake the pie crust and fill with the lemon filling; cover and refrigerate. Prepare the soup and chill. Soak the black-eyed peas. Measure out the dry ingredients for the corn bread. Trim and cut the squash; seal in a plastic container and refrigerate.

SUNDAY MORNING

Top the pie with meringue and bake. Stuff the fish, place in the baking dish, cover with plastic and refrigerate.

gelatin until smooth and then slowly blend the yolks back into the lemon mixture. Stir over low heat for about 2 minutes. Remove the pan from heat to cool; after 3 to 4 minutes stir in the butter a tablespoon at a time. Cool uncovered for 5 minutes.

~ **THIRD,** pour the hot filling into the baked pie shell. To keep a skin from forming, cover the top with a piece of waxed paper that has been brushed with a little melted butter. Cool the pie to room temperature and then refrigerate until just a couple of hours before you plan to serve—wait until then to top the pie with the meringue.

MERINGUE

4 large egg whites, room temperature
¼ teaspoon cream of tartar
8 tablespoons superfine sugar

PREPARE THE MERINGUE:

~ Beat the egg whites until foamy in the bowl of a mixer fitted with a clean dry whisk. Add in the cream of tartar and 4 tablespoons of the superfine sugar and beat until stiff peaks form. Gently fold in the remaining 4 tablespoons of superfine sugar.

ASSEMBLE THE PIE:

~ Preheat the oven to 375°F. Remove the waxed paper from the surface of the lemon-lime filling. Use a pastry bag to pipe rosettes of meringue over the surface of the pie, or spoon the meringue over the pie and create peaks using a spatula or pastry knife. Be sure to spread the meringue so that it seals the entire edge of the crust to keep the meringue from shrinking as it bakes. Bake until golden and set, about 12 minutes. Cool the meringue by placing the pie on an open rack in the freezer for 10 to 15 minutes. Keep the pie refrigerated until 10 to 15 minutes before serving, at which point you can let it rest at room temperature.

A Homespun Gathering

≫ ≫ ≫ | BUTTERMILK-FRIED CHICKEN
with COUNTRY CREAM GRAVY

HOMINY SPOON BREAD

GREEN BEANS WITH SMOKED BACON AND ONIONS

FLAKY BUTTERMILK BISCUITS

MOLASSES PECAN CAKE WITH BURNT-SUGAR FROSTING

Fried chicken! Golden-crispy, moist in the middle, tender and juicy: It's the perennial Sunday dinner favorite. Indeed, Sunday dinner is every bit about simple homespun meals rooted deep in rural American life. These are the favorite foods our grandparents and great-grandparents made with wholesome ingredients such as farmhouse eggs, prized chickens, and produce fresh from the garden.

Not so long ago, most Americans lived on family farms or in towns that sprang up along the railroad lines and winding U.S. highways. Daily routines centered on the simple tasks of sustaining life. People sewed their own clothes from homemade patterns, canned their own vegetables, and raised enough chickens and hogs to provide meat for their own tables.

The center of this homespun society was typically church. Under the welcome shade of ancient cottonwoods and oaks, around the bustling town squares, and up and down quiet streets, neighbors met up with neighbors on the way to Sunday worship. Farm families made the drive to town along dusty roads, often planning to stay for evening services as well. In white clapboard churches with plain wooden pews and hand-pumped organs, time-honored hymns were sung with grateful hearts. Back home, the dinner table was already set, waiting to be shared with friends, relatives, or the guest preacher.

Styles of cooking in this simpler era, of course, had to conform to the foods that were available. Beef was often a luxury, but most everyone could raise a few chickens, and the best young and tender ones were saved for Sunday dinner. Fried chicken with cream gravy has long been one of the standards for this midday meal. This humble dish was born of necessity, yet it has taken its place as a classic American treat.

Whether you treasure memories of your own, cherish stories passed down from long ago, or reflect on images captured in old photographs, it's easy to feel the tug of that homespun life. Like the smell of a freshly baked pie cooling on an open windowsill, the invitation is irresistible.

Just picture a checkered tablecloth, set with an old milk bottle full of wildflowers. Beside it a basket of hot biscuits, a crock of sweet-cream butter, a glistening pitcher of sweetened iced tea, platters piled high with buttered mashed potatoes, delicately browned spoon bread, country-style green beans, succulent homegrown tomatoes, and, of course, that crisp golden chicken! On the sideboard, a beautiful, mouthwatering cake proudly stands in wait. All bid us home—like the welcome call hollered from the screened front door:

"Come on in. Dinner's ready!"

COUNTRY STORE

SUMMER
Squash
Beets
Leaf Lettuce
Swiss Chard

Pok Choi

BUTTERMILK-FRIED CHICKEN
WITH COUNTRY CREAM GRAVY
8 SERVINGS

Fried chicken has long been an American Sunday favorite. When I was young, my family would often visit my father's parents, who owned a general store out in the high desert of Southern California. Grandma Cronkhite always made fried chicken for Sunday dinner, and she always fried up just drumsticks—a treat for us kids, because we could eat with our fingers and it was easy to dip the chicken into the creamy gravy. My grandpa used to tell us these platters of drumsticks came from twelve-legged chickens—he called them "desert chickens." No matter how many times he told us the same story, we'd laugh as though we'd never heard it before.

BUTTERMILK-FRIED CHICKEN

2 3-pound frying chickens
2 cups buttermilk
2 cups all-purpose flour
½ teaspoon granulated garlic
2 teaspoons onion powder
2 teaspoons dried parsley or summer savory
2 tablespoons dry rubbed sage
1 teaspoon ground thyme
2 tablespoon salt
2 teaspoons ground black pepper
Pinch of cayenne pepper
Vegetable shortening for frying

PREPARE THE CHICKEN:

~ **FIRST,** rinse the chickens thoroughly under cold running water and pat dry with paper towels. Use a sharp knife to cut each chicken into 8 serving pieces and transfer them to a 13x9-inch baking dish. Pour the buttermilk over the chicken, turning to coat each piece thoroughly, and refrigerate covered for at least 8 hours or overnight.

~ **SECOND,** whisk together the flour, granulated garlic, onion powder, parsley or savory, sage, thyme, salt, black pepper and cayenne pepper in a wide bowl. One by one, dredge the pieces of chicken in the seasoned flour until they are heavily coated and lay the pieces out on a wire rack or baking sheet while the oil is heating.

~ **THIRD,** place a large cast-iron or heavy-bottomed skillet over medium-high heat and melt enough shortening to cover the bottom about ⅓-inch deep; heat until an instant thermometer reads 300°F or until a small cube of fresh bread or a pinch of flour sizzles instantly when added.

FRY THE CHICKEN:

~ **FIRST,** drop the chicken breasts, skin side down, into the hot oil. Adjust the heat to maintain an even temperature of around 275°F. Fry the breasts undisturbed for 5 minutes, then add the wings to the skillet. When the breasts and wings have developed a nice golden crust on the bottom, 5 to 7 minutes more, turn them over; then cover the skillet with a tight-fitting lid, reduce the heat slightly and simmer until the pieces are fully cooked and the juices run clear when tested with a knife, 20 to 25 minutes (a little less for the wings). Transfer the pieces to a paper towel–lined platter and place in a warm oven.

~ **SECOND,** add more shortening to the skillet, if needed, and return to 300°F; then drop the legs and thighs into the hot oil. Adjust the heat to maintain an even temperature of around 275°F and fry undisturbed until the legs and thighs have developed a nice golden crust on the bottom, 10 to 12 minutes. Turn them over, cover the skillet, reduce the heat slightly and simmer for about 25 minutes. For crispy chicken, remove the lid from the skillet during the last 10 to 15 minutes of cooking.

CREAM GRAVY

3 tablespoons all-purpose flour
1 cup whole milk
2 cups chicken broth
Salt and pepper to taste

MAKE THE CREAM GRAVY:

~ Pour off all but 3 to 4 tablespoons of the oil in the skillet and return to medium-high heat. Sprinkle 3 tablespoons of flour over the oil and stir to form a *roux.* Slowly pour in the milk and chicken broth, whisking constantly and scraping the brown meaty pieces from the bottom of the skillet. Continue whisking until the liquid blends with the flour and oil to form the gravy. Turn the heat to low and let the gravy simmer for a few minutes; just before serving, season to taste with salt and pepper.

HOMINY SPOON BREAD
8 SERVINGS

*H*ominy, made from boiled white corn, is a truly American product. In many areas of the country, hominy is served baked in a casserole with squash and cheese. Grits, which are often served for breakfast, are made from ground hominy. One of my favorite ways of serving grits is in this spoon bread, which is very much like a soufflé or a baked Indian pudding. This wonderfully creamy custardlike spoon bread is a great alternative to mashed potatoes or steamed rice.

SPOON BREAD

1 cup cornmeal
1 tablespoon baking powder
2 tablespoons cornstarch
½ teaspoon salt
½ teaspoon pepper
4 cups prepared hominy grits, cooled
2 tablespoon unsalted butter
5 large egg yolks, room temperature
1 cup whole milk
½ teaspoon Tabasco sauce
5 large egg whites, room temperature
½ teaspoon cream of tartar

~ Adjust the rack to the center of the oven and preheat to 375°F.

PREPARE THE SPOON BREAD:

~ **FIRST,** butter a 2-quart ceramic baking dish or casserole.

~ **SECOND,** combine the cornmeal with the baking powder, cornstarch, salt and pepper in a small bowl; whisk together thoroughly and set aside.

~ **THIRD,** use a wooden spoon to beat the butter into the cooked grits in a large mixing bowl. Next, stir in the egg yolks until they are fully incorporated, then fold in the milk and Tabasco sauce. Finally, add the combined dry ingredients in 2 batches, mixing until smooth.

~ **FOURTH,** use an electric handheld mixer to beat the egg whites with the cream of tartar in a separate bowl until they hold stiff peaks—to achieve the best results, be sure that your egg whites are at room temperature and the clean bowl is thoroughly dry. Gently fold the egg whites into the cornmeal mixture using a rubber spatula; stir until just combined.

~ **FIFTH,** pour the batter into the prepared pan and bake until puffed and golden, about 45 minutes. Serve immediately, smothered with generous ladlefuls of country cream gravy.

GREEN BEANS WITH
SMOKED BACON AND ONIONS
8 SERVINGS

My grandmother always cooked her homegrown pole beans with bacon and onions. True to her generation, however, they were usually boiled. I prefer mine sautéed and bright green, with just a little snap left to them.

GREEN BEANS

2 pounds green beans
4 strips thick-cut smoked bacon, diced
1 medium onion, thinly sliced
Pinch of salt

PREPARE THE GREEN BEANS:

~ **FIRST,** use a sharp paring knife to trim the ends and pull any tough strings from the green beans.

~ **SECOND,** blanch the beans in a large saucepan filled with boiling salted water. They should cook just long enough to become tender and turn bright green, about 3 to 4 minutes. Drain the beans and immediately plunge them into ice water to stop the cooking process.

~ **THIRD,** cook the bacon in a large skillet over medium-high heat until it begins to brown, then add the blanched beans and onion slices and season with a pinch of salt. Toss thoroughly with the bacon fat.

~ **FOURTH,** reduce the heat to medium and sauté until the beans are cooked through and the onions have begun to caramelize, 4 to 5 minutes.

Easy time-saving
AND DO-AHEAD TIPS:

FRIDAY EVENING
Cook the hominy grits and refrigerate them. Bake the cake layers, cool and wrap in plastic.

SATURDAY
Prepare the filling and frosting. Refrigerate the chicken pieces in the buttermilk marinade. Assemble the cake. Sift the dry ingredients for the spoon bread and the biscuits. Blanch the green beans and refrigerate.

SUNDAY MORNING
Prepare the spoon bread mixture and the bicuits for baking.

FLAKY BUTTERMILK BISCUITS
18 BISCUITS

On a nineteenth-century farm, you would have churned your own butter and afterward enjoyed a tall glass of cold buttermilk—sweet, creamy, and with bits of butter floating on the surface. Cultured buttermilk is not nearly as good, but it still makes for some of the best, flakiest biscuits ever.

BUTTERMILK BISCUITS

4 cups all-purpose flour
5 teaspoons baking powder
1 teaspoon baking soda
1 teaspoon salt
1 cup shortening, chilled
1½ cups buttermilk

~ Adjust the rack to the center of the oven and preheat to 425°F.

MAKE THE BISCUITS:

~ **FIRST,** sift the flour, baking powder, baking soda and salt into a large bowl. Slice the chilled shortening into pieces and add to the dry ingredients. Use a pastry cutter to cut in the shortening, or pulse for several seconds in a food processor, until the mixture resembles coarse crumbly meal. Add the buttermilk and stir with a fork until the dough just holds together.

~ **SECOND,** turn the dough out onto a lightly floured surface. Knead gently for 1 minute, adding a little extra flour as necessary to incorporate all the ingredients and ensure that the biscuits will rise evenly. Pat into a ½-inch-thick circle and let the dough rest, covered with a clean tea towel, for 10 to 15 minutes.

THIRD, cut the biscuits with a 2-inch round cutter dipped in flour. Arrange them about ¾-inch apart on an ungreased baking sheet and brush the tops with a little buttermilk. Bake in the center of the oven until golden, 10 to 12 minutes. Cool the biscuits on wire racks and brush them with melted butter, if desired.

Alcohol and honky-tonks weren't topics of conversation in the 1950s. So let's just say my mother's "nerves" kept my family from enjoying Norman Rockwell Sunday dinners.

But in 1954, when we moved to McGregor, Texas, I was initiated into the Sunday Dinner Society. The church ladies all came with invitations to join their respective congregations, and I accepted the Methodists' because my new first-grade pals went there. When my friend Stephanie's mom invited me to Sunday dinner, Mother warned that they might have fancier dishes than our Appleware. I told Mother later that they used rags for napkins (fringed cloth napkins) and played 33⅓-rpm records without any words, which they called "classical."

I loved that Sunday dinner experience at my friend's house. Stephanie refused to eat her green beans, stuck her tongue out at her mother, splashed her potatoes with a fork—and still got dessert! Here was a world where children, not parents, could be the source of drama. I hadn't seen such sport since the dish ran away with the spoon.

During the next twelve years, I accepted every invitation to Sunday dinner and cherished in my heart what I saw: siblings squabbling, dads talking, lots of laughing, frozen peas, Monopoly, and quiet afternoons. The food wasn't the most important thing to me because nobody made fried chicken as well as my mother. But the families in that small Texas town gave me a gift that became a birthright for our five now-grown children: nurturing, fun, and family dinners—Sunday or otherwise.

❧ LINDA JACKS ☙

MOLASSES PECAN CAKE
WITH BURNT-SUGAR FROSTING
12 SERVINGS

Pecan trees still grow wild throughout the southern United States, where they were planted by various Native American tribes from Mississippi to the Texas hill country. There are many different kinds of pecan desserts and so many scrumptious variations that it is difficult to choose just one.

NOTE: *There has to be one recipe more challenging than the rest in every cookbook, and this is it. Butter-rich, densely textured, with a gooey-nutty caramel flavor—this is some kind of cake!*

CAKE

3 cups cake flour	¼ cup molasses
1 tablespoon baking powder	1 teaspoon pure vanilla extract
½ teaspoon salt	4 large eggs, room temperature
1 cup (2 sticks) unsalted butter, softened	¾ cup strong-brewed coffee
1½ cups granulated sugar	1 cup finely ground pecans
½ cup packed dark brown sugar	

Adjust the rack to the center of the oven and preheat to 350°F.

MAKE THE CAKE:

FIRST, butter and flour two 9-inch round cake pans with 2-inch sides, tapping out the excess flour.

SECOND, sift the cake flour, baking powder and salt into a small bowl and set aside.

THIRD, thoroughly cream the butter with the granulated sugar and brown sugar until light and fluffy, 6 to 8 minutes. Beat in the molasses and vanilla. Add the eggs one at a time, beating well after each addition. Scrape down the sides of the bowl with a rubber spatula.

FOURTH, with the mixer running at low speed, alternately add the flour mixture and strong-brewed coffee in batches, beginning and ending with the flour; mix until each addition of flour is fully combined. Increase the mixer speed to medium and beat for 1 minute, then gently fold in the ground pecans.

FIFTH, divide the batter evenly between the 2 pans and bake until the cakes are beginning to shrink from the edges of the pans and the centers spring back when pressed gently, 30 to 35 minutes. Transfer to baking racks and cool for 10 minutes. Loosen the cakes from their pans by running a thin knife around the edges, then turn out onto the racks to cool completely.

FILLING

1 cup (2 sticks) unsalted butter

5 large egg yolks, room temperature
(reserve egg whites for frosting)

1 14-ounce can sweetened condensed milk

1 teaspoon pure vanilla extract

1⅓ cups (6 ounces) roughly chopped pecans

⅔ cup toasted flaked coconut

MAKE THE FILLING:

~ FIRST, combine the butter, egg yolks and sweetened condensed milk in a stainless mixing bowl or in the top of a double boiler. Beat with a stiff wire whisk or an electric hand-held mixer until smooth.

~ SECOND, place the mixing bowl over a pan of simmering water (do not let the bowl touch the water) and stir constantly to fully melt the butter. As the butter melts, the mixture will become thin; continue to cook the filling, stirring continually, until it thickens to the consistency of thick custard, about 12 minutes. Stir in the vanilla, then beat for 1 minute with an electric hand-held mixer set at medium speed. Fold in the chopped pecans and coconut; cool. (*Note:* The filling can be made a day ahead and refrigerated.)

BURNT-SUGAR FROSTING

1½ cups (3 sticks) unsalted butter, room temperature

¼ cup superfine sugar

5 large egg whites, room temperature

⅛ teaspoon cream of tartar

⅔ cup granulated sugar

½ cup boiling water

MAKE THE FROSTING:

~ FIRST, beat the butter until light and fluffy; set aside. Combine the superfine sugar, unbeaten egg whites and cream of tartar in a double boiler set over a pan of simmering water. Whisk by hand until the sugar is dissolved and the whites are warm, thick and frothy, about 2 minutes. Transfer the mixture to the bowl of a mixer and beat on medium-high speed until soft peaks form, about 3 minutes.

~ SECOND, heat the granulated sugar in a small heavy-bottomed saucepan over medium-high heat until it begins to melt around the edges. Stir with a wooden spoon, breaking up any large pieces that form, until all the crystals have dissolved and the liquid is amber in color. Carefully begin pouring the ½ cup boiling water over the sugar, a little at a time to avoid splattering. As you pour, the melted sugar will bubble rapidly; stir until the sugar is completely dissolved. Continue cooking over medium-high heat until the liquid reaches 240°F and has achieved the consistency of syrup, 2 to 3 minutes.

~ THIRD, slowly pour the sugar syrup into the beaten egg white mixture in a slow, steady stream; avoid pouring the sugar syrup onto the beaters. Beat at medium-high speed until the frosting begins to cool and firm peaks start to form, 15 to 20 minutes. Cool to room temperature.

~ FOURTH, add in the beaten butter ⅓ at a time, beating well after each addition. If the first addition of butter begin to melt, cool a little longer, then continue mixing until the frosting is smooth and creamy.

ASSEMBLE THE CAKE:

~ Use a sharp serrated knife to split each of the cake layers in half horizontally. Put one of the layers on a cake plate and spread ⅓ of the filling over it. Top with a second layer, spread with ⅓ more filling, and repeat once more, using all of the filling in the process. Top with the fourth layer, then frost the top and sides of the cake with the cooled burnt-sugar frosting.

NOTE: *This cake is best when it is made the day before and kept at moderate room temperature, covered.*

Mountain's Majesty

PAN-FRIED RAINBOW TROUT WITH BACON AND PECANS
DRY-RUBBED PEPPERCORN STEAKS
STUFFED BAKED POTATOES
CUCUMBER-RANCH SALAD RING
ROASTED CORN ON THE COB
WARM PEACH COBBLER
VANILLA ICE CREAM

In 1893, Katherine Lee Bates stood atop 14,000-foot-tall Pikes Peak with a group of fellow professors summering in Colorado. Electrified by the majesty that lay before her, she wrote "America the Beautiful."

That same scene of mountain majesty has inspired me many times. For years my family lived high in the mountains of Colorado, surrounded by the Pike National Forest, where I worked at a guest ranch and family retreat. Three of my four children were born in Colorado. We lived in, and around, the small Western towns with their wood-planked sidewalks, tack shops, general stores, and small cozy cafés.

What a spectacular place to live! In the summer we'd picnic under the mountains' glorious gaze, and in the winter we'd ski the backwoods on never-touched white powder. We'd hunt and fish in some of the best places in the country, often overcome by the sheer grandeur of God's incredible creation. At night, the black velvet sky would twinkle with so many stars that we couldn't begin to count them.

This is ranch country, where some of the finest beef in the nation is raised. Here a 4x4 is a valuable tool and horses are a way of life. It's not a life for the faint of heart or feeble of body. It's just plain hard work. It's hard enough to make you hungry!

My family often attended worship services in a small country church that sat just on the edge of town. In the warmer months we'd gather in a great meadow outside beneath the aspens or beside a small lake that reflected the still-snowcapped peaks. And Sunday dinner after church was always a multifamily affair. Women brought pies and cobblers; men grilled beef, half-chickens, or venison; teenage boys showed off by hand-churning ice cream; the smaller kids helped set the table. After grace (when those ever-present cowboy hats would finally come off), the food-laden platters would make their way around great knotty-pine tables. There would be fresh-caught trout, grilled meats, fried potatoes, molded salads, corn on the cob, and peach cobbler with ice cream.

Life, however, is seldom just beautiful streams, peaceful meadows, and towering mountain peaks. We also buried our first child in that land of majestic mountains. She was just 16 weeks old. Each year, on the anniversary of her death, our hearts break yet again. Yet each year our hearts find comfort in the memories of the breathtaking beauty of that place and the community life we shared with those who gave us so much more than Sunday afternoons.

PAN-FRIED RAINBOW TROUT
WITH BACON AND PECANS
8 SERVINGS

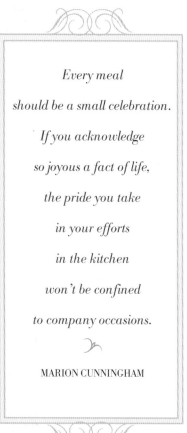

It's always nice to have freshly caught trout—their flesh is firm and pink and ever so succulent. The combination of tangy buttermilk, lemon pepper, smoky bacon and toasted pecans takes me back to days of streamside cooking in the great outdoors!

TROUT

4 12-ounce fresh boneless rainbow trout
1 cup buttermilk
2 tablespoons lemon pepper
½ teaspoon salt
1 cup finely ground pecans
1 cup cracker crumbs
8 strips bacon

PREPARE THE TROUT:

- **FIRST,** cut the head and tail from each boneless trout and discard; split each trout lengthwise down the back into 2 fillets and remove the fins.

- **SECOND,** whisk the buttermilk with the lemon pepper and salt and pour into a flat dish or pie plate. Combine the ground pecans with the cracker crumbs in a second flat dish or pie plate. Cook the bacon in a large skillet over medium heat until it just begins to crisp, then remove with a slotted spoon and drain on a paper towel; leave the bacon fat in the skillet.

- **THIRD,** dip each fillet in the seasoned buttermilk and then in the crumb mixture, pressing the crumbs gently into the fillets to form a thick even coating.

- **FOURTH,** reheat the bacon fat in the skillet over medium-high heat. Working in 2 batches, place the fillets skin side up in the skillet and brown for 3 to 4 minutes. Carefully turn the fillets over and brown for 2 to 3 minutes more, then transfer to a baking sheet and repeat the process with the remaining fillets. When you are done, broil the fillets on the baking sheet for 1 minute to finish the cooking process.

- **FIFTH,** transfer the fish to a platter with the skin side down; crumble the crisp bacon over the top and garnish, if desired, with lemon wedges. Serve immediately.

DRY-RUBBED PEPPERCORN STEAKS
8 SERVINGS

Steaks are cut thick out West, where beef is dry-rubbed and grilled to perfection. I prefer serving thick-cut sirloins, then slicing them across the grain like a London broil. The greater size of the steaks means longer grilling time, which creates a well-seasoned crust and juicy, mouth-watering slices.

NOTE: *Have your butcher select thick-cut top sirloin steaks that weigh 1½ to 2 pounds each and measure between 1 and 1½ inches thick. Make sure that the steaks are well trimmed and have a good amount of marbled fat.*

STEAKS

2 tablespoons mixed peppercorns
2 teaspoons granulated garlic
2 teaspoons onion powder
1 tablespoon paprika
1 tablespoon coarse salt
1 tablespoon packed brown sugar
2 1½ to 2-pound thick-cut sirloin steaks
2 tablespoons Worcestershire sauce

PREPARE THE DRY RUB:

~ Use a mortar and pestle or the bottom of a flat skillet to crush the peppercorns. Combine in a small bowl with the granulated garlic, onion powder, paprika, coarse salt and brown sugar.

GRILL THE STEAKS:

~ **FIRST,** remove the steaks from the refrigerator. Rub the Worcestershire sauce into the meat and then coat with the dry rub. Transfer to a large platter and allow the seasoned steaks to rest at room temperature for 20 minutes.

~ **SECOND,** if you are grilling the steaks, brush the grate with oil. Grill directly over medium-high heat, about 8 to 10 minutes on each side for medium-rare steaks. If you're using a broiler, first heat the broiler pan, then brush the steaks with a little oil. Broil the steaks 3 inches below the heat for 5 to 6 minutes. Turn them over and broil for an additional 5 to 6 minutes for medium-rare. Allow the steaks to rest at room temperature for 10 minutes before slicing, then serve immediately.

STUFFED BAKED POTATOES
8 SERVINGS

I find that russets are the best potatoes for baking. These savory twice-baked potatoes, stuffed with green onions, peppers and cheddar cheese, are wonderfully simple to make. The potatoes are baked and scooped out, mashed with butter and sour cream, then refilled. One of the best parts is that they can be made oven-ready a full day ahead.

STUFFED POTATOES

8 medium baking potatoes
2 tablespoons butter
½ cup diced green bell pepper
2 cloves garlic, minced
½ cup chopped green onions
½ cup (1 stick) butter
½ cup sour cream
½ cup whole milk, as needed
Salt and pepper to taste
1 cup grated cheddar cheese

Adjust the rack to the center of the oven and preheat to 375°F.

PREPARE THE POTATOES:

FIRST, scrub the potatoes and pat dry. Bake the potatoes directly on the oven rack until they are done and easily give way when pressed gently, 60 to 70 minutes. Once they have cooled enough to handle, gently roll each potato back and forth on a flat surface (this will make them nice and mealy inside). Cut the top third from each potato and scoop out the inside, leaving a shell that is sturdy enough to hold its shape.

SECOND, melt 2 tablespoons of butter in a small skillet over medium heat and add the bell pepper and garlic; sauté until the peppers are soft, 3 to 4 minutes, then fold in the chopped green onions and set aside to cool.

THIRD, use a potato masher or stiff wire whisk to thoroughly mash the potato insides in an up-and-down motion. Add in ½ cup of butter and the sour cream and mash until they are smooth, about 1 minute. Whip in enough of the milk so that the potatoes become fluffy but still hold their shape. Fold in the sautéed peppers and onions and season to taste with salt and pepper.

FOURTH, mound the seasoned mashed potatoes back into the empty shells and transfer to a lightly oiled baking sheet. Bake in a 375°F oven for 20 to 25 minutes; sprinkle with cheese during the final 5 minutes of baking.

Easy time-saving
AND DO-AHEAD TIPS:

FRIDAY EVENING
Prepare the vanilla ice cream base; cool to room temperature and refrigerate. Prepare the ranch dressing and refrigerate.

SATURDAY
Bake, hollow and stuff the potatoes, then cover and refrigerate. Prepare the cucumber salad and refrigerate. Cut the trout into fillets. Finely grind the pecans. Process the ice cream.

SUNDAY MORNING
Clean and season the ears of corn and wrap in foil. Prepare the peach cobbler to be oven-ready. Mix together the dry rub for the steaks.

CUCUMBER-RANCH SALAD RING

8 TO 10 SERVINGS

Molded salads made with fruit or vegetables were once a standard on the American table, and you can still find wonderful recipes in Junior League and church cookbooks. They are a wonderful accompaniment to any family meal. This cool, tangy cucumber mold is hard to beat, especially when garnished with crisp cucumbers, tender leaves of butter lettuce and a touch of homemade ranch dressing.

CUCUMBER SALAD

2 tablespoons unflavored gelatin
¼ cup water
2 tablespoons lime juice
2 large seedless English cucumbers
½ teaspoon salt
1 cup cottage cheese
¼ cup finely chopped green onions
¼ cup finely diced celery
2 cups Ranch dressing, recipe follows

MAKE THE CUCUMBER SALAD:

~ **FIRST,** combine the unflavored gelatin and the water in a small saucepan. Stir over medium heat until the gelatin is completely dissolved, then add in the lime juice and remove from heat.

~ **SECOND,** peel the cucumbers and cut into large chunks; transfer to the bowl of a food processor fitted with a steel blade and pulse until the cucumbers are almost smooth, then season with the salt.

~ **THIRD,** combine the cottage cheese with 2 cups of the ranch dressing and whisk until nearly smooth. Combine the dissolved gelatin with the cucumber purée and whip into the cottage cheese mixture; then fold in the green onions and celery. Transfer to a 5-cup salad ring or ceramic dish and cover with plastic wrap. Chill until the salad is set, at least 8 hours or overnight.

RANCH DRESSING

1 cup mayonnaise
1 cup sour cream
1 tablespoon Dijon mustard
1 teaspoon salt
2 teaspoons pepper
1 teaspoon Worcestershire sauce
2 cups buttermilk

MAKE THE RANCH DRESSING:

~ Blend the mayonnaise and sour cream together in a mixing bowl. Whisk in the mustard, salt, pepper and Worcestershire sauce; then fold in the buttermilk. Cover and refrigerate for at least 8 hours or overnight.

GARNISH

2 heads butter lettuce, rinsed
Sliced cucumbers
2 bunches watercress, rinsed
Additional ranch dressing

PRESENT THE SALAD:

~ Dip the bottom into hot water to loosen the gelatin. Remove the plastic wrap and carefully invert the salad onto a decorative plate lined with lettuce leaves. Garnish the outside with fresh cucumber slices and fill the center with bunches of watercress. Pass additional ranch dressing alongside the salad.

ROASTED CORN ON THE COB

8 SERVINGS

hether it is dripping with melted butter on the cob or added to a crunchy, savory salad, corn is hard to beat. The sweet native grain lends a contrast of texture and flavor to the seasoned sirloin and delicate trout in this menu. Wrapping the cobs in foil steams the corn in its own natural sugars and allows the butter to permeate each tender kernel.

ROASTED CORN

8 ears sweet corn
Salt for seasoning
8 tablespoons (1 stick) butter

ROAST THE CORN:

~ **FIRST,** shuck the corn and trim the ends, then rinse off all the stringy silk. Lay each ear on a 12-inch square of foil and season with salt; if desired, season with a pinch of chili powder. Cut each tablespoon of butter into 4 or 5 pieces and lay alongside the corn on the foil. Roll the foil tightly around the corn and crimp the ends to seal.

~ **SECOND,** if grilling, place the foil-wrapped ears directly over medium heat and roast for 12 to 15 minutes, turning 2 or 3 times; or roast the ears on the center rack of a 375°F oven for 15 to 18 minutes. As they cook, the ears of corn will steam in the butter.

~ **THIRD,** carefully unwrap the roasted ears from the foil and serve.

WARM PEACH COBBLER

12 SERVINGS

Peaches ripen slowly in the summer sun and grow juicy as the fall sap begins to sweeten. Few things are as satisfying as warm fruit cobbler topped with fresh homemade ice cream.

PEACH FILLING

8 cups fresh sliced peaches or frozen peaches, thawed
1 tablespoon fresh lemon juice
1 teaspoon ground cinnamon
Pinch of ground nutmeg or mace
3 tablespoons cornstarch
½ cup packed light brown sugar
½ cup granulated sugar
¼ cup (½ stick) unsalted butter

Preheat the oven to 375°F.

MAKE THE FILLING:

Combine the sliced peaches with the lemon juice, cinnamon and nutmeg or mace in a large mixing bowl; toss together with the cornstarch, brown sugar and granulated sugar. Cut the butter into little pieces and combine with the peaches. Transfer to a buttered 13x9-inch baking dish.

COBBLER TOPPING

1½ cups all-purpose flour
1 cup cake flour
4 teaspoons baking powder
½ teaspoon salt
8 tablespoons (1 stick) unsalted butter
⅓ cup granulated sugar
2 large eggs, room temperature, lightly beaten
¾ cup whole milk

MAKE THE TOPPING:

FIRST, sift the all-purpose flour, cake flour, baking powder and salt into a mixing bowl. Slice 8 tablespoons of butter into 1-inch pieces and scatter the pieces over the flour mixture; sprinkle with the sugar, then cut all of the ingredients together with a pastry cutter until the mixture resembles coarse crumbly meal.

SECOND, whisk the egg and milk together in a separate bowl, then add to the crumbly mixture. Stir with a wooden spoon until the dough just blends together and reaches the consistency of a wet biscuit dough.

THIRD, spoon the topping into 12 mounds over the peach filling. Brush the mounds with a little milk and sprinkle with a little granulated sugar. Bake until the topping is golden and the fruit is bubbling, 40 to 45 minutes.

VANILLA ICE CREAM
MAKES ABOUT 1½ QUARTS

Just "plain" vanilla? I don't think so! In this recipe, rich vanilla custard is frozen into smooth ice cream. At Blair House, I made my own ice cream; I had a small but powerful commercial machine, which saved me from having to crank by hand!

ICE CREAM

6 large egg yolks, room temperature
¾ cup granulated sugar
1 vanilla bean
2 cups half-and-half
2 cups heavy whipping cream

MAKE THE CUSTARD BASE:

- **FIRST,** place the egg yolks in a stainless bowl or in the top of a double boiler. Slowly beat in the sugar with a wire whisk—it's important that the sugar dissolves slowly and completely into the yolks and that you do not beat the mixture too rapidly, which will make the yolks frothy and full of air.

- **SECOND,** split the vanilla bean in half lengthwise and combine with the half-and-half in a saucepan. Heat slowly over medium heat until the half-and-half just begins to boil, then remove from heat immediately.

- **THIRD,** temper the yolks by whisking ½ cup of the hot half-and-half into the yolk mixture until fully blended; then whisk in the remaining hot half-and-half. Place the bowl over a pan of simmering water, making sure that the bowl does not touch the water. Cook the custard, stirring constantly with a heat-resistant rubber spatula, until thickened, 6 to 8 minutes. To test for thickness: Dip a spoon into the sauce and hold it horizontally over the pan, making sure that the sauce coats the spoon evenly; then run your finger through the sauce on the spoon—if the line doesn't fill back up, it has thickened enough.

- **FOURTH,** remove the vanilla bean and strain the custard through a fine sieve into a stainless bowl. Cool by partially submerging the bowl in a second bowl of ice water; stir gently until cool. Stir in the cream, then scrape all of the tiny seeds from the vanilla bean into the ice cream. Whisk the custard thoroughly, then process in an ice cream freezer according to the manufacturer's instructions.

The King of Desserts,

when made aright,

this frozen delicacy of delight,

the exacting Epicure

with smiles galore,

like Oliver Twist,

will ask for more!

AUTHOR UNKNOWN

Rising to Meet You

"May the road rise to meet you…"

That traditional Gaelic blessing must have haunted three Irish brothers who made their way through the squalor and din of nineteenth-century New York. Two ventured north to Boston; the other headed south and found his way to Georgia. The story of James Cross, my great-great-grandfather, is all too familiar. It's the story of the Irish in America.

Under English rule, the Irish people had essentially become serfs in their own country. The potato, most likely imported from Virginia by Sir Walter Raleigh, had turned out to be a plentiful and inexpensive food staple for these peasants. Then, however, came the great potato famine of the 1840s, which caused the deaths of more than a million Irish and forced another 2 million to emigrate. These are staggering statistics for a country of fewer than 8 million people.

Those who fled to America found conditions not much better than at home. Undereducated and dirt poor, they had to take the lowest-paying jobs as housemaids, factory laborers, and miners. Long workweeks, unsafe conditions, and child labor all but guaranteed a continuance of poverty. Yet these tough, lively people prevailed and made their mark. Today some 30 million Americans consider themselves of Irish descent and rich traditions of storytelling, music, and handcraftsmanship still thrive today. So do the close bonds of family and church that have always sustained the Irish American community. It is close-knit, but with a strong sense of feisty independence, and built on a foundation of unshakable faith.

Corned beef and cabbage have long been associated with the Irish, and in particular with their favorite holiday, St. Patrick's Day. But this wonderful dish of salt-preserved meat, also known as New England boiled dinner, was enjoyed in this country for more than a century before the mass Irish immigration began. Beef, in fact, was not common fare in Ireland, where cattle were raised almost exclusively for dairy products. The traditional Irish dish of bacon and cabbage, however, was readily changed to use corned beef, which kept well over the winter months and was easy to come by on St. Patrick's Day in March.

As Americans began moving west—the Irish among them—they quickly grew to appreciate cured meats such as corned beef, which traveled well. Later, during World War I, the Great Depression, and World War II, economical corned beef and cabbage became one the most popular dishes throughout the country—especially for Sunday dinner. Today this down-to-earth dish still blesses a Sunday table with a bit of an Irish lilt:

"Until we meet again, may God hold you in the hollow of His hand."

FRESH SWEET PEA SOUP

6 SERVINGS

Using fresh peas instead of dried is the traditional Irish version of this soup. It is seasoned with thick-cut bacon, smoked ham broth and leeks. You can serve this light, satisfying soup as a simple supper, accompanied by the soda bread.

PEA SOUP

4 tablespoons (½ stick) butter
½ cup diced sweet onion
4 cups fresh blanched peas or frozen peas, thawed
2 cups ham or chicken broth
4 strips thick-cut smoked bacon, julienned
1 cup thinly sliced leeks, white part only
Salt and white pepper to taste
½ cup sour cream or crème fraîche
1 tablespoon fresh snipped chives

MAKE THE PEA SOUP:

FIRST, melt 2 tablespoons of the butter in a saucepan over medium-low heat. When the butter begins to bubble, add in the diced onion, being careful not to let the butter brown. Sauté the onions until they are soft and translucent, about 2 to 3 minutes. Then add in the remaining 2 tablespoons butter, let it melt, and add in the peas. Cook the peas, stirring frequently, for 2 to 3 minutes. Pour in the ham or chicken broth, increase the heat to medium-high and simmer until the peas are fully cooked, tender and still bright green, 6 to 8 minutes. Remove the pan from heat to cool slightly.

SECOND, strain the peas through a sieve, reserving the peas and liquid separately. Transfer the peas to a food processor fitted with a steel blade and pulse until the peas are coarsely chopped. Slowly add in the reserved cooking liquid and pulse to a smooth purée.

THIRD, sauté the bacon over medium heat until it just begins to crisp, 2 to 3 minutes (you can use the same pan that the peas were cooked in). Drain off all but 1 tablespoon of the bacon grease and add in the sliced leeks. Sauté the leeks until they are tender and translucent in color, 3 to 4 minutes. Add in the pea purée, season to taste with salt and white pepper, and simmer for another 5 minutes to blend all the flavors.

SERVE THE SOUP:

Ladle the soup into wide bowls and top each serving with a generous spoonful of sour cream or crème fraîche, then sprinkle with chives. Serve immediately.

Easy time-saving
AND DO AHEAD TIPS:

FRIDAY EVENING

Prepare the soup to be reheated on Sunday. Prepare the lemon curd and the raspberry sauce and refrigerate separately in well-sealed containers.

SATURDAY

Bake and completely assemble the jelly roll. Sift dry ingredients for the soda bread.

SUNDAY MORNING

Prepare the vegetables and refrigerate in well-sealed containers. Cook the corned beef and prepare the mustard glaze.

MUSTARD-GLAZED CORNED BEEF WITH CABBAGE AND BRAISED ROOT VEGETABLES
6 SERVINGS

Corned beef gets its name from the coarse grains of salt ("corns") that were once used to cure the meat. In Vermont, corned beef is glazed with maple syrup and baked in the oven after being boiled. In other parts of New England, the glaze is made with mustard or horseradish and just a touch of honey or brown sugar. Either way, this "Irish" dish is a truly American classic—influenced by the many immigrants who helped make our nation diverse.

CORNED BEEF

1 3-pound corned beef brisket
1 medium onion
1 bay leaf
2 whole cloves
2 whole cloves garlic
1 teaspoon mustard seeds
½ teaspoon black peppercorns

PREPARE THE CORNED BEEF:

~ **FIRST,** rinse the corned beef thoroughly under cold running water. Place fat side up in a large pot or Dutch oven and pour in enough cold water to cover all but an inch of the meat.

~ **SECOND,** peel and quarter the onion, then add the onion, bay leaf, whole cloves, garlic, mustard seeds and peppercorns into the pot with the corned beef. Bring to a boil over medium-high heat, reduce the heat to low and skim off any residue that floats to the surface. Place the lid on the pot and simmer until the meat is fork-tender, about 2 hours.

VEGETABLES

1 head green cabbage
6 medium carrots
10 to 12 small boiling onions
4 parsnips
12 to 18 small boiling potatoes
3 large turnips
¼ cup (½ stick) butter
1 tablespoon fresh chopped parsley
Salt to taste

PREPARE THE VEGETABLES:

∽ **FIRST,** cut the cabbage in half and then into 6 equal wedges; cut out the core. Peel the carrots and slice them into 2-inch rounds. Cut the root end from each of the boiling onions with a paring knife and peel, leaving the pointed shoot end intact to keep them from falling apart when they are cooked. Peel the parsnips and cut into 2-inch pieces. Scrub the potatoes to be cooked in their jackets. Peel the turnips and cut into quarters.

∽ **SECOND,** when the brisket is fork-tender, remove it from the pot and place it in a shallow roasting pan, this time with the fat side down. Use a small strainer to remove the onion, bay leaf, cloves, garlic, mustard seeds and peppercorns from the liquid. Remove and set aside about 1 cup of the cooking liquid.

∽ **THIRD,** add the carrots, onions, parsnips and turnips to the remaining cooking liquid in the pot. Cover with the lid, place on the stovetop and bring to a boil; then reduce the heat to medium-low and simmer for 20 minutes. Add in the potatoes and cook until the potatoes are tender, another 15 to 20 minutes.

∽ **MEANWHILE,** place the cabbage in a casserole or covered skillet large enough to easily hold all of the wedges. Add in enough of the reserved cooking liquid to cover the bottom of the skillet by a little more than ½ inch. Cover the skillet with a tight-fitting lid, set the heat to high and steam until tender, about 15 minutes.

GLAZE

2 teaspoons prepared horseradish
2 tablespoons spicy brown mustard
2 tablespoons packed brown sugar

PREPARE THE GLAZE:

∽ Whisk together the horseradish, mustard and brown sugar in a small bowl. While the vegetables are still cooking, use a pastry brush to coat the corned beef with the glaze; transfer to a 325°F oven and bake until the glaze is bubbling hot, about 30 minutes. Allow the corned beef to rest in the roasting pan at room temperature until you are ready to slice, so that it stays juicy.

SERVE THE CORNED BEEF:

∽ Place the corned beef on a clean cutting board and slice thinly against the grain with a sharp carving knife. Arrange the slices on a warm platter with the steamed cabbage and drizzle with a little of the cooking liquid. Serve the carrots, onions, parsnips and turnips in a separate bowl drizzled with a little more of the cooking liquid. Toss the potatoes with the butter and chopped parsley; season them with salt and serve in a separate bowl.

IRISH SODA BREAD
MAKES 2 SMALL LOAVES

There are many variations of traditional Irish soda bread, including tea bread with raisins and brown bread made with whole wheat flour and perhaps a little oatmeal. The basic method of preparation, however, is always the same. This variation is both hearty and rustic.

NOTE: *Today's all-purpose flour is made with a blend of soft and hard wheat, which have stronger gluten than Irish flour; I've substituted a little cake flour for a lighter, more authentic bread. I also find the addition of a little butter, missing from our commercial buttermilk, will give the bread the added moisture it should have.*

SODA BREAD

2 cups unbleached all-purpose flour
1 cup cake flour
3 cups whole wheat flour
2 teaspoons baking soda
1 teaspoon salt
¼ cup (½ stick) unsalted butter, chilled
2 cups buttermilk

Adjust the rack to the center of the oven and preheat to 450°F.

MAKE THE SODA BREAD:

FIRST, combine the unbleached flour, cake flour and whole wheat flour in a large bowl and whisk well; then sift together with the baking soda and salt.

SECOND, rub the butter into the flour mixture with the tips of your fingers until the butter is fully incorporated and "disappears" into the flour mix. Make a well in the center, pour in the buttermilk and beat with a wooden spoon until the dough just holds together and is slightly sticky. Turn out onto a lightly floured work surface, or place in the bowl of an electric mixer fitted with a dough hook, and knead by hand or on low speed until smooth, about 6 minutes.

THIRD, form the dough into two 6-inch rounds and pat smooth. Dust the bottoms with a little all-purpose flour and transfer to a lightly greased baking sheet. Use a sharp thin knife to mark 6 equal wedges by scoring a ⅓-inch-deep pattern into the top of each loaf.

FOURTH, bake for 10 minutes, then lower the temperature to 400°F and continue baking for 30 to 35 minutes. The loaves should sound hollow when tapped on the bottom. Cool completely on racks before serving.

A curious mix of lingering warmth and growing chill, the bitter-sweet incense of burning leaves hanging in the air—that's what I remember about October Sundays in New Hampshire when I was young. I'd shuffle home after church to a bout of neighborhood football or watch the game on television with Dad, who would often doze between quarters. Sundays were the only day I could really hang out with him. The grocery business was more than a full-time job, but thankfully the store was closed on Sundays.

While we watched, the aroma of Mom's good Irish-American cooking would slowly fill the house. Just as Saturday night meant beans and franks and brown bread, Sunday dinner always meant pot roast, corned beef and cabbage, or leg of lamb. No other meal, not even Thanksgiving dinner, has left such vivid memories. Long after dinner, the smells would linger throughout the house like a pleasant melody that slowly fades away. Then family conversations and fun-filled games would keep us occupied as early darkness fell. Finally, we would gather for our Sunday evening tradition, watching *The Ed Sullivan Show* on TV.

❦ GEORGE KNIGHT ❧

RASPBERRY-LEMON JELLY ROLL

6 SERVINGS

This is a wonderful, easy-to-prepare dessert made with sponge cake, raspberry jam and lemon curd. I love serving it with fresh strawberries, fresh strawberry sauce and a dollop of sweetened whipped cream.

LEMON CURD

2 lemons
½ cup (1 stick) unsalted butter
2 large eggs, room temperature
⅔ cup granulated sugar

MAKE THE LEMON CURD:

~ **FIRST,** scrape the outer yellow zest from each lemon. (*Note:* Be careful not to scrape any of the bitter white pith underneath.) Then cut each lemon in half and squeeze out the juice. Combine the lemon zest, lemon juice, butter, eggs and sugar in a stainless mixing bowl or in the top of a double boiler. Fill the bottom of a double boiler or medium pot with just enough water so the bowl will barely touch the water, and bring the water to a slow boil over medium heat. Place the double boiler or stainless mixing bowl over the boiling water. Stir the lemon curd with a wooden spoon or heat-resistant rubber spatula until the butter is melted.

~ **SECOND,** turn the heat to high. Stir the lemon curd constantly until the curd has thickened and is bubbling, 8 to 10 minutes.

~ **THIRD,** strain the lemon curd through a fine sieve into a glass or ceramic dish. Cover the top with a piece of plastic wrap laid directly on the curd (to prevent a skin from forming) and cool to room temperature. When the curd has cooled to room temperature, refrigerate for 2 hours or until it is completely set. The lemon curd may be made in advance and kept, tightly sealed, for up to 2 weeks in the refrigerator.

JELLY ROLL

⅔ cup cake flour
3 tablespoons cornstarch
¼ teaspoon salt
4 large egg yolks, room temperature
Zest of 1 lemon
¾ cup superfine sugar
1 teaspoon pure vanilla extract
4 large egg whites, room temperature
Pinch cream of tartar
Powdered sugar for dusting
½ cup seedless raspberry jam

MAKE THE SPONGE CAKE:

~ **FIRST,** preheat the oven to 425°F. Line a standard jelly roll pan or 10x15-inch rimmed baking sheet with parchment paper that has been greased on both sides.

~ **SECOND,** sift the cake flour, cornstarch and salt into a small bowl.

~ **THIRD,** combine the 4 egg yolks with the zest, ½ cup of the superfine sugar and the vanilla in a separate larger bowl. Beat vigorously by hand or with a mixer on medium-high speed until the mixture is thick and pale yellow, about 3 minutes.

~ **FOURTH,** place the egg whites in a stainless bowl and add a pinch of cream of tartar. Whip the mixture with clean dry beaters until it holds soft peaks; slowly add in the remaining ¼ cup superfine sugar and continue beating until the mixture holds stiff peaks.

~ **FIFTH,** stir ⅓ of the beaten egg white mixture into the yolk mixture, then fold the sifted flour mixture into the yolk mixture until it is fully incorporated. Finally, fold in the remaining beaten egg whites (do this gently so the batter does not deflate). Spread the batter evenly in the prepared pan.

~ **SIXTH,** bake in the preheated oven until the cake is golden and springs back when gently pressed in the center, 8 to 10 minutes. Remove the sponge cake from the oven and dust it with powdered sugar. Lay out a piece of parchment paper or a clean tea towel that has also been dusted with powdered sugar and invert the cake onto it. Carefully peel away the parchment paper that the cake was baked on and loosely roll the cake up lengthwise (along the long edge). Allow the cake to rest at room temperature for 30 minutes.

ASSEMBLE THE JELLY ROLL:

~ Carefully unroll the cake onto a clean dry surface. Heat the raspberry jam with a few drops of water (so that it will spread easily across the entire surface of the sponge cake). Spread the jam on the cake and allow it to soak in and cool completely. Spread the lemon curd over all but the last 2 inches of the cake along the long edge of the roll. Sprinkle the jelly roll with more powdered sugar, then roll tightly in plastic wrap and refrigerate for at least 1 day and up to 3 days.

RASPBERRY SAUCE

2 cups fresh or frozen raspberries
½ cup granulated sugar
2 tablespoons framboise or raspberry syrup

MAKE THE RASPBERRY SAUCE:

~ In a saucepan, combine the raspberries with the sugar and framboise or raspberry syrup. Bring the mixture to a boil over medium heat. Stirring constantly, boil the mixture for 3 minutes, until the berries are beginning to break apart and the sugar is dissolved. Reduce the heat to low and simmer for 10 to 15 minutes. Remove from heat and pass through a fine sieve, pressing all the pulp firmly through the sieve with a rubber spatula. Discard the seeds that remain in the sieve and let the sauce cool.

GLAZE

1 tablespoon fresh lemon juice
½ cup powdered sugar

MAKE THE LEMON GLAZE:

~ Take the jelly roll out of the refrigerator and unwrap. In a small bowl, blend the lemon juice into the powdered sugar. Use a pastry brush to glaze the top and sides of the roll with the syrup. Keep the jelly roll uncovered and at room temperature until ready to serve.

SERVE THE JELLY ROLL:

~ Trim away each end of the roll with a thin serrated knife, then cut the jelly roll into 6 even slices. Arrange the slices on plates and pour a little raspberry sauce over each; dust with powdered sugar and serve immediately.

Agape: A Love Feast

❧ ❧ ❧

SALAD OF SPINACH, CUCUMBER AND RADISH
with LEMON YOGURT DRESSING

SUCCULENT BUTTERFLIED LEG OF SPRING LAMB
with ROASTED RED-SKINNED POTATOES

GRILLED ZUCCHINI WITH EGGPLANT, FETA AND TOMATOES

RUSTIC VILLAGE BREAD

ORANGE-SOAKED HONEY-WALNUT CAKE

Agape is the Greek word for God's kind of love. This is the love that binds us in holy communion and bids us to gather, hand in hand, for yet another kind of feast around the Sunday dinner table.

Perhaps no other Christian holiday better exemplifies God's never-ending love than Easter. It's the original Sunday dinner because it celebrates the Sunday morning when the risen Christ appeared to His friends. Easter is also the quintessential springtime celebration, universal in its appeal. For just as the spring brings us newness of life, fresh possibilities, and hope for the future, this yearly feast gives testament to the earth's regeneration, mirrored in the Easter story itself, and the promise of spiritual rebirth.

For many Americans, especially those whose ancestry springs from the ancient civilizations of Lebanon, Syria, Greece, Turkey, Cyprus, and Macedonia, Easter is the most significant holiday of the year, more family-centered and wonder-filled even than Christmas, a time of rich and meaningful tradition. If you were raised in a Greek Orthodox home, for instance, you would prepare for Easter by following a traditional Lenten 40-day-long fast.

The solemn Holy Week leading up to Easter Sunday would be filled with a myriad of activities, for yours is a faith rich in symbolic liturgy and customs. On Holy Thursday, for example, you would eat an austere meal of lentil soup seasoned with herbs and vinegar as a way of partaking in Christ's sorrow. The next day, Good Friday, would be devoted to prayer. On Saturday you would attend a solemn midnight service, at the end of which a priest would bless a supply of Easter eggs dyed red to symbolize the blood of Christ.

Then on Easter Sunday all your fasting would be over and the celebration would begin. After a joyous church service, you would gather with friends and family for the feast: roast lamb, dripping and juicy, seasoned with heady Mediterranean herbs and paired with potatoes or baked orzo, and deliciously supplemented with briny olives, stuffed grape leaves, fresh and roasted vegetables, a bounty of cheeses, and rustic breads. Your mouth would water as you prepared to enjoy the meal with those you love. But first, everyone around the festive table would take a brightly colored egg and crack it against that held by one's neighbor, celebrating the sound echoing that of the stone rolled away from the tomb. As you broke the eggs, you also would exchange a traditional blessing, emphasizing the *agape* joy of the Easter feast:

"*Christos Anesti*"—Christ is risen!

"*Alithos Anesti*"—Indeed, He is risen!

SALAD OF SPINACH, CUCUMBER AND RADISH
WITH LEMON YOGURT DRESSING
8 SERVINGS

Crisp salads made with fresh vegetables are served in nearly every country. Generally they are simply dressed, like this one—with olive oil, lemon and herbs. Serve this salad with thick slices of rustic village bread accompanied by tiny bowls of extra-virgin olive oil for dipping the bread into and a variety of cured olives for all to enjoy.

SALAD

2 8-ounce bags baby spinach leaves
1 cucumber, peeled and thinly sliced
8 radishes, trimmed and thinly sliced
1 bunch green onions, thinly sliced

MAKE THE SALAD:

Thoroughly rinse the spinach leaves in cold water to refresh them and discard any tough stems or wilted leaves. Shake the spinach dry in a colander covered with a clean tea towel or in a salad spinner. Toss the spinach with the sliced cucumber, radishes and green onions. Refrigerate in a salad bowl covered with a damp paper towel or plastic wrap until you are ready to serve.

DRESSING

2 cloves garlic
½ teaspoon coarse salt
1 teaspoon granulated sugar
2 tablespoons fresh lemon juice
1 cup plain yogurt
¼ cup extra-virgin olive oil
¼ teaspoon coarse-ground black pepper
1 tablespoon fresh chopped dill
1 tablespoon fresh chopped parsley

PREPARE THE DRESSING:

Combine the garlic cloves in a small mixing bowl with the salt and sugar; use a fork to mash them into a paste. Whisk in the lemon juice and the yogurt; then slowly whisk in the extra-virgin olive oil until blended. Season to taste with the pepper.

SERVE THE SALAD:

Just before serving, add the fresh chopped dill and parsley to the refrigerated salad and lightly toss together with the dressing.

SUCCULENT BUTTERFLIED LEG OF SPRING LAMB WITH ROASTED RED-SKINNED POTATOES

8 SERVINGS

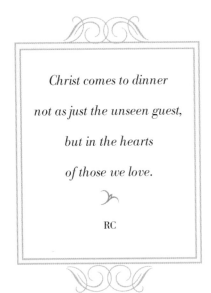

Christ comes to dinner

not as just the unseen guest,

but in the hearts

of those we love.

RC

There was a time when many Americans ignored lamb. We were, after all, a wide-open country known for raising and eating beef. That has changed somewhat in the past decade or two, and once you've tasted this seasoned lamb you'll understand why. Lamb is a traditional Easter dish throughout much of the world. Certainly it is perfect in spring, but lamb is wonderful any time of the year.

NOTE: *Have your butcher bone out the leg of lamb, keeping the shank attached and trimming away any excess fat, and then butterfly it for easy preparation.*

LAMB

1 6-pound leg of lamb, butterflied
6 whole cloves garlic
Pinch of coarse salt
2 tablespoons fresh chopped rosemary
½ cup packed fresh basil leaves
¼ cup packed fresh mint leaves
2 tablespoons cracked peppercorns
2 lemons, halved, seeds removed
¼ cup olive oil
Coarse salt to season

MAKE THE LAMB:

FIRST, place the lamb cut side up on a clean work surface. Sprinkle the garlic with a pinch of salt in a small mixing bowl and use a fork to mash the garlic to a paste; spread the mashed garlic evenly over the inside of the lamb and sprinkle with half of the chopped rosemary. Lay the basil and mint leaves over the rosemary, then roll the lamb leg back into its natural shape.

SECOND, tie the lamb securely with kitchen twine, knotting it every 2 inches; then tie lengthwise. Rub the remaining rosemary and the cracked peppercorns into the exterior surface of the lamb. Squeeze the halved lemons over the lamb and drizzle with the olive oil. Cover with plastic wrap and marinate overnight or for up to 24 hours in the refrigerator.

THIRD, adjust the lower rack near the bottom of the oven, leaving enough room on the top rack for the vegetable casserole. Remove the lamb from the refrigerator. Sprinkle it with coarse salt and allow it to rest for 45 minutes at room temperature. *(Note:* Now is a good time to grill the vegetables for the casserole.)

∽ **FOURTH,** place the lamb in a shallow roasting pan and transfer to a 450°F oven. Roast the lamb for 15 minutes, then reduce the heat to 325°F and cook for 1 hour longer—the roast should be rare at this point.

POTATOES

2 pounds small red-skinned potatoes
2 tablespoons olive oil
2 cloves garlic, thinly sliced
1 tablespoon fresh chopped rosemary
Salt and pepper to taste

PREPARE THE POTATOES:

∽ **FIRST,** cut the potatoes in half and toss them with the olive oil, garlic and rosemary in a mixing bowl. After the lamb has roasted for 1 hour, scatter the potatoes around the roasting pan, sprinkle with salt and pepper and continue baking with the roast until a meat thermometer inserted into the thickest part

of the lamb reaches 140°F, about 20 to 25 minutes. Remove the lamb from the pan and place it on a clean cutting board; allow it to rest for 15 minutes before slicing.

∽ **SECOND,** increase the oven temperature to 400°F and spread the potatoes evenly in the bottom of the roasting pan. Return the potatoes to the oven and let them continue baking until they are fully cooked and nicely browned, 15 to 20 minutes.

SERVE THE LAMB AND POTATOES:

∽ Carefully cut away the kitchen twine. Hold the lamb at the shank end and evenly slice the meat with a sharp carving knife. Transfer the shank to a warm platter and fan the slices out from the shank across the middle of the platter. Scatter the potatoes around the meat; if desired, garnish the platter with fresh herbs. Pour the juices from the pan and the cutting board over the meat and potatoes.

GRILLED ZUCCHINI WITH EGGPLANT, FETA AND TOMATOES

8 SERVINGS

Mediterranean flavors are celebrated in this tantalizing, easy-to-prepare dish. The sweetness of the grilled onion, eggplant and zucchini, coupled with the garlicky tomato and mint, underscores the sharpness of the feta cheese. This is a wonderfully sensuous dish!

VEGETABLES

4 medium zucchini
2 medium onions
2 medium eggplants
¼ cup olive oil
Coarse salt

PREPARE THE VEGETABLES:

～ **FIRST,** trim the ends from the zucchini and cut lengthwise into ⅓-inch-thick slices. Peel the onions and cut into ⅓-inch-thick slices. Hold at room temperature while you prepare the eggplant.

～ **SECOND,** use a sharp knife to cut the stem and ends off each eggplant; then peel and cut lengthwise into ½-inch-thick slices. Sprinkle the eggplant slices with coarse salt and place in a colander for 30 minutes to drain the bitter juices; then rinse and pat dry with paper towels. Brush the slices of zucchini, onion and eggplant with olive oil and season with a little salt.

～ **THIRD,** grill the vegetables directly over high heat, turning them once: 6 to 8 minutes for the eggplant, 4 to 5 minutes for the onion, and 2 to 3 minutes for the zucchini; or lay the vegetables on lightly oiled baking sheets, turn your oven heat to high and broil for the prescribed times listed above.

TOPPING

2 tablespoons extra-virgin olive oil
2 cloves garlic, minced
2 tablespoons diced onion
4 cups peeled, seeded and diced tomatoes
2 teaspoons fresh chopped mint leaves
Salt and pepper to taste
2 cups crumbled feta cheese

PREPARE THE TOPPING:

～ Heat the extra-virgin olive oil in a skillet over medium heat. Sauté the garlic and onion until translucent, 2 to 3 minutes. Toss in the tomatoes and simmer until the liquid is reduced, 4 to 5 minutes. Add in the chopped mint leaves, season to taste with salt and pepper and remove from heat; set aside.

ASSEMBLE THE CASSEROLE:

～ Arrange the grilled slices of eggplant on the bottom of a lightly oiled 13x9-inch casserole, followed by the onion and then the zucchini. Cover with 1⅓ cups of the crumbled feta cheese and lace the dish with the tomato topping. Place the casserole in the oven at the same time that you add the potatoes to the lamb roast; bake at 325°F for 20 to 25 minutes. Increase the temperature to 400°F, sprinkle the top of the casserole with the remaining ⅔ cup feta and continue baking for an additional 10 to 15 minutes.

RUSTIC VILLAGE BREAD
1 ROUND LOAF

Making great bread is a simple act of love; it takes time, patience and nurturing. This rustic loaf is even more reminiscent of village life when it is baked on a pizza stone. As with all breads that are made with whole-grain flour, additional rising time is required—but the reward is well worth the wait!

BREAD

1 package (2¼ teaspoons) active dry yeast
¼ cup warm water, about 110°F
1 tablespoon honey
1 tablespoon olive oil
¼ cup plain yogurt
1 cup water, room temperature
1 cup whole wheat flour
1½ cups bread flour
½ cup wheat germ
½ tablespoon coarse salt

MAKE THE BREAD:

FIRST, sprinkle the yeast over the ¼ cup of water and let stand for 1 minute. Then stir with a wooden spoon until the yeast is dissolved.

SECOND, whisk the honey, olive oil and yogurt together in a mixing bowl until blended; whisk in the additional 1 cup of water and the dissolved yeast. Use a wooden spoon to stir in the whole wheat flour and ½ cup of the bread flour; continue stirring until the mixture is smooth and elastic, about 200 strokes. The dough will now have the consistency of a thick batter. Scrape down the sides of the bowl with a rubber spatula. Cover with a clean tea towel and set in a draft-free place until the dough is bubbly and has doubled in volume, about 1½ hours.

THIRD, whisk the remaining bread flour together with the wheat germ and salt in a separate bowl. Use an electric mixer fitted with a dough hook to slowly incorporate the flour mixture into the bubbly dough, adding in extra flour as needed, a tablespoon at a time, until the dough pulls away from the bowl and forms a ball. Knead on low speed for about 8 minutes—the dough should be densely textured and stiff enough to hold its shape.

FOURTH, lightly coat the dough with a little olive oil, place it into a clean bowl and cover with a clean tea towel. Allow it to rise in a warm, draft-free place until it has doubled in volume, about 1 hour.

FIFTH, place the dough on a lightly floured work surface and knead for about 1 minute. Shape into a smooth ball. Flatten the ball into a 7-inch round loaf and score a ¼-inch-deep cross cut on the top, using a sharp knife. Brush with a little water. Cover the loaf with a clean tea towel and let it rise for 45 minutes.

SIXTH, preheat the oven to 400°F. Brush lightly with olive oil and sprinkle with a pinch of coarse salt. Transfer the loaf to a pizza stone or a baking sheet dusted with cornmeal and bake for 30 to 35 minutes. When it is done, the bread will have a dark brown crust and sound hollow when tapped on the bottom.

Easy time saving

AND DO-AHEAD TIPS:

SATURDAY

Bake the honey-walnut cake and
soak with the orange syrup.
Marinate the lamb. Bake the
bread. Prepare the salad dressing
and refrigerate. Prepare and grill
the vegetables for the casserole;
refrigerate in well-sealed containers.

SUNDAY MORNING

Prepare the salad vegetables and
refrigerate. Assemble the vegetable
casserole.

ORANGE-SOAKED HONEY-WALNUT CAKE
12 SERVINGS

*This moist, delicious, traditional cake is made without butter or milk, making
it a perfect choice for Lent. It is an example of the various recipes found throughout the ancient world that have been added to the ever-changing American table,
where they are savored and served as a "taste of home" on holidays and at family
gatherings. Sunday dinner is one such time.*

CAKE

2½ cups all-purpose flour
½ cup fresh white bread crumbs
2 teaspoons baking powder
1 teaspoon baking soda
½ teaspoon cinnamon
¼ teaspoon salt
4 large egg whites, room temperature
Pinch cream of tartar
1 cup vegetable oil
1½ cups granulated sugar
¼ cup honey
4 large egg yolks, room temperature
1 cup freshly squeezed orange juice
1 cup finely ground walnuts

~ Adjust the rack to the center of the oven and preheat to 350°F.

MAKE THE CAKE:

~ **FIRST,** combine the flour and fresh bread crumbs with the baking powder, baking soda, cinnamon and salt in a mixing bowl; whisk together thoroughly.

~ **SECOND,** combine the egg whites with the cream of tartar in a separate bowl.
Beat the whites using an electric mixer and clean dry beaters until they hold
their peaks and are stiff but not dry.

~ **THIRD,** combine the vegetable oil, sugar and honey in the bowl of an electric mixer fitted with a balloon whisk; blend on medium speed until the sugar and honey are dissolved; then blend in the egg yolks. Fit the electric mixer with a paddle attachment and slowly add the dry ingredients in 3 batches alternately with the orange juice, mixing just enough after each addition for all the ingredients to fully blend together. Then use a rubber spatula to gently fold in the beaten egg whites, followed by the ground walnuts.

~ **FOURTH,** spoon the batter into a lightly greased and floured 10-inch bundt pan. Bake until a wooden pick comes out clean when inserted into the center of the cake, about 50 minutes. When the cake is done, remove it from the oven and place on a cooling rack for 10 minutes; then turn the cake out onto a rack and let it cool for 20 to 30 minutes while you prepare the orange syrup.

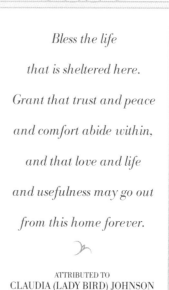

Bless the life

that is sheltered here.

Grant that trust and peace

and comfort abide within,

and that love and life

and usefulness may go out

from this home forever.

ATTRIBUTED TO
CLAUDIA (LADY BIRD) JOHNSON

ORANGE SYRUP

¾ cup granulated sugar
½ cup water
1 cinnamon stick
2 tablespoons honey
¾ cup freshly squeezed orange juice
Zest of 1 orange

PREPARE THE ORANGE SYRUP:

~ Mix the sugar into the water and bring to a boil, stirring constantly to dissolve all the sugar. Add in the cinnamon stick, honey, orange juice and orange zest. Turn the heat down to medium and simmer until the liquid reduces to 1 cup of syrup, about 20 minutes. Discard the cinnamon stick.

GLAZE THE CAKE:

~ Brush the warm syrup over the outside of the warm cake, allowing it to soak in; continue to brush on the glaze until all of the syrup is absorbed.

God's Country: Sunday in the Northwest

> GOLDEN MUSHROOM AND ONION SOUP
> BAKED PACIFIC HALIBUT WITH LEMON-CAPER BUTTER
> BUTTERED NEW POTATOES
> DILL STEAMED ASPARAGUS SPEARS
> STRAWBERRY POPPYSEED SHORTCAKES

My grandmother always called the Pacific Northwest "God's country," and I can understand why. From the vast wilderness of Alaska down through the settled greenery of Oregon, this region offers untold bounty in a world of wonder. There are snow capped mountain peaks, cascading whitewater streams, giant red cedars piercing forest canopies, and the crashing white-edged ocean. The contrast to the dusty red flatlands of her native west Texas must have taken my grandmother's breath away!

It takes my breath away, too, every time I visit. I've traveled extensively through this beautiful region, where I used to live. I've hiked in the Cascades, climbed great driftwood piles along the rugged coast, and watched the sunset off Oregon's spectacular Coos Bay. I've followed the headwaters of the Spokane River from Idaho into Washington, crossed the mighty Columbia, and traversed the pastoral Willamette Valley. Each memory is a tie of affection, a call to return to a place that is like no other.

When it comes to food, each state in this bountiful region boasts something special. Washington is known for great apples and sweet onions; Alaska for deepwater crab and halibut; Oregon for fine fruit and cheese, especially Anjou pears and the excellent Tillamook cheddar. Berries abound everywhere in the cool climate; untamed rivers teem with salmon, steelhead, and rainbow trout; wild asparagus sprout along a river's edge; and earthy mushrooms shoot up through fern-covered forest floors.

At one time this was all Russian territory, stretching south from the Bering Sea to California's Monterey coast. Fur trapping was the main endeavor here, though missionaries also aspired to convert the natives (the first Russian Orthodox mission was established on Kodiak Island in 1794). Over the course of the nineteenth century, however, Russia's grip on the region loosened. Treaties extended U.S. and Canadian territory west to the Pacific, opening Washington and Oregon to flocks of American settlers who traveled west along the Oregon Trail. Finally, in 1867, the United States purchased the remaining Russian territory in the New World—what is now Alaska.

The Russian influence continued in the Pacific Northwest, however. Many of today's Alaskans are of Russian-Native descent. Portland, Oregon, is also home to one of the largest Russian populations in our country. Some sixty thousand Russians fleeing Communist persecution—Baptists, Pentecostals, and Orthodox—have found a welcome homeland here.

You'll find a welcome, too, in the beautiful Pacific Northwest. You'll also find a bounty made for a Sunday celebration. Here is a menu that reflects both the natural abundance of the region and its unique history with unpretentious, delicately seasoned foods that boast rich yet natural unadorned flavors.

God's country indeed!

Easy time-saving

AND DO-AHEAD TIPS:

FRIDAY EVENING

Prepare the strawberry sauce. Prepare the lemon-caper butter for the halibut.

SATURDAY

Prepare the soup and refrigerate. Cut the halibut into serving portions. Blanch the asparagus and prepare the leeks.

SUNDAY MORNING

Bake the poppy seed shortcakes.

GOLDEN MUSHROOM AND ONION SOUP
6 SERVINGS

ild mushrooms are abundant throughout the Northwest, especially in the spring and early fall, and their aroma and earthy flavors are intense and heady. The variety of wild forest mushrooms being foraged and brought to market has dramatically increased over the past several years. For this lovely soup, I like to combine fresh button, crimini, shiitake, wood ear and chanterelle mushrooms. (Do not use portabellos—their dark juices will make for an unappealing soup.) I prefer to use sweet Walla Walla or Vidalia for the onions.

MUSHROOM SOUP

1 pound assorted fresh mushrooms
1 rib celery with leaves, chopped
1 leek, white part only, chopped
1 sprig fresh thyme
6 cups chicken broth
2 medium sweet onions
8 tablespoons (1 stick) butter
4 cloves garlic, thinly sliced
Pinch of salt
½ cup fruity white wine or white grape juice
2 chicken bouillon cubes
1½ tablespoons cornstarch
1½ cups half-and-half
Salt to taste
1 tablespoon fresh snipped chives

MAKE THE SOUP:

~ **FIRST,** clean the mushrooms with a damp paper towel and remove the stems. Combine the mushroom stems, celery, leek and thyme with the chicken broth in a 4-quart saucepan and bring to a boil over medium heat. Let the broth boil for 2 to 3 minutes, then remove from heat, cover with a tight-fitting lid and steep for about 25 minutes to infuse the broth with the mushroom flavor. Strain the seasoned broth through a fine sieve into a bowl and discard the stems and vegetables.

~ **SECOND,** cut the onions in half crosswise and then slice the halves into slivers. Slice the mushrooms into varying thicknesses. Heat 4 tablespoons of the butter in a heavy-bottomed skillet over high heat until it just begins to brown. Sprinkle the slivered onions in the butter, reduce the heat to medium-high, add in the garlic and caramelize until the onions are amber in color, 6 to 8 minutes.

~ **THIRD,** make a well in the middle of the caramelized onions by pushing them to the edges of the skillet. Melt the remaining 4 tablespoons of butter in the well, add in the sliced mushrooms and toss lightly with the butter. Sauté for 3 to 4 minutes without stirring, then toss the mushrooms together with the onions and season with a pinch of salt.

~ **FOURTH,** add the wine or grape juice to the skillet and scrape the bottom to loosen any browned bits, then pour in the reserved mushroom broth. Simmer until the mushrooms are tender but still meaty and firm-fleshed, about 5 minutes. Strain the soup through a fine sieve into a bowl; reserve the mushrooms and onions. Return the strained liquid to the skillet and place over medium heat. When it begins to simmer, add the chicken bouillon cubes.

~ **FIFTH,** thoroughly whisk the cornstarch with the half-and-half in a small bowl, then pour into the broth. Simmer for 4 to 5 minutes, stirring occasionally. Add in the reserved mushrooms and onions and simmer for a few minutes more. Season to taste with salt, fold in the snipped chives and serve immediately.

Hospitality is a wonderful gift. We don't need a grand palace or a dream home—few of us have those. To make others feel truly welcome, we only need an open heart and the greater beauty of love expressed.

RC

BAKED PACIFIC HALIBUT
WITH LEMON-CAPER BUTTER
6 SERVINGS

Pacific halibut run from the Bering Straits to the Santa Barbara Islands. These flat-fish weigh an average of 70 pounds in California, but they can grow up to 800 pounds and measure 9 feet long in the cold, clear waters of Alaska. Halibut's flavor, firm texture and snow-white color make it one of the most delectable fish anywhere.

LEMON-CAPER BUTTER

½ cup (1 stick) unsalted butter
1 tablespoon minced capers
2 tablespoons minced green onion
2 tablespoons fresh lemon juice

~ Adjust the rack to the center of the oven and preheat to 400°F.

PREPARE THE LEMON-CAPER BUTTER:
~ Combine the butter, capers, green onion and lemon juice in the bowl of a food processor fitted with a steel blade; pulse to blend.

HALIBUT

6 6-ounce halibut fillets
1 teaspoon coarse salt
3 tablespoons Dijon mustard
1½ cups fresh white bread crumbs
1 tablespoon chopped parsley
2 lemons, halved

PREPARE THE HALIBUT:
~ FIRST, place each fillet on a clean dry surface and sprinkle with a little coarse salt. Smear the Dijon mustard over the top and sides of each fillet and coat with the bread crumbs and parsley.

~ SECOND, coat the bottom of a baking sheet with half of the lemon-caper butter. Place the fillets, skin side down, on the buttered pan and dot the top of each fillet with the remaining lemon-caper butter. Bake until the fish is crusty and golden on the outside and moist and flaky in the middle, 15 to 20 minutes.

~ THIRD, carefully transfer the baked fish to a warm platter. Squeeze the lemons into the butter and drippings that remain on the baking sheet and transfer to a small stainless bowl; whisk together thoroughly. Pour over the fish and serve immediately.

BUTTERED
NEW POTATOES
6 SERVINGS

We often take potatoes for granted by dressing them up and effectively masking their subtle and wonderful flavor. A simple potato dish is a wonderful treat all by itself, and this one pairs well with the delicate halibut. White spring potatoes or baby Yukon Golds are best when gently boiled and smothered in butter—simple is sometimes best.

POTATOES

18 to 24 small new potatoes
Salt and white pepper to taste
½ cup (1 stick) butter

MAKE THE POTATOES:

~ **FIRST,** one by one, peel the potatoes and submerge in a bowl of cold water; then drain and transfer the potatoes to a large pot. Cover with fresh water and season with a little salt.

~ **SECOND,** bring the water to a boil over high heat, reduce the heat to medium and simmer until you can just pierce the potatoes with the tip of a knife, 12 to 15 minutes. Drain and season the potatoes with salt and white pepper, then add the butter into the pot and cover to let the butter melt. Toss the potatoes with the melted butter just before serving.

DILL STEAMED
ASPARAGUS SPEARS
6 SERVINGS

Though we have grown accustomed to finding good-quality asparagus year-round, the very best spears can be found from late March through early June. Tender asparagus seem like they were made to accompany delicate fish—why else would we serve them together so often?

ASPARAGUS

1½ pounds fresh asparagus spears
2 tablespoons butter
1 leek, white part only, thinly sliced
1 tablespoon fresh chopped dill
Pinch of salt

PREPARE THE ASPARAGUS:

~ **FIRST,** trim the woody ends from the asparagus and then, for a more decorative look, carefully peel about 1 inch of the cut ends with a vegetable peeler. Blanch the asparagus by dropping them into a shallow pan filled with boiling salted water; cook for 3 to 4 minutes, then immediately plunge into a bowl of ice water to stop the cooking process. Remove the spears after 2 minutes; drain and dry thoroughly. (*Note:* You can blanch the asparagus spears up to 2 days ahead and refrigerate in a well-sealed container.)

~ **SECOND,** spread the butter over the bottom of a skillet and sprinkle the sliced leek evenly onto the butter. Lay the blanched asparagus over the leek and season with the chopped dill and a pinch of salt. Cover with a tight-fitting lid and steam just enough to heat the asparagus through, 2 to 3 minutes.

*B*ecause ours was a small family—just my brother, mom, dad, grandma, and me—we tended to supplement our Sunday get-togethers by inviting good friends over for dinner. Many lifelong friendships began that way during my high school years in Oregon's Willamette Valley.

On Saturdays, two of my girlfriends and I would make pies together. Then in the evening, after the baking was done, we would have game night, inviting neighbors and friends from the farm community to come over and play games like Rook or Pictionary or whatever we felt like. This was a regular weekend routine—we even have home movies of all of us playing games together.

On Sundays we would come home from church and finish preparing our Sunday meal. My grandmother always made the mashed potatoes, I made the salad, and my mom and dad worked on the main dish—fresh salmon or halibut, roast beef, or pork loin.

Then we would sit around the table for hours, eating and talking as only a family can do. Dessert would be presented after we had cleared the table and served everyone coffee and tea. Then we would sit some more, eat some more, and just laugh—sometimes we laughed until we cried. I will never forget the joy and laughter in that household.

ELLEN DONNELLY

STRAWBERRY POPPY SEED SHORTCAKES
6 SERVINGS

I often made shortcakes at Blair House for special guests that I knew would enjoy a truly all-American treat. These are very special: They are tender and buttery—sublime when served with the fresh strawberry sauce and mounds of sweetened whipped cream!

POPPY SEED SHORTCAKES

1½ tablespoons pure vanilla extract	¼ teaspoon salt
1 tablespoon poppy seeds	10 tablespoons (1¼ sticks) unsalted butter
1 cup all-purpose flour	6 tablespoons superfine sugar
1 cup cake flour	1 teaspoon orange zest
2 teaspoons baking powder	1 large egg, room temperature
¾ teaspoon baking soda	⅓ cup heavy cream

MAKE THE SHORTCAKES:

⌁ **FIRST,** warm the vanilla extract over low heat in a small stainless pan or in a glass dish in the microwave. Add the poppy seeds to the warm vanilla and soak them for 2 hours; this will soften the poppy seeds and allow them to absorb the vanilla flavor.

⌁ **SECOND,** preheat the oven to 425°F. Sift the all-purpose flour, cake flour, baking powder, baking soda and salt into a mixing bowl.

⌁ **THIRD,** slice the butter into 1-inch pieces and scatter the pieces over the top of the flour mixture; sprinkle the superfine sugar, vanilla-soaked poppy seeds and orange zest over the top. Cut all the ingredients together with a pastry cutter until the mixture resembles coarse crumbly meal.

⌁ **FOURTH,** combine the egg and cream in a separate bowl and whisk until frothy, about 1 minute; then add to the crumbly mixture and stir until the dough holds together and attains the consistency of moist biscuit dough. Knead gently until smooth, about 1 minute.

⌁ **FIFTH,** dust the dough with a little flour and form into a log that is about 6 inches long and 2½ inches in diameter. Place the log on a clean, lightly floured work surface and cut into 6 even slices. Gently reshape the slices into flat rounds and pat smooth. Brush the tops with a little heavy cream and sprinkle with a little granulated sugar.

⌁ **SIXTH,** transfer the shortcakes to an ungreased baking sheet and bake until fully risen, 12 to 15 minutes. They should spread and rise until doubled in size with golden cracked tops. Cool completely on the baking sheet before serving.

STRAWBERRY SAUCE

1 dry pint strawberries
¼ cup granulated sugar

MAKE THE STRAWBERRY SAUCE:

~ FIRST, wash and then hull the strawberries; slice into halves. Bring the berries and sugar to a simmer in a saucepan over medium heat and stir continuously until the sugar is dissolved, about 3 minutes.

~ SECOND, simmer undisturbed until the berries begin to fall apart, about 20 minutes; then remove from heat and strain through a sieve into a small stainless bowl. Use a wooden spoon to press on the berries, scraping hard to extract all of the pulp; leave the solids in the sieve. Scrape the pulp from the outside of the sieve and add to the sauce, then cover and refrigerate.

SHORTCAKE FILLING

1 dry pint strawberries
Granulated sugar to taste
1½ cups heavy whipping cream
6 tablespoons granulated sugar
Powdered sugar for dusting

PREPARE THE FILLING:

~ FIRST, wash and hull the strawberries, then slice into a stainless mixing bowl and sweeten to taste with sugar. Allow the berries to rest at room temperature for 20 minutes, so that the berries absorb the sweetness of the sugar and the juices combine to form a syrup.

~ SECOND, pour the cream into the chilled bowl of a mixer and add the sugar; mix with a chilled balloon whisk at medium speed until the sugar has dissolved, 3 to 4 minutes. Then whip on high until stiff peaks hold, about 2 more minutes. Cover and refrigerate until ready to use.

ASSEMBLE THE SHORTCAKES:

~ Use a thin serrated knife to split each shortcake horizontally in half. Place the bottom layers on dessert plates and spoon a little strawberry sauce over each, letting it run onto the plate. Follow with a dollop of whipped cream. Divide the strawberries between the shortcakes and drizzle a little of their natural syrup over each. Mound with more whipped cream, then replace the biscuit tops. Drizzle the remaining strawberry sauce around the assembled shortcakes and dust the tops with powdered sugar. If desired, garnish with rosettes of the whipped cream and a whole fresh strawberry. Serve immediately.

Along the King's Highway

CHILLED SHRIMP GAZPACHO
GAME HENS AND RICE WITH OLIVES AND ALMONDS
SALAD OF JICAMA, RED ONION, ORANGE AND AVOCADO
BAKED CARAMEL CUSTARD

It's called the King's Highway, but it's really the mission road.

California's El Camino Real connects past and present just as it connects one centuries-old Franciscan mission to another. Twenty-one of these self-sufficient outposts once marked this beautiful byway, each a long day's journey from the other across rugged California ranch country, each an oasis for the weary traveler. Most still stand today. The King's Highway winds its way between them from San Diego to Sonoma County, its 600 miles marked by bells cast in concrete and cast iron. They are mute reminders of the mission bells that once echoed across the sunny landscape.

For vast areas of the American Southwest, Sunday-morning church bells used to mean Spanish mission bells. The open arid lands of this region, from west Texas and New Mexico across the Arizona desert to the stunning California coast, were first explored by the Spanish and were later part of Mexico. In the late 1700s, in fact, while our English-speaking founding fathers fought to establish their own country, Spanish-speaking churchmen in the Southwest were laboring to establish a different kind of society. In the name of their faith, these sturdy priests ministered to the natives, taught them to read and write and farm, planted vineyards and olive trees, and endeavored to protect their charges from persecution and conquest.

The Spanish culture still thrives in these areas, a heritage resplendent with tradition. *Siesta,* or a daily time of rest, figures strongly in this way of life. And Sunday is a siesta in itself, a day of rest honored with a leisurely midday meal, which spices local traditional fare with the lively flavors of Mexico and the Mediterranean. The ingredients and flavors vary with the locale. Along El Camino Real, however, California ranch cookery prevails: red ripe tomatoes, peppers and briny olives, sweet oranges and almonds, buttery avocados, game birds and succulent tender shrimp. All are simply prepared and richly enjoyed.

We all seek refuge from an encroaching world, a place of rest along the highway of life. Like the tranquil missions along El Camino Real, Sunday offers us a respite, an opportunity to lay down our burdens and truly relax. So why not take your siesta somewhere along the King's Highway? Spend time beneath the bay laurel trees, caressed by the gentle breeze. Enjoy the dignity and grace of this once-agrarian world. Feel the fine hand-tooled leather. See the skills of the equestrian. Sit back on the veranda under a red-tiled roof. And be sure to stop in the sleepy midday quiet to listen once more for the sound of mission bells.

Easy time-saving

AND DO-AHEAD TIPS:

FRIDAY EVENING

Clean and marinate the shrimp
and refrigerate.

SATURDAY

Bake the custard, wrap in plastic
and refrigerate. Prepare the gazpacho,
cover and chill. Prepare the salad
dressing. Season the game hens and
tie their legs together; cover and
refrigerate. Cook the shrimp; cover
and refrigerate.

CHILLED SHRIMP GAZPACHO
6 SERVINGS

Gazpacho is a cold soup that is often thought to have originated in Spain, but the traditional ingredients—tomatoes and peppers—found their way to Spain from Mexico during the age of exploration. There are countless ways to prepare this classic summer soup. I like to caramelize the garlic and onions to bring out their sweetness. You'll find some older recipes that call for bread, which is used to bind the juices and give the soup body, but I prefer using tomato paste as the binder instead.

SHRIMP

18 medium shrimp (about 1 pound)
¼ cup extra-virgin olive oil
4 cloves garlic, minced
1 teaspoon crushed red pepper
2 tablespoons fresh chopped basil
Pinch of salt
1 lemon, halved

MARINATE THE SHRIMP:

~ **FIRST,** carefully cut down the back of each shell with a pair of poultry shears or a sharp knife. Remove the shell and the vein that runs along the back of each shrimp; then rinse the shrimp thoroughly under cold running water.

~ **SECOND,** whisk together the extra-virgin olive oil, garlic, crushed red pepper and basil in a stainless mixing bowl. Coat the shrimp thoroughly and spread evenly in a ceramic dish. Cover and marinate in the refrigerator for at least 4 hours and up to 24 hours.

COOK THE SHRIMP:

~ Heat a skillet over medium-high heat and quickly add in the shrimp and marinade; sauté undisturbed for 2 to 3 minutes. Season with a pinch of salt, and turn each of the shrimp using a pair of kitchen tongs. Squeeze the lemon halves over the shrimp and continue cooking until the shrimp are firm, pink and just cooked, about 1 minute. Transfer the contents of the skillet to a clean ceramic dish and cool to room temperature. Then cover tightly with plastic film and refrigerate.

GAZPACHO

¼ cup extra-virgin olive oil
4 whole cloves garlic
1 medium onion, diced
2 cups peeled, seeded and diced tomatoes
1 tablespoon fresh chopped basil
½ teaspoon chili powder
Pinch of salt
Pinch of pepper
2 cups tomato juice or V-8 juice

1 tablespoon tomato paste
1 teaspoon red wine vinegar
1 teaspoon Worcestershire sauce
1½ cups peeled, seeded and diced cucumber
¾ cup diced green bell pepper
¾ cup diced yellow bell pepper
½ cup chopped green onions
Salt and pepper to taste

MAKE THE GAZPACHO:

~ **FIRST,** heat the extra-virgin olive oil in a heavy skillet over medium-high heat. Sauté the whole garlic cloves, turning every so often until they just begin to brown, 3 to 4 minutes. Add in the onion and continue cooking until the garlic and onion begin to caramelize, 4 to 5 minutes. Stir in the diced tomatoes and sauté for 2 minutes. Add the chopped basil and season with the chili powder and a pinch of salt and pepper, then pour in the tomato juice and simmer for 1 minute. Whisk in the tomato paste and add the vinegar and the Worcestershire sauce. Remove the skillet from heat and cool to room temperature.

~ **SECOND,** pour the cooled mixture into the bowl of a food processor fitted with a steel blade; pulse just enough to blend (it should be chunky).

~ **THIRD,** combine the diced cucumber, bell peppers and green onions in a stainless mixing bowl. Mix all but 6 tablespoons of the combined vegetables into the soup mixture and adjust the seasoning to taste with salt and pepper. Cover and chill in the refrigerator for at least 4 hours and up to 24 hours.

~ **FOURTH,** ladle the soup into chilled bowls (glass bowls make a stunning presentation). Mound 1 tablespoon of the reserved vegetables into the center of each bowl of soup and set 3 of the cooked shrimp around the little mound of vegetables. If desired, garnish the soup with fresh basil leaves.

A world without a Sabbath would be like a man without a smile, like a summer without flowers, and like a homestead without a garden. It is the joyous day of the whole week.

HENRY WARD BEECHER

GAME HENS AND RICE WITH OLIVES AND ALMONDS
6 SERVINGS

The Spanish-mission influence is evident throughout California, where monks planted vineyards, olive groves and oranges. This simple, peasant-style dish—called arroz con pollo—*captures and celebrates a bygone era with its harmony of natural flavors. This is a childhood favorite of mine that my mom used to make and serve with a festive salad.*

MARINADE

¼ cup olive oil
2 cloves garlic, minced
1 tablespoon fresh chopped oregano
1 tablespoon fresh chopped sage
½ teaspoon crushed red pepper
1 tablespoon cracked white peppercorns
6 whole game hens, 18 to 20 ounces each
3 small lemons, halved
3 small onions, halved
6 sprigs fresh oregano

MAKE THE MARINADE:

~ Combine the olive oil with the garlic, oregano, sage, crushed red pepper and cracked white peppercorns in a small mixing bowl.

MARINATE THE GAME HENS:

~ Trim and discard the wing tips from each hen. Evenly spread the marinade all over the outside and inside of each hen. Insert half a lemon, half an onion and a sprig of oregano inside each game hen, then tie their legs together with kitchen twine. Place the hens in a ceramic dish, cover and refrigerate for 24 hours.

GAME HENS AND RICE

Coarse salt for seasoning
¼ cup olive oil
1½ cups long-grain or basmati rice
½ cup slivered almonds
6 whole cloves garlic
3 small onions, quartered
3 cups chicken broth
½ cup pitted black olives
½ cup pitted green olives
1 bay leaf

~ **FIRST,** remove the hens from the refrigerator about 20 minutes before they're to be browned and season with coarse salt. Preheat the oven to 325°F.

~ **SECOND,** heat the olive oil over medium heat in a large ovenproof skillet or Dutch oven. Working in 2 batches, brown the game hens evenly until they are golden, 4 to 5 minutes on each side, for a total of 16 to 20 minutes. Return the cooked hens to the ceramic dish.

~ **THIRD,** add the rice, almonds, garlic and onions to the skillet. Sauté the mixture, stirring often, until the rice and almonds are beginning to brown and the garlic has begun to caramelize, 4 to 5 minutes. Pour in the chicken broth and stir; then add in the black olives, green olives and the bay leaf.

~ **FOURTH,** place the game hens on top of the rice and cover with a tight-fitting lid. Transfer to the preheated oven and bake until the juices run clear, the rice is tender, and a meat thermometer registers 160°F when inserted between the leg and the thigh, 40 to 45 minutes.

~ **FIFTH,** when the game hens are fully cooked, remove the kitchen twine. Mound the rice on a platter and arrange the hens around it.

SALAD OF JICAMA, RED ONION, ORANGE AND AVOCADO

6 SERVINGS

I really love a crisp salad. Perhaps it comes from growing up in California, where we enjoyed warm weather and fresh produce year-round. It helped that we had an avocado tree in our backyard! This salad has it all: crunchy romaine, spicy jicama and sweet red onion, perfectly balanced with buttery avocado and dressed with the tang of honey mustard and citrus.

DRESSING

1½ teaspoons honey
1 tablespoon fresh lime juice
1 tablespoon Dijon mustard
1 tablespoon tarragon vinegar
1 tablespoon fresh snipped chives
1 tablespoon fresh chopped tarragon
⅓ cup vegetable oil
Salt to taste

PREPARE THE DRESSING:

~ Combine the honey, lime juice, mustard and vinegar in a blender. Add in the chives and tarragon and pulse until well blended. Turn the blender on low speed and slowly pour in the vegetable oil to emulsify. Season the dressing to taste with salt.

SALAD

2 ripe avocados
1 lime, halved
Pinch of salt
1 small head of romaine lettuce
2 cups julienned jicama
4 oranges, peeled and sectioned
1 red onion, thinly sliced

PREPARE THE SALAD:

~ **FIRST,** cut the avocados into halves with a sharp paring knife and remove their pits. Scoop the avocado flesh from each half with a large spoon and slice into a small bowl. Squeeze the lime halves over the avocado slices and season with a pinch of salt; set aside.

~ **SECOND,** rinse, spin dry and chop the romaine. Combine the jicama and orange sections with the red onion slices; mix with the chopped romaine in a large salad bowl. Toss with the dressing and then gently fold in the avocado slices. Serve immediately.

BAKED CARAMEL CUSTARD

6 SERVINGS

Baked custard, or flan, is rich yet simple. It makes a wonderful dessert for Sunday dinner because of its ease and simplicity. You can make this custard without the caramel, if you wish, and serve it in festive custard cups.

CARAMEL

½ cup granulated sugar
1 tablespoon water

PREPARE THE CARAMEL:

Heat ½ cup of sugar undisturbed in a heavy skillet over low heat until it begins to melt; then gently move the pan in a back-and-forth motion to help all of the sugar evenly melt. When the melted sugar turns a light caramel color after 2 to 3 minutes, quickly add in the water and shake the pan a bit until the bubbling subsides. Immediately divide the caramel between six 5-ounce custard cups or pour into a 1-quart custard dish. Tip the dish (or dishes) to swirl the caramel so that it evenly coats the bottom and about ½-inch up the sides of each dish.

CUSTARD

4 large eggs, room temperature
2 large egg yolks, room temperature
1 teaspoon pure vanilla extract
⅔ cup granulated sugar
2 cups half-and-half

MAKE THE CUSTARD:

FIRST, combine the eggs, egg yolks and vanilla in a stainless bowl. Slowly beat in the sugar with a wire whisk. It's important that the sugar dissolves slowly and completely into the eggs. Do not beat the mixture too rapidly; it will make the custard frothy and full of air.

SECOND, scald the half-and-half in a small saucepan by placing it over medium heat just to the point of boiling; then remove from heat immediately. Temper the yolks by whisking ½ cup of the hot half-and-half into the egg mixture until fully blended; then whisk in the remaining half-and-half.

THIRD, pour the mixture into the prepared custard cups or baking dish and place in a second, larger pan; fill the pan with enough warm water to come nearly all the way up the sides of each dish. Bake in a 325°F oven until a knife comes out clean when inserted into the center of the custard, about 40 minutes for the small dishes or 60 minutes for the larger dish. Carefully remove the pan from the oven and then remove each dish from the water to cool until they reach room temperature. The custards can be served at room temperature or covered tightly with plastic wrap and refrigerated overnight.

FOURTH, loosen the edges of the custard by running a thin sharp knife around the inside rim of the dish. Set the dish in a pan of warm water for 5 minutes and invert onto individual dessert plates or a large serving dish; the custard should slide out easily with the caramel syrup running down onto the plate.

Southern Traditions

> > > | GLAZED COUNTRY-BAKED HAM
> GINGER-PEACH CHUTNEY
> THYME-SCENTED SCALLOPED POTATOES
> BAKED SPAGHETTI SQUASH
> SALLY LUNN BREAD
> PINEAPPLE MANGO UPSIDE-DOWN CAKE

Baked ham has long been a Sunday dinner favorite. In the Southeast, especially, where traditions run deep and where roots are buried firmly in the soil of our early American colonies, a baked-ham dinner is standard Sunday fare. Different varieties of American hams, each with their distinct flavor and style, were created throughout these developing lands—from Virginia, home of the famous Smithfield hams, down to the Carolinas and Georgia, and over the mountains to Kentucky and Tennessee.

Smoking as a way to preserve meats is an ancient practice. In America on family farms, plantations, and in local communities, it became an art form. During the fall after the fattened hogs were slaughtered, the cured, whole bone-in legs were then sewn into muslin bags and hung in smokehouses to pick up the smoke's rich flavor and develop a deep terra-cotta color. Each region created a distinct flavor by using a variety of methods for feeding, curing, and smoking. Feeding hogs on corn, peanuts, or even peaches; brine-curing the meat and rubbing it with various spices, salt, and sugar; and finally smoking the joints over the choicest woods gave each farmer's meaty and succulent creation a signature aroma and taste. A great ham was cured for months and became a long-anticipated treat, along with the garden's first offerings for springtime dinners—especially on Easter Sunday.

Thomas Jefferson, America's third president and one of the authors of the Declaration of Independence, was also famous for his fine hams, his gardens, and his hospitality. He grew more than 250 kinds of vegetables at his Virginia home, Monticello, including a great variety of squash, beans, and peas. His table was often filled with the good company of friends and family. The hours spent attending to his farm and enjoying his loved ones and guests were among his happiest. Shouldn't that be true for us all?

The tradition of an open door is not simply a sign of Southern hospitality, of course, but is a quintessentially American habit. When we open our homes, we open our hearts. And when we offer our best and welcome our guests to the bounty of our table, we continue this fine tradition, a tradition well worth keeping. Surely the best Sunday dinners are those where visitors become part of the family.

We all have our favorite expressions of hospitality, just as each of us has our favorite way to serve baked ham. In the colonial years, a favorite symbol of welcome and ease was the pineapple, a rare and prized treat. What could be a more appropriate choice to finish this time-honored meal, then, than a moist pineapple mango upside-down cake?

Easy time saving
AND DO-AHEAD TIPS:

FRIDAY EVENING
Prepare the chutney.

SATURDAY
Bake the pineapple mango cake.
Bake the bread.

SUNDAY MORNING
Slice the onion for the scalloped
potatoes; refrigerate in a well-sealed
container. Trim and score the ham.
Prepare the glaze. Peel the potatoes
and cover with cold water.

GLAZED COUNTRY-BAKED HAM
12 SERVINGS

Most hams found in grocery stores today are water-added, and while they can be used for making this delicious ham dinner, taking the time to find a hand-cured, bone-in, fully cooked ham with natural juices is well worth the effort. Not only does the ham have a better natural flavor; it will also be less processed. The ham bone can later be used to make a delicious meal, such as split pea soup or baked beans.

BAKED HAM

1 10-pound sugar-cured smoked ham

~ Adjust the lower rack to near the bottom of the oven and preheat to 325°F.

MAKE THE HAM:

~ **FIRST,** rinse the ham under cool running water and dry it thoroughly with paper towels. Use a sharp knife to carefully trim away the outer skin from the ham, leaving a layer of fat and a collar of skin around the shank bone. You may trim away some of the fat as well, but leave a ½-inch layer. Score the fat on the top of the ham in a 1- to 2-inch diamond pattern, cutting just slightly into the meat.

~ **SECOND,** place the ham in a shallow roasting pan and bake in the preheated oven until the ham reaches an internal temperature of 140°F, about 1 hour and 45 minutes.

GLAZE

¼ teaspoon ground cinnamon
¼ teaspoon ground cloves
2 tablespoons deli-style mustard
½ cup packed dark brown sugar

PREPARE THE GLAZE:

~ Thoroughly combine the cinnamon, cloves, mustard and brown sugar in a small mixing bowl. When the ham has baked for the prescribed amount of time, brush the top and sides evenly with the glaze. Increase the oven temperature to 350°F and continue baking until the glaze is bubbly, 20 to 30 additional minutes.

SERVE THE HAM:

~ Carefully remove the ham from the roasting pan and transfer it to a clean cutting board. Let it rest at room temperature for 15 to 20 minutes, then use a sharp carving knife to slice. Transfer the slices to a warm platter and serve immediately.

GINGER-PEACH CHUTNEY
12 SERVINGS

Though generally associated with Indian cuisine, chutney is actually English in origin and during colonial times was one of the best ways to preserve exotic fruits. This wonderful, tangy, gingery chutney is a perfect complement to the smoky ham. It is also excellent when nectarines, apricots or plums are substituted for the peaches.

CHUTNEY

¼ cup packed dark brown sugar
2 tablespoons cider vinegar
1 cup peach juice or nectar
1 cup peach preserves
4 cups fresh sliced peaches or frozen sliced peaches, thawed
1 tablespoon fresh minced ginger
1 small red chili pepper, seeded and minced
1 cinnamon stick

PREPARE THE CHUTNEY:

~ **FIRST,** combine the brown sugar, vinegar, peach juice or nectar and preserves in a heavy-bottomed saucepan; bring to a boil over medium-high heat. Add in the peach slices, ginger, chili pepper and cinnamon stick. Lower the heat to medium and simmer, stirring frequently, until the peaches are fully cooked and the liquid is thick and bubbling, 30 to 40 minutes.

~ **SECOND,** remove the pan from the stove and cool to room temperature. Remove and discard the cinnamon stick. Spoon the chutney into a stainless or glass bowl. Cover and refrigerate for at least 2 hours and up to 3 days before serving.

> *It seems to me that our three basic needs for food and security and love are so mingled and entwined that we cannot straightly think of one without the other, so it happens that when I write of hunger I am really writing about love and the hunger for it....*
>
> M. K. FISHER

THYME-SCENTED SCALLOPED POTATOES

12 SERVINGS

One can hardly think of ham without thinking of scalloped potatoes—the two are simply made for each other, and these potatoes are truly exceptional. Using sharp cheddar cheese at the end adds extra zing to this creamy casserole.

POTATOES

10 medium potatoes
1 medium onion, thinly sliced
1 tablespoon fresh chopped thyme
½ cup (1 stick) butter
4 cups whole milk
¼ cup all-purpose flour
1½ teaspoons salt
½ teaspoon white pepper
½ cup grated sharp cheddar cheese

~ Preheat the oven to 325°F.

MAKE THE SCALLOPED POTATOES:

~ **FIRST,** working with one potato at a time, peel and slice into ¼-inch-thick slices; then transfer to a bowl of cold water. Continue this process until all of the potatoes are sliced. Drain thoroughly.

~ **SECOND,** butter the bottom and sides of a 13x9-inch baking dish. Arrange a single layer of the potato slices on the bottom of the buttered dish, then sprinkle with onion slices and a little thyme. Dot with butter and repeat for several layers; finish with a final layer of potatoes dotted with butter.

~ **THIRD,** whisk the milk and flour together until smooth. Season with the salt and white pepper. Slowly pour the mixture over the potatoes to fill the casserole a little more than halfway. (The potatoes will cook down as they are baked.)

~ **FOURTH,** cover the dish tightly with nonstick foil or foil that has been sprayed with oil. Place the 13x9-inch baking dish on a baking sheet and transfer to the oven. Bake until the potatoes are tender when tested with the tip of a knife, about 1½ hours.

~ **FIFTH,** remove the foil. Increase the oven temperature to 350°F and bake until the top is golden brown and the casserole is bubbling, about 30 more minutes. Sprinkle with ½ cup of grated cheddar just before serving.

BAKED SPAGHETTI SQUASH
12 SERVINGS

Spaghetti squash has gained popularity only recently, though it has been around for over five thousand years. English colonists called it "vegetable squash" because its unique crunch and tender texture resembles a vegetable more than do other squash varieties. Because of its hard shell, it is mostly thought of as a winter squash, so named because they keep well into the winter months. Many people think, however, that the spaghetti squash is really the origin of the canary-yellow summer squash.

SPAGHETTI SQUASH

1 large spaghetti squash
2 tablespoons butter
Salt and pepper to taste

PREPARE THE SQUASH:

~ **FIRST,** cut the squash in half lengthwise and scoop the seeds from the center. Rub the center of each half with a tablespoon of butter and season with salt and pepper. Place the squash directly onto the top rack of the oven or on a baking sheet and bake along with the potatoes and ham in a 325°F oven for 50 to 60 minutes.

~ **SECOND,** remove the squash from the oven and transfer to wire racks until they are cool enough to handle, about 10 minutes. Scrape the flesh from the shells with a fork, twisting a little as you do to separate the yellow strands. Transfer immediately to a wide serving bowl and serve with additional butter, or cool and then reheat in the microwave in a covered casserole.

Mama and I always had a book to read while eating our meals, and this became a lifetime habit for my own family and me. The only exception was Sunday dinner, which, for some reason, had too formal an atmosphere for literature at the table.

JIMMY CARTER

SALLY LUNN BREAD

MAKES 1 BUNDT LOAF

This creamy-textured bread, popular in the southern colonies and traditionally baked in a fluted tube or bundt pan, makes a beautiful centerpiece. Legend has it that Sally Lunn was a young girl from eighteenth-century Bath, England, who cried sweet tears into the bread that bears her name. Most likely the name came from the French bakers who pushed their carts through the streets of this once-fashionable British spa, crying "Soleil lune!" ("sun and moon") to describe the bread's golden crust and soft, creamy center.

BREAD

1 package (2¼ teaspoons) active dry yeast
¼ cup warm whole milk, about 110°F
1 cup whole milk
¼ cup granulated sugar
½ cup (1 stick) unsalted butter
½ cup shortening
3 cups all-purpose flour
3 large eggs, room temperature, lightly beaten
1 cup cake flour
1 teaspoon salt

MAKE THE BREAD:

- **FIRST,** sprinkle the yeast over the ¼ cup warm milk and let stand for 1 minute, then stir until the yeast is dissolved.

- **SECOND,** scald 1 cup of milk with the sugar by heating it in a small saucepan just to the point of boiling. Remove it from heat, add in the butter and shortening and swirl until they are melted. Cool in the pan until lukewarm.

- **THIRD,** combine the dissolved yeast with the lukewarm milk in the bowl of a mixer fitted with a paddle. Turn the mixer on low speed and gradually add in 2 cups of the all-purpose flour, ½ cup at a time, until the flour is fully incorporated. Continue mixing until the batter is smooth and elastic, about 2 minutes. Scrape down the sides of the bowl with a rubber spatula.

- **FOURTH,** turn the mixer to low speed and gradually add in the 3 lightly beaten eggs until they are fully incorporated. Then add in the remaining 1 cup of all-purpose flour, ¼ cup at a time; continue to beat on low speed until the dough is once again smooth, about 2 more minutes.

- **FIFTH,** whisk the cake flour together with the salt in a separate bowl. Turn the mixer to low speed and slowly add the mixture into the dough, ¼ cup at a time. Scrape down the sides of the bowl with a rubber spatula. Replace the paddle with a dough hook and knead on low speed for 5 minutes. The dough will now have a buttery-smooth, silky texture. It will be much softer than traditional bread dough. Cover the dough with a clean tea towel and set in a draft-free place until it has doubled in volume, about 1½ hours.

- **SIXTH,** lightly butter a 10-inch bundt pan. Beat the raised dough down with a spatula or wooden spoon and turn evenly into the buttered pan. Cover with a clean tea towel and let rise until the dough has doubled in volume by half, about 40 minutes. Brush the top with a little milk and bake in a 350°F oven for 50 to 60 minutes. As it bakes, the bread will rise above the rim of the pan.

- **SEVENTH,** when the bread is done baking, it will have a deep golden hue on the outside and a dense, soft feel to it when squeezed gently. Cool in the pan for 5 minutes, then turn the loaf onto a baking rack to cool.

I'll never forget the day my uncle told my mother and me that both my father and my brother had been killed in a tragic plane crash. And I'll never forget that feeling of being so alone. What would my life be like now? Would anything ever be the same again?

Certainly many things in my life were never the same after that. But one thing remained consistent, something I later recognized as a source of solace: Sunday was still the same—and Sunday dinner became a renewing source of comfort. Even though my father and brother would never again be present at Sunday dinner, others were there to comfort with their presence. Family members, neighbors, and church friends who came and brought us their famous family dishes communicated stability and security without words.

Although many things in life change, some never do. In this broken, often grief-filled world, it helps to know that Sunday is always there. Until the end of time, Sunday will show up every seventh day, bringing with it the reminder that the Lord of the Sabbath is the same yesterday, today, and forever.

JOHN HUTCHINSON

PINEAPPLE MANGO UPSIDE-DOWN CAKE

12 SERVINGS

Fruit upside-down cakes have been around for ages—especially those made with pineapples, which were a symbol of hospitality throughout colonial America. There was a time when not everyone had an oven and cakes were baked in skillets set off to the side of an open hearth. The fruit on the bottom protected the cake from burning and gave it needed moisture.

NOTE: *You can substitute two 14-ounce cans of whole pineapple rings in syrup for the fresh pineapple. If you do, skip the "prepare the pineapple" steps in the recipe.*

FRUIT

1 medium fresh pineapple
¾ cup granulated sugar
1 cup water
2 cups mango chunks

PREPARE THE PINEAPPLE:

~ **FIRST,** cut the top and bottom from the pineapple and discard; stand the pineapple on one end and use a sharp knife to cut the peel away by slicing down toward the cutting board. Once peeled, cut the pineapple into ½-inch-thick slices. Use a 1-inch biscuit cutter to remove the core from each slice to create rings; if you wish, use a 4-inch biscuit cutter to cut the rings into uniform rounds; set aside.

~ **SECOND,** dissolve the sugar into the water by whisking together thoroughly in a large saucepan. Bring the liquid to a boil over medium heat and simmer for 5 minutes. Place the pineapple rings into the sugar syrup in 2 separate batches, turning once and simmering each batch for 3 to 4 minutes; transfer the slices from the syrup into a glass dish and let the pineapple rings cool to room temperature. When you are done simmering the pineapple, remove the pan from heat and add the fresh mango chunks to the pineapple syrup. Cool to room temperature, then drain the mango chunks and reserve the syrup. (*Note:* You should have about ¾ cup reserved syrup.)

CAKE

2¼ cups cake flour
2½ teaspoons baking powder
½ teaspoon salt
⅔ cup unsalted butter
1 cup granulated sugar
3 large eggs, room temperature
1½ teaspoons pure vanilla extract
½ cup whole milk
½ cup reserved pineapple syrup

MAKE THE CAKE BATTER:

~ **FIRST,** adjust the rack to the middle of the oven and preheat to 350°F. Then sift together the cake flour, baking powder and salt; set aside.

~ **SECOND,** use a mixer fitted with a paddle to cream the butter with the sugar until light and fluffy, 6 to 8 minutes. Scrape down the sides of the bowl with a rubber spatula. Turn the speed to medium and add in the eggs one at a time, mixing well after each addition; then add in the vanilla.

~ **THIRD,** reduce the mixer speed to low and add in the dry ingredients in 3 stages alternately with the milk; mix long enough to form a smooth batter. Increase the mixer speed to medium and pour in ½ cup of the reserved pineapple syrup; beat for 1 minute.

TOPPING

3 tablespoons unsalted butter
½ cup packed light brown sugar
¼ cup reserved pineapple syrup

MAKE THE TOPPING:

~ Melt the butter over medium heat in a 10-inch round ovenproof skillet with 2¼-inch sides. Remove the skillet from heat, sprinkle the brown sugar evenly over the bottom and pour in the remaining ¼ cup reserved pineapple syrup.

ASSEMBLE THE CAKE:

~ Crowd the pineapple slices into the bottom of the skillet and cut any remaining slices to fit around the edges and up the sides of the skillet. Place a chunk of mango in the center of each pineapple ring and in any spaces between the rings. Slowly spread the cake batter over the fruit. Bake in the preheated oven until a wooden pick comes out clean when inserted in the middle, 40 to 45 minutes. Cool on a wire rack for 5 minutes; then invert onto your favorite serving plate. Serve slices topped with freshly whipped cream.

Coming Home

> ɤ ɤ ɤ | *He will also send you rain*
>
> *for the seed you sow in the ground,*
>
> *and the food that comes from the land*
>
> *will be rich and plentiful.*
>
> ISAIAH 30:23

Coming home. The words warm our hearts with memories and with anticipation.

Picture an entire family that has joined together, crowding into the living room, settling into those old familiar chairs. Listen to the laughter that spills from the kitchen. Inhale the distinct aromas of favorite home-cooked dishes. Perhaps it is a holiday, like Thanksgiving, Christmas, or Easter. It could be the celebration of an accomplishment or a milestone, like a graduation or a golden anniversary. It might even be a solemn occasion, like a funeral, with the family all gathered to share their sorrow and support as well as their treasured memories.

The Sunday table is like that—it is a weekly occasion for homecoming, a time and place where everyone in the family knows they will be welcomed with open arms.

When I was growing up, Grandma's Sunday dinner table was where the whole family gathered when an announcement was to be made, when a baby had been born, or when one of my uncles had bought a new automobile. (Our family albums are filled with pictures of kids and cars!) It was the place to remember birthdays, too. Once a month the whole clan would gather to celebrate all of the birthdays that fell in that particular month. Special occasions—a graduation, a baptism, a new house—were recognized as a family. Like the bright pieces that form a mosaic, those singular moments created memories that will last a lifetime.

Not all of us have large families living nearby. Some have parents who have passed on. Others have let many years go by since they last came together. But Sunday celebrations can still be a time for opening our hearts and our table to those who are family by choice as well as birth.

The Sunday dinner table is the ideal place to build extended family. Church friends, neighbors, coworkers, childhood pals, and college classmates who are invited for Sunday dinner often become cherished friends with whom we take vacations and celebrate special occasions. These are the friendships that endure through challenge and triumph. And Sunday dinner is where it all begins, nurturing an investment far beyond any earthly value, creating a world we are glad to come home to.

There was always extra room at my grandmother's and my mother's tables, and my wife and I wanted to recreate that sense of openness in our home. From the time they were very small, each of our children knew that their friends were welcome to join us. Sunday dinner became the natural place to bring new acquaintances and an easy way for them to introduce the special people in their lives.

Even after our children ventured off to college, using their weekends home to run around and see their friends, we knew they'd be at our house for Sunday dinner. When they brought friends with them, they usually phoned ahead—but not always. There were a few times when our kids would simply show up and expect a warm family welcome for whomever they brought with them. And though we occasionally needed to run to the market or creatively raid the refrigerator, we still managed to make room at the Sunday table.

Now our children are grown and have embarked on lives of their own. God willing, we will live to see our family of five grow to include grandchildren. Then, like my grandparents, we will be ready to expand our table and our open invitation to Sunday dinner. Whatever happens in our family's lives, we hope our children and, someday, their children will know they can always bring their friends home to Sunday dinner.

Yes, the Sunday dinner table is a touchstone to our past. Yet it can also be the stepping-stone on which to build memories—a place to share, grow, laugh, weep, and, most of all, come home to. It's a time to see God's blessings more clearly, to celebrate His bounty, and to share our love through careful preparation and heartfelt welcome.

Isn't it nice to know we can always come home? Even those who have ventured forth and squandered their inheritance, like the Prodigal Son in the Bible, can still find a place to return to—a place of acceptance, a place where the language of unconditional love is spoken.

So join us, if you will. Set the table with your Sunday best, prepare the feast with loving hands, and open the front door wide. The family is coming home!

In a Pinch...

BAKING POWDER

1 teaspoon baking powder = ¼ teaspoon baking soda + ½ teaspoon cream of tartar + ¼ teaspoon cornstarch.

BUTTER

Butter = butter. (There is no substitution!)

BUTTERMILK

1 cup buttermilk = 1 tablespoon lemon juice *or* white vinegar + enough milk to equal 1 cup. Stir the mixture well, then let stand for 5 to 10 minutes before using.

CAKE FLOUR

1 cup cake flour = ¾ cup all-purpose flour + 2 tablespoons cornstarch.

BITTERSWEET CHOCOLATE

1 ounce bittersweet chocolate = ½ ounce unsweetened chocolate + 1 tablespoon granulated sugar.

UNSWEETENED CHOCOLATE

1 square (1 ounce) unsweetened chocolate = 3 tablespoons natural cocoa powder (not Dutch-processed) + 1 tablespoon vegetable oil *or* shortening.

STRONG-BREWED COFFEE

½ cup strong-brewed coffee = ¼ cup instant espresso powder dissolved in 6 tablespoons hot water.

CORNMEAL

1 cup stone-ground cornmeal = 1 cup regular cornmeal *or* corn grits *or* polenta.

CORNSTARCH

When used as a thickener, 1 tablespoon cornstarch = 2 tablespoons flour.

CURRANTS

¼ cup currants = ¼ cup chopped dark raisins.

POWDERED GELATIN

1 envelope (¼ ounce) powdered gelatin = 2 ½ teaspoons.

FRESH HERBS

1 tablespoon fresh chopped herbs = 1 teaspoon dried herbs.

DARK BROWN SUGAR

1 cup dark brown sugar = 1 cup granulated sugar + ¼ cup molasses.

LIGHT BROWN SUGAR

1 cup light brown sugar = ½ cup dark brown sugar + ½ cup granulated sugar.

SUPERFINE SUGAR

1 cup superfine sugar = 1 cup granulated sugar, processed in a food processor or blender until very fine.

DARK CORN SYRUP

1 cup dark corn syrup = ¾ cup light corn syrup + ¼ cup molasses.

ACTIVE DRY YEAST

1 envelope (¼ ounce) active dry yeast = 1 cake ($^3/_5$ ounce) fresh compressed yeast.

Kitchen Math

Pinch . . . . less than ⅛ teaspoon

3 teaspoons . . . . 1 tablespoon

4 tablespoons . . . . ¼ cup

5 ⅓ tablespoons . . . . ⅓ cup

8 tablespoons . . . . ½ cup

12 tablespoons . . . . ¾ cup

16 tablespoons . . . . 1 cup

LIQUID MEASUREMENTS

2 tablespoons . . . . 1 liquid ounce

8 ounces . . . . 1 cup

1 cup . . . . ½ pint

2 cups . . . . 1 pint

4 cups . . . . 1 quart

2 quarts . . . . ½ gallon

4 quarts . . . . 1 gallon

DRY MEASUREMENTS

1 pound flour . . . . 4 cups

1 pound sugar . . . . 2 cups

With Gratitude

❧ ❧ ❧

*T*aking on a project like this is not a single-handed effort. So many people leave their fingerprints on each and every page. The writer, like a great chef, is more a conductor or composer than a practiced instrumentalist filling out an orchestra.

My heartfelt appreciation to Kay and Charles James for their generosity—thanks, Kay, for making the introduction and giving me the big push.

Friends are one of God's greatest gifts, and without the encouragement of wonderful people like Bob and Jean Baldwin, March and Mariam Bell, Glenn and Dana Elsnick, Carl and Kay Meyer, and Dick and Ellen Osborne, this book would never have been written.

Steffany Woolsey, you are the best—let's do this again.

A big thank-you to all those working behind the curtain at Multnomah who gave so much of their time testing recipe after recipe. And to our many other friends who gave so generously from their own memories and came over so willingly for all those midweek Sunday dinner sessions.

Hats off to the incredible design team at Koechel Peterson, especially Heather Rohm and Tom Henry, who captured the vision so beautifully and gave so much more than was required.

Marina…for those 1,650 Sunday afternoons (perhaps you should have written this instead of me). ❧

Acknowledgments

Vignette on page 35 by Sandra Yoder Smallman © 2003.
Used by permission of the author.
Sandra Yoder Smallman is a pastor's wife and homemaker.

Vignette on page 57 © 2003 by Kay Coles James. Used by permission of the author.

Vignette on page 79 © 2003 by Mary Ann Bell. Used by permission of the author.
Mary Reeves Bell writes young adult fiction.

Vignette on page 103 © 2002 by Gina Vos. Used by permission of the author.
Gina grew up in Pella, where Vos is equivalent to Smith. She now lives
in Nashville with her husband and three preschool children.

Vignette on page 127 © 2003 by Lenore E. Same. Used by permission of the author.

Vignette on page 143 © 2003 by Guy N. Faucheux. Used by permission of the author.

Vignette on page 159 © 2003 by Linda Jacks. Used by permission of the author.
Linda Jacks: Writer, born in Oklahoma, nurtured in Texas, transplanted to Virginia.

Vignette on page 179 © 2003 by George F. Knight. Used by permission of the author.

Vignette on page 199 © 2003 by Ellen J. Donnelly. Used by permission of the author.
To my small, wonderful family! Love, Ellen Donnelly.

Vignette on page 217 © 2003 by John R. Hutchinson. Used by permission of the author.
John R. Hutchinson, Senior Pastor, McLean Presbyterian Church, McLean, Virginia.

Back cover quote by Corrie ten Boom, taken from *In My Father's House*, by Corrie ten Boom and C. C. Carlson.
Published by Fleming H. Revell Company, a division of Baker Book House Company.
© 1976 by Corrie ten Boom and Carole C. Carlson. Used by permission of Baker Book House Company.